Escape PRISONS OF THE MIND

by

Kaziah May Hancock,

A granddaughter of Mosiah Hancock, a Mormon pioneer

DORRANCE PUBLISHING CO
EST. 1920
PITTSBURGH, PENNSYLVANIA 15238

The contents of this work, including, but not limited to, the accuracy of events, people, and places depicted; opinions expressed; permission to use previously published materials included; and any advice given or actions advocated are solely the responsibility of the author, who assumes all liability for said work and indemnifies the publisher against any claims stemming from publication of the work.

All Rights Reserved
Copyright © 2022 by Kaziah May Hancock

No part of this book may be reproduced or transmitted, downloaded, distributed, reverse engineered, or stored in or introduced into any information storage and retrieval system, in any form or by any means, including photocopying and recording, whether electronic or mechanical, now known or hereinafter invented without permission in writing from the publisher.

Dorrance Publishing Co
585 Alpha Drive
Pittsburgh, PA 15238
Visit our website at *www.dorrancebookstore.com*

ISBN: 978-1-6366-1360-4
eISBN: 978-1-6366-1939-2

DISCLAIMER FOR RELIGIOUS AND HISTORICAL CLARIFICATION

Dear Reader, please carefully read the following information in order to clearly understand the organization described in this book:

Escape Prisons of the Mind is an autobiography by Kaziah Hancock, largely about her forced marriage and controlled life by members and leaders of the FLDS church cult, which originated in Short Crick, Arizona, with current headquarters in Hildale, Utah and Colorado City, Arizona. The Fundamentalist Church of Jesus Christ of Latter-Day Saints was founded in 1929 by Lorin C. Woolley, and was a break-off religion created by a group of people who completely left, and were excommunicated from the LDS Church, which church is known worldwide as the Mormon Church. The widely known Mormon Church is officially named The Church of Jesus Christ of Latter-Day Saints and founded by Joseph Smith in 1830 in Fayette, New York, with current headquarters in Salt Lake City, Utah. The FLDS church cult that is told about in this story IS NOT part of, and NOT to be confused with, the church known as the Mormon Church. The FLDS cult religion is NOT the same religion or organization as The Church of Jesus Christ of Latter-Day Saints. Although the FLDS church cult uses the Book of Mormon, and their own different interpretation of said book, they do not practice the same principles or doctrine as the LDS (Mormon) church. The FLDS church is in NO WAY associated with The Church of Jesus Christ of Latter-Day Saints (Mormon church). Although the author often mentions the "Mormon church," and Book of Mormon, she is speaking of the break-off religion who only claimed to be Mormons, but continued to practice polygamy long after The Church of Jesus Christ of Latter-Day Saints had ended that practice. Additionally, the FLDS church further corrupted that practice to include forced marriage, including forced marriage of teenage girls, a practice that completely goes against the doctrine of the LDS/Mormon Church.

In comparison of the two separate religions, the FLDS church described in this book, was led by founder Lorin C. Woolley (1929-54), Leslie Broadbent, John Y. Barlow, Charles Zitting, Joseph White Musser, LeGrand Woolley, and Louis A. Kelsch, and around the time of the death of leader LeRoy S. Johnson (1954-86) there were more splinter groups of the FLDS church, including that led by Rulon Jeffs (1986-2002), Warren Jeffs (2002-07), Merril Jessop, William Jessop, and Wendel L. Nielson. HOWEVER, in contrast, the only LDS (Mormon) Church was led in succession by founder Joseph Smith (1830-44), Brigham Young (1844-77), John Taylor (1880-87), Wilford Woodruff (1889-98), Lorenzo Snow (1898-1901), Joseph F. Smith (1901-18), Heber J. Grant (1918-45), George Albert Smith (1945-51), David O. McKay (1951-70), Joseph Fielding Smith (1970-72), Harold B. Lee (1972-73), Spencer W. Kimball (1973-85), Ezra Taft Benson (1985-94), Howard W. Hunter (1994-1995), Gordon B. Hinckley (1995-2008), Thomas S. Monson (2008-18), and Russell M. Nelson (2018-present day 2021).

Please be aware and be sure that the FLDS church cult (including any offshoot groups), and The Church of Jesus Christ of Latter-Day Saints are two completely different and separate organizations, and are NOT associated in ANY way.

PREFACE

As a kid I knew nothing about the power of words, or scriptures. The only book I had read was about George Washington Carver. He was always working on inventions and finding uses for waste products, and every day I would walk around thinking and wishing I could invent something. I was trying to find a smart way to make a few bucks. On Sunday, my mother always wanted me to go to meeting with her. The Church meeting lead by the polygamist brethren where they would sit on an elevated platform and look down upon us, and I thought the meetings were way to long and boring. Also, it was demoralizing to woman. The way they would go on and on talking of men having to marry more than one wife so he could go to the Celestial glory as though women had no more value than a man buying a bunch of cattle. And then they would say that the young boys and girls needed to come to the feet of the priesthood to be placed in marriage where God supposedly wanted them to go, rather than finding a mate on their own.

This one Sunday I refused to go and went out that day to try to earn some money. I thought I was going out to dig cacti and load them in a truck for people who wanted rock gardens. I had been out earning money doing this before with my boyfriend at that time, Frankie. But Frankie's boss said Frankie was sick and could not come with us. But I went with him anyway. I was so naive. He drove way out into the southern Utah desert then demanded sexual favors, which I refused. He pulled out a nine-inch dagger and threatened to run it thru me. I escaped from being raped and murdered.

I told God while running away as fast as I could. "If You save me from this, I will attend the meeting's, I will obey the brethren, GOD SAVE ME."

Well God did save me. Shaken to my core, when I got back home, I had to live by what I had promised God under extreme duress. Nevertheless, a promise is a promise, and I became a changed girl. I began to study early book of Mormon history called the Journal of Discourses and attend meetings. Primed, I was ripe for the picking as I was determined to serve God even if it killed me. Mother had drilled into me that the priesthood brethren were 'Holy Apostles' that spoke for God. They would use phrases like thus saith the Lord. Preaching that whatever they would bless God would bless, and whatever they would curse God would curse. Quite frankly, that scared the pee out of me I knew I had no priesthood or special powers. I was but a recipient of God's goodness. And I was told that if I did not obey the priesthood brethren and give my consent to live polygamy that I would be eternally damned. That even my very soul would be destroyed and I would cease to exist. They read the words of Joseph Smith out of the book the Doctrine and Covenants section 132 verse 6:

And as pertaining to the new and everlasting covenant, it was instituted for the fullness of my glory, and he that receiveth a fullness thereof must and shall abide this law or he shall be damned, saith the Lord God.

How horrible—I could see no way out. I had not read in the Bible, Matthew 19 verses 4, 5, and 6, where Jesus said that a man and woman should leave father and mother and the two should become one. I thought a lot about before Jesus went on the cross, He asked God if the bitter cup could be taken from Him. But then said Father not my will but thine be done. And then in the book of Mormon what Nephi said, that God will never ask you to do anything that he would not help you with. It is said that fools rush in where angels fear to tread. I am no fool but I knew I was going where angels would not want to be.

At 15 I was given in marriage as a third wife to a man I had hated my whole life. My mood was so grim, like being in a prison walking towards my execution. And all I could say after the ceremony was "I hope I can endure" for it is the worst form of slavery for a woman to have to give her body to a man where there is no love.

The husband had massive pimples on his face and blood shot eyes, and a foul odor from the lack of bathing. You could smell him coming before you could see him. But worse than that was his rude, and domineering personality. I wanted to hide. Years later I found out he had paid a lot of tithing, like a good boy getting brownie points, they added up and I was the sacrifice to payback. You see young female flesh is the grease that keeps the wheels of these off-shoot groups of Mormonism spinning.

I found myself thrust into a very strange environment. The first wife was always making up stuff to get me in trouble. She resented me, and rightfully so. In the darkness of oppressive degradation, I was not allowed to make phone calls to family or friends never did I have a room or my own bed. My bed was his bed that was the only place I was allowed to lay on. But he would not let me sleep, until his sex desires were satisfied. He was such a control freak I was not allowed to have time by myself. I was either eating, working, or having sex, or listening to this man's shouting what he called scriptures. There's nothing I can say if You don't get the picture of this man-made hell hole by now. So, I preferred work. It gave me a sense of worth and self-respect. And the whole Mormon mindset has always been, by their works you shall know them. Fine my plan was to work myself to death, like a form of suicide then God would know how much I love Him, and I would be out of that hell. And for a kid that only prayed maybe three times a year, I was praying five to seven or more times a day to get thru each hour. So, I became a workaholic working 14 to 16 hours of physical labor in the little business they had, five and six days a week. It was my escape. A way to avoid the constant contention of false doctrine.

One day I made a comment that he had twisted the scriptures, and he shouted "This is how It is supposed to read," then he said in a commanding tone of voice "You are to forget everything and everyone that you have known before you came here. Erase it all from your mind. And put nothing in your head except what I tell you! Have you got that!?"

As he stared at me, I had no comment.

Then he told me that I would be held responsible for the support of his family. I asked, "Why ME?"

He said, "Because you are the one the God has given the body and the brains. No one else here has that."

I was five feet five inches tall, and 103 lbs. My dear Mother, fearing that I was being worked to death, sold her home and handed over the monies thinking that would buy her some respect. Then she came to live in this caustic environment to work with me in the little business. But she was given no respect; just the opposite. Looking back, it was like a concentration camp of the Hitler Regime.

I had the radio on while working and when the song 'The House of the Rising Sun' came on I always listened, not that I thought I was damned, but I sure could relate to the words.

I focused on trying to invent jigs and things to find a better, faster, and a more economical way to do a job. I was determined to build a business from nothing to something. But what I ended up building along with the business was my self-confidence. Even then, it took 18 years for me to come to the conclusion. How can I be sent to hell? I am already in hell.

The man and his first wife took all of my earnings and put the money into their social security accounts as though I did not even exist.

He said to me, "Well social security will be broke by the time you are old enough to collect anything."

I had to trust that my love for, and my belief in, Jesus was enough to save me. I could not stand it another day. All the preaching of hell and damnation was like water on a duck's back. I had indeed grown a spine, I ESCAPED, and I took driving lessons! Every day out of that hellish environment was wonderful! I thanked God over and over again. I had a new mind set of maintaining my FREEDOM. A spiritual war zone, the battle between good and evil was not over.

They would do prayer rituals asking God to curse and destroy me for my apostacy from their insanity. I was on the look-out, always aware of my surroundings, for I knew they believed in blood atonement. I bought a 38-caliber revolver. I was out of the damn mess of Mormon dogma. And nothing they could say or do could make me return.

It was crazy they (Reed, the husband) tried suing me for support. Why? Because I had been the bread winner. The trial went on for two and a half years. After all I had suffered and witnessed, what my mother had suffered, along from what was stolen from us, I would not yield to them another dime. Then on December 13, 1985 the verdict came in at the Salt Lake County Courthouse, in Salt Lake City, Utah.

As I walked down the steps of the courthouse, the cool winter breeze on my face, I stopped for a moment with immense appreciation and joy in my heart as I thought of the courtroom scene I had just left. I burst into tears. "Thank you, God," I murmured as I looked into the heavens.

Just then a young man ran up from behind. "Uh, pardon me, ma'am. That was an incredible hearing! Do you think it possible that I could get a copy of the court transcript?"

"Well, I don't know," I replied, shaking his hand.

Some time has passed since that day, and it was only the first of such reactions. There have been many friends who have suggested that I write this story of my life. I have thought to do so but have hesitated, for every time I began to tell someone what went on, they would look at me like, I was nuts. Because if you attend Sunday service at a main stream Mormon Church, members just pay 10% tithing. They have one wife and get married in the temple. They go on with their life, and they never look back at the trunk of the tree, the roots where their religion came from. The 132nd section in the Doctrine and Covenants is still part of their scriptures. It has never been deleted.

I asked a good Mormon man, "Do you know how many wives Joseph Smith had?"

He answered "No, and I don't want to know."

Well ok, there you have it.

And we have all heard of Churches where priests molest altar boys. Then there are Churches where men twist scriptures to intimidate a child so they think they are serving God by allowing someone to rape them, mentally, physically, spiritually, and financially.

Now as I look back after the fact, I view the brethren as whitened sepulcher full of dead men's bones. No priesthood or power at all. I am now a Christion and as I study the Bible. I try to give heed to what Jesus said, 'KNOW THE TRUTH AND THE TRUTH SHALL MAKE YOU FREE.' And when God sets you free you are free indeed.

So now before I get stuck on a view of something, I go find out what Jesus said. Then I can make a stand. This story happened because of my lack of knowledge at age 15.

CHAPTER ONE

A person of an honest heart and contrite spirit seeking for truth may find themselves entangled in the dark side of Mormon Doctrine. My Father was one caught up in that dilemma.

My mother, Edith Kaziah Soderberg Hancock, was the second wife of my father, Joseph Heber Hancock. Father's first wife was married to him by the laws of the land, but she told father that she did not want to have children because she had epilepsy and was afraid their offspring might inherit the problem. Father did not want to give her a divorce but told her that he would have to remarry and she gave her consent. Now because of this, father was not able to marry Mother by the laws of the land. They had discussed the issue of plural marriage but father was not certain as to who held the keys of authority having the right to perform plural marriages. He was searching and believing in a strong delusion, for HOW CAN ANYONE HAVE THE RIGHT TO AUTHORIZE SOMEONE TO COMMIT A WRONG? But he had bought into the Joseph Smith story that a man must have more than one wife to receive the highest degree of Celestial glory, So, Father and Mother wrote up a marriage contract that they both signed, and with the hope that if they ever could find the man who had sealing authority, they would be married properly by him. Nevertheless, they stayed true to their covenants. To support and keep his second wife, my mother, hopefully without incurring the wrath from the federal government, Father took my mother to live on the prairie 50 miles from Short Crick, Arizona, where he had squatter rights on a 180-acre mining claim. Father had hired a man with a truck to bring lumber and building materials along with water, and food supplies. Each month Father would walk the 50 miles to Short Crick, more commonly known now as Colorado City, to pick up his government check as he had served in the Army in WW1 as a Post Chaplin. A bullet had grazed his skull leaving him with the necessity of having a steel plate in his head. The money he received monthly along with what he could earn by chopping wood, planting gardens, and repairing things for the folks in town would be used for supplies, including cement for laying a concrete bottom for a water reservoir. The water would run in to form a little pond when it rained so they could catch it for drinking and cooking, but not for bathing. That luxury was when there came a down pour. However, through his continual trips, he built a one room house for Mother where she raised four children. Water, however, was always a problem. During one particularly dry spell, Mother worriedly discussed the situation with my father.

"Hon, what are we going to do? We are almost out of water. It hasn't rained for almost two weeks."

"The Lord will provide," he said. "Why don't you pray about it?"

There were no clouds in the sky.

She prayed, "Oh, God, our Eternal Father. Please look down upon us as we are out here on this desert trying to serve you the best we can. We have no more water. Would you let rain come? In the name of Jesus Christ, Amen."

Half an hour passed. There came a cloud just over their land. It rained just long enough to water the garden and replenish the reservoir, thus keeping their little family alive and well. However, on another dry spell Mr. Eaton, a sheepherder in the area came upon an old water hole that was green and stagnant. A dead coyote lay on the one edge while my father and Joe Jr. was on the other side. In desperation Daddy was kneeling down trying to strain water and fill a little flask hoping to boil it to kill the deadly bacteria. Mr. Eaton came the next day with 4 barrels of water. Daddy was so thankful for this delivery he wanted to pay him. But Mr. Eaton refused. During those years, they had been studying the literature put out by the different fundamentalist groups, mainly the books called truth put out by Joseph White Musser, embellishing and encouraging men to in-delve into what Joseph Smith taught in secret meetings. Proof is the volumes of the History of the Church put out in the 1800's, so in their minds they were the real Mormons.

After reading the news of the month, Mother said, "What in the world is the matter with Heber J. Grant saying he hopes the polygamists get the full extent of the law, then he's caught having a second wife on the side? Why, I'd just like to write him a letter and tell him what I think of him."

"Well, why don't you do it then?"

"Ok I will." So, she sat down and wrote him a long letter telling him what a hypocrite he was. "There. It's finished. Will you mail it?"

"I sure will. But I don't know if it will do him any good."

"I don't know if it will either, but I sure feel a lot better now. He needs to be told."

That is how strongly they believed in what they were doing. See, the polygamist leaders try to justify their actions by saying polygamy is in the Bible. Yes, it is right along with adultery, child molesting, rape, and murder. The Bible has it all, but it does not make it right, but back to their story.

Far away from the rule of the Church, they believed it was better to live in the desert than in town, although Father owned a house with water and one and one-half acres in Murray, Utah. He had kept this information secret from Mother, but near the end of a long illness during which he had progressively grown worse, he called her to his bedside late one afternoon.

"My mission on earth is not finished so If I die. I hope God will let me return within three days. But if I do not resurrect, then I want you to move to a house in Murray, Utah. Here is the deed and all the information you'll need to be able to find it. The Veterans check will be of support to you and the children. Without me there, the law will give you no trouble with our religion but I want you to promise me something—that you won't surrender so much as your little finger to anything except the teachings of Joseph White Musser." (This is Guy Musser's father.)

Mother knelt beside his bed and prayed that he would be healed, but her prayers were not answered. Father passed away three days later, just one week before I was born.

Pregnant, Mother worked with the help of her four children Joe Jr. the oldest, then Sarah, Ester, Haisa ages 9 to 4, to bury father and prepare herself for my birth. At four o'clock in the morning, May 10, 1948, by the light of kerosene lanterns and the help of her four children, Mother gave birth to her baby. Mother's heart filled with sorrow from her loss of Daddy and filled with joy from her giving birth. I was welcomed into this world into loving arms. But destitute for water, Mother had no milk for me. My brother Joe milked a goat that had just had kids, and that kept me alive. Now think about this, if you can imagine, NO car, NO horses, NO phone or any other means of transportation or communication. Father was the family's only link to the outside world, no one else could walk that distance, and Mother refused to think that God would leave us out there to parish. She was praying and taught all of the children to pray. And told them to keep praying. All while listening to the wolves and coyotes howling off in the distance every night, waiting for something to die, or an easy kill, so they eat and drink. So, Mother did the unthinkable, she went out and began removing the maggots from Daddy's dead body every day, praying that he would resurrect. Joe Jr. helped. He wanted to believe Mother that Daddy could return, but as the stench became beyond bearable, on the third day Mother gave Joe Jr. permission to bury his father the best he could. Joe had a hard time believing in anything that Mother would tell him after that horrible traumatic experience.

Three weeks after Daddy's death a figure darkened the doorway. Mother, delirious from thrush cried out "Hon is that you?"

"No mam its Mr. Eaton."

"Mr. Eaton?"

"Yes Kelly Eaton"

"Oh, thank God."

Then as she moved into the light, he could see her face. Her lips were so dry that they had turned inside out. Sarah later described this as so traumatic, being extremely thirsty day after day. God had answered Mother's prayers. He came just in time to save all six of us from certain death. Mother asked if he would help move us to the home in Murry. He said he would. Mr. Eaton brought Mrs. Eaton out to help with the rescue. They brought food and water not only to drink but to also bath the children. She removed the old Army shirts they were dressed in they then were given clothes. Years later Mother told me that I was wrapped in an old piece of holey Army canvas and my cradle was an empty gun powder wood box.

Then while loading he asked "What of this is junk and what isn't?

Mother laughed.

"I mean what do you want loaded and what is to be left here?"

Everyone was happy, and Mother then prayed over Father's grave that God would protect it from being ravaged by the wild animals.

Mother asked "Can you come back and haul the goats to Murry also?"

He answered "No, it is all I can do to rescue you from this God forsaken place."

Mother hoped that some of the Krikers would come and get the goats to save them from coyotes.

Mother settled with her little family at 4255 South 500 East, near other polygamists in the area—the Kunz's, Kelches, and the Zittings. When the Veterans check came in, we all went with Mother to town to buy groceries. At three, my little legs would get so tired. Mother and Sarah would take turns carrying me on their backs. Then Mother would hire a taxi to bring us and the groceries home.

We became acquainted with families in the area and associated especially with Charles Zitting and his wife, Francis, and their ten children. They had a large old home approximately a block and a half away from where we lived.

One afternoon when Charles was taking his children on an outing, we straggly little Hancock kids were there wishing we could go, but did not say much, because

ESCAPE PRISONS OF THE MIND

his car was already loaded with his own kids. He came out to drive away and saw us standing there.

A big smile came upon his face. "Well, come on and get in."

We made a dash to squeeze in somehow. I heard him laughing as he said, "There's always room for one more even if I have to part my hair and take off my shoes."

I wound up somewhere near the floor in the middle. Looking up, I could see a few small patches of light.

Charles's children and Mother's children would play together nearly every day. I could always be found following the bunch of kids searching through VaNoy's pasture with our noses downward. After rainstorms we looked for mushrooms. "I found one, I found one," I exclaimed. We would look some more then Charles's daughter, Lucy, would shout, "I found one and there's another one," as we both dashed for it. "Hey, there's another one." We walked along.

"What are you going to do with yours?" Lucy asked.

"I don't know. Sumpin'. Watcha' gonna do?"

"I'm giving mine to Daddy."

"How come?"

We stopped and she looked as though this was an important mission, "My daddy just loves mushrooms and my daddy is in the Priesthood Council."

"Hum." We kept looking. I was thinking to myself, Golly, I sure wish I had a daddy.

When we got back to her house with our goodies, she ran to her father who was by the barn door. "Daddy, daddy. I found you some mushrooms."

He picked her up and gave her a kiss. "You sweet little thing. Thank you so much."

As I watched I felt so selfish and worthless with my little bag. As he walked towards the house, I got up enough nerve to look up at him as he was passing. I held out my little bag and asked, "Would you want these too?"

He said, "Why, thank you." And a smile broke across my face. Then we scurried off to a nearby creek to play in the water.

One day Mama was over at Charles's with her wheelbarrow. Francis said that Mom could have the pears on the ground. I was eating some when Charles came home.

He got out of his car and waved, "Hello, Mrs. Hancock," as he came over shaking her hand.

Mom said, "I sure appreciate these pears you're letting me have."

"Oh, you're welcome." Then looking into the wheelbarrow, he said, "Those don't look too hot." He dumped out the wheelbarrow. "Let's get you some good ones." He began to pick the fruit off the tree.

"My, that's sure nice of you," Mom said. "Are you sure you have enough for your big family too?"

"Oh, yes. The Lord will provide. We will be OK."

I took some good ones. "Gee thanks, Mr. Zitting."

"You're welcome, little lady. Mrs. Hancock, what are you going to have for Thanksgiving?"

"Uh well, I don't know," Mom replied while scratching her head and looking into the distance. "Let's see. I've got some chickens we could have." She stopped talking, as though in deep thought.

"I have a splendid idea," he said. "Why don't you bring your little bunch down here for Thanksgiving and eat with my family?"

Mom smiled, "You really mean that?"

"I certainly do."

"But you have so many to feed already."

"Nonsense. Don't you worry about a thing. I want you to know, Mrs. Hancock, that you and your little bunch are always welcome at my table."

Tears came to Mama's eyes as she said, "We love you too, Charles. Thank you very much."

He hugged Mom for a few seconds, then he said, "Let's load this little wheelbarrow," as he continued to pick.

We were soon on our way home.

Mama said, "Imagine that. He already has I don't know how many to feed, but it's quite a few, he's got Bonnie and her ten children, and Edna and he don't say how many others. We don't even know how many children he has."

"He sure is a good man to take care of so many,"

As we walked further, Mom said, "And he helps Delone and Doris too, because they don't have any husband, and all their children.

"Mom, how come you can't marry him so I can have a daddy?"

"You just pipe down and never mind, just never mind."

While I was skipping, my little heart was happy.

Mama took her family to the meetings whenever they were held, sometimes in one home, sometimes in another. I would look at the brethren who were talking but did not understand them much until I would get really tired and fall asleep on Mama's lap. Mom would try to get Joe to attend the meeting but he refused. He would say things like "To hell with all their bull shit, I don't believe a damn thing they say."

Mother tried to raise a garden but Mr. Wright's pig would get loose, and come over and up root and eat everything. Mother Told Mr. Wright to keep his pig home. He did not, so after the pig came destroying her garden for the fourth time, she killed it cleaned it and we ate pork instead of vegetables. Then when Mr. Wright found out what happened to his little piggy he was cussing and called Mother 'ole lady screwball.'

Sarah had a baby-sitting job, and one sunny day we walked over to a hot dog stand and she bought one for me. I would always remember her and that simple act of kindness.

Winter came and with it all this talk of Santa Claus. I was wondering if we were going to get candy, or would I get an onion or a lump of coal in my sock, because Joe and Sarah had been teasing me. I was so hoping for a coloring book and crayons. I loved to draw and was in total awe as I looked at the artist images in the Bible and would spend hours trying to understand the story by seeing the images. On Christmas Eve I heard singing outside our house and I jumped up and looked out the window. There were the boys and girls from the high school in Sarah's classroom with the snow coming down on their faces, singing Christmas carols sounding like heavenly angels. I was delighted when the door opened and in came Santa, "Ho, ho, ho!" Mama was laughing. He picked me up and put me on his knee. I sat there looking at him like his face looked so familiar, but the white fuzzy thing hanging down made it hard to recognize who he was. So, I pulled it down. "Oh! It's Mr. Wright!" His face went red. I began crying out loud. But when he left, he had given me candy, nuts, a ball and jacks, a jump rope, a doll, and some crayons with a coloring book.

On Christmas Day I headed down to the Zittings to see what Lucy and Irene got. We were in the front room playing with the toys that Sub for Santa had brought them when the outside door to the kitchen opened and there stood Francis in her white uniform and coat. Our attention was immediately turned to a loud voice that nearly shook the house.

"All right, you kids. You either shut up or get outside. Do you hear me? I've been working all night and I'm tired."

I put my coat on, chucked my crayons in the box, and took off running, about a block and a half away through the snow. I was so glad to get home. When in the house, Mama was in the kitchen where the oven door was open and her back turned to the heat.

"Oh, Mama. I'm sooo cold."

"I'll get ya warm," she smiled as she opened up her hands for me to put my small hands into hers."

"Uh, that feels good."

We stood there for a moment.

"Let's get a chair over here," she said. Then she sat down and I sat on her lap. Mama put her arms around me. I folded my hands and wedged them between our bodies soaking up her warmth.

In wonderment I asked, "Does it cost lotsa money to buy toys 'n stuff?"

While rocking me back and forth with my feet towards the oven door, she said, "Yes. I think so."

"How did they get the money?"

"Do you want to know? It wasn't money, I mean it was really cute. Sarah took a can of beans to school for an assignment to help out a needy family and come to find out all the things in the box that the boys and girls brought were from her classroom. Each student brought something. Sarah was amongst the children singing." Mom's voice choked up as she continued, "And the neighbors gave you children the toys you've got."

I sat there for some time in silence as my little mind was trying to comprehend what she had said. Then I asked, "Mama, how do people get money?"

"Well, there are different ways. Like some people work so they can get a little money. And sometimes a person has something they can sell. Like my father, your grandfather had a farm and he would raise sugar beets to sell. Now us, we don't have too much to sell, but if we had more chickens, we could sell eggs. People would buy them."

I was trying to think of what we might have we could sell. The thought occurred to me the only thing Mama had was a bunch of kids. A strange feeling came over me and I asked, "If someone had lotsa money and wanted to buy me, would you sell me to them?"

"Sell you? Why, I should say not. You are more precious than any amount of money."

"Even a million dollars?" I asked.

"I should say so. You're more precious than two million," she smiled.

"Well, what about three million?"

She laughed, "Oh you're funny. Do you think I would sell my baby? Why, there is no amount I would take for you."

I was feeling so happy. I just kinda' needed to hear it.

Then she went on, "When you were born just after your father passed away, you were like a little ray of sun coming through dark clouds and I have cherished you ever since. Would you like me to tell you a story?"

"Uh huh."

"There was a wealthy woman who couldn't have children and she asked me, 'Mrs. Hancock, you have so many children, and I can't have any. Do you think you would be willing to give me that little girl?' That was you. 'I would take real good care of her,' she said. 'Why I should say not, I told her. She wanted you so bad and I told her, 'Give up my baby? I would never give up my baby.'"

Still sitting on Mother's lap, laying my head on her bosom, I looked up at Mama's smiling face. "I love you. I'm glad that you didn't give me away because I want you for my mama."

Sarah and Ester and the Zitting girls would have what they called a slumber party and would sleep at our house. They were telling stories one night as I sat up listening. The one story was called "The Little Match Girl," a story about a girl whose mother was very sick and they had no money for food, so the little girl would go out in the ice and snow to stand on a street corner all day to sell enough matches to maybe get only two or three cents. As the story went on to about the end of it, I cried, "Does anybody know where they are 'cause we could take them some potatoes." Tears of sorrow were streaming down my face. Sarah laughed as she looked at me and said, "Poor little wire head" (that was her nickname for me) "You would believe anything. It's just a story."

"What do ya mean?"

"Well, somebody made it up. There ain't no little match girl freezing on a street corner."

"Oh," I sighed.

She finished the story and I was sure thankful that we were not that poor.

Winter and Spring passed and Summer brought with it a day that even the small children would remember. Mother was busy making bread when the door flew open. It was Louie, Charles's boy, panting as he got the words out, "Daddy died."

Mama wiped the bread dough off onto her apron. "Oh, no!" she exclaimed as she began to cry. "Is this true?"

"Yes, it is," he cried as we left the house, walking and running as fast as we could, the clouds blackening the sky and the air thundering. We arrived at Zittings only to see confusion and grief everywhere. Mama went to Francis crying. She put her arm around her while they wept together.

Laurie was bawling and her sisters were trying to comfort her and control their own emotions at the same time by saying, "Honey, Daddy's gone to heaven. He's happy now 'cause he's with Heavenly Father."

Her tears of grief continued to flow along with theirs. I knelt down in some weeds watching everyone.

I cried, as I thought, What does this mean? He died? What does it mean? It was like they were implying that we would not see him again. I had not known anyone who had died before that time. I was six years old.

There were quite a few people coming and going. We stayed until after dark then Mom and I walked home. That night after supper I shook Mom's arm to get her attention.

"What does it mean? Charles died. Huh?"

Sarah had fixed some potatoes and gravy, but no one seemed very hungry. Mama pushed her tin plate out in front of her as she rested her head in her hands. She sat in silence for some time. I ate some potatoes then stopped, looked at Mom and asked,

"Ya goin' to tell me? What happened?" as I clung to her arm.

She turned to me and said, "I need to take you children to meeting so you could learn all these things."

"Can't you just tell me, Mom? I got to know."

"Well, his spirit left his body because God wanted him on the other side."

"What's a spirit?"

"Your spirit is what helps you think and move so you can do things. Everyone that's living has a spirit, and if you follow the priesthood's teachings, like Charles did, his spirit is in heaven."

"You mean someday I'm gonna die, too?"

"Yes, everyone has to die."

My mind was thinking about our collie dog that got hit by a car and Joe dug a hole and put the dog in it and covered it over.

I asked, "Are they going to put Charles in a dirt hole?"

"Yes, they will bury his body."

"Oh, but it's dark in the ground."

"He won't see the dark ground because he has gone where it is light and beautiful, where there's pretty grass and sunshine where Heavenly Father lives. That's where your father is and maybe Charles and your father are friends, like you and Lucy are friends. I showed you the picture of your father, haven't I?"

"Uh huh. I want to see it again."

We went to find her Book of Remembrance. In Mom's bedroom we sat on the bed. While I was looking at Father's picture for the longest time, Mom said, "I hope they do meet up there. Your father was a good man, but Charles could teach him a lot about the Gospel." Mom was still crying. "If you be a good girl and me too, I've got to do good also so we can go to heaven, we will see Uncle Charles and your daddy again."

After thinking a while I said, "I hope God don't take you to heaven and leave me here alone with no mama."

I felt that would be more than I could stand.

Mama took me with her to the funeral. I looked out over the steps and could see people standing all up and down the stairs along the street in the parking lot when they began his funeral. They said it was one of the largest funerals that Larkin Mortuary ever had. We were standing until a man got up and gave Mother his seat. I squeezed in next to her for a little spot of the bench. We were so far back we could hear very little, almost like the people in the parking lot. They could not hear anything either but they stayed there to show reverence.

For weeks after that I would go to Zittings to play with Lucy and Irene. This one day we were playing outside when Francis hollered to Lucille,

"Can you come in for a minute?"

She did. then when she came out, she asked Irene to go in the house. I asked "What did your mother want?" "Oh she just wanted me to eat." I learned that day everyone was not like Mother who would share with any child at our house whatever she had. Even at that age. I was kinda a tuff kid. My attitude was, Fine, if you don't want to feed me. I don't want to be fed.

I got up and went home, I said to Mother. "I am so hungry I think I am going to die."

"Well come on, I'll fry you some potatoes." I stood on a chair, stabbing each piece as it got a little brown on the edges. Soon after that I did not see Irene or Lucy. I was told that they went to live with their sister while another said they went to live with Aunt Edna, one of their other mothers.

I ended up playing by myself. Through the summer months I often went to Pills Pond to catch polliwogs or water skeeters, along with climbing trees, going through fences, or chasing butterflies so I could see how pretty they were when they landed. I was in the field one afternoon when I heard mother calling me.

"Kaziah, oh, Kaziah May."

The echo was sweet on my ears. It sounded just like the voice of an angel calling me, and I went running happily to meet her.

When she saw me, she laughed, "Ho, ho, ho. You look funny."

I looked at myself. I had mud here and there and everywhere. Then I exclaimed, "Look what I found!"

"Uh huh. If we had 20 acres and one mud hole, you'd find it. It's time to come in and have some supper before the others eat it all."

I passed by the table. "Mmm. Bread and beans."

After half washing, I sat down thinking, Boy this is really nice of Mama to have this fixed tonight. It's so good.

Several months after the death of Charles, an Elder named Walt came to our house. Mother said he was sent to help us learn the Gospel. He had a car that looked like a big black stink bug. Anyway, we could all fit into it. So, on Sunday he took us to meeting held by the fundamentalist brethren in a small white house. We went into the living room and sat down. No sooner did a man get up to speak than I fell asleep leaning over on Mama. When it was over and we were on our way home, Mom and Haisa were up front while Sarah, Ester and I were in back.

As I sat there the two girls began talking over me.

Sarah said, "Did you hear that one guy say we're not supposed to cut our hair?"

"Yeah, and you're not supposed to wear lipstick."

Sarah thought for a while. "I wonder if makeup is ok to cover my freckles?"

"I don't know, but we can't wear fingernail polish anymore."

"I don't care. My bottle's empty anyway."

"What about not wearing short sleeved dresses or short skirts?"

Sarah shook her head, "I don't have any short skirts anyway."

"Yeah, but what are you going to do with that purple and white blouse? It's got short sleeves."

After a while Sarah replied, "I just won't wear it to meeting. That's all." Walt turned the car into a Dairy Queen. His deep voice asked, "Would you girls like some ice cream?"

"Oh, yes!" I jumped up and looked over the seat, as a happy little thrill came over me. "Mmm, ice cream. Uh, can we have some root beer, too?"

"Let's see how much money I've got." Walt was digging into a little black purse. Moving his coins back and forth, he ordered six ice cream cones and six small root beers.

"Oh, for good."

Mama laughed. "Thank you, Walt."

He nodded as if to say, "You're welcome."

As we were licking our cones, we all thanked him.

When school started again, Mama seemed more concerned with just having clothes for us rather than if they were short or long sleeved or not. Being the youngest, it seemed I would always fall heir to the other children's clothes, even Joe's T-shirts Mama put on me. My appearance left much to be desired. The dress I had was somewhat long for me, but the worst part seemed to be the T-shirt sleeves protruded underneath the sleeves of my dress coming nearly to my elbows. The other children, mainly boys, would make fun of me while I sat there and would sweat.

One day a boy called me "little witchy." I wished that Mama could find a dress that actually fit me, one with long sleeves so the T-shirt sleeves would not show. And long enough, too.

One day Haisa put her slip on me, then pinned up the straps as high as she could but it was still quite long. And with Sarah doing my hair, I was quite content. She took an interest in me most of the time, and sometimes we would skip school together.

One day Sarah said, "Kaziah May, how about skipping school with me today?"

"No, I want to go to school."

"Oh, please."

"Nope."

"I won't do your hair then."

"OK. I'll just do it myself then." So I went into the bathroom and put some water on my hair and pushed it up a little in front as an attempt to make waves, then I stuck bobby pins in it and just let the rest go. When I got to school, the teacher said, "We are going to have our pictures taken today."

Oh, no! I thought. I should have skipped. Now what? As I sat there so self-conscious, the time got closer and I was just hoping the teacher would see my predicament and take care of the situation. But she did not. Oh dear, they took my picture.

When Spring came, I turned eight. There was a lot of hurrying around the house the day I was to be baptized. They borrowed a white dress from one of the neighbors that was really big on me and Sarah handed me some white socks and said, "Put these on." Then I put on my holey canvas shoes that once were white.

We all got in Walt's car and went up in the canyon to a little creek that ran next to Edna Zittings house, one of Charles's wives. There was an Elder there to baptize me. When we got out, he came over smiling and said, "How are you, young lady? Do you know what this is about?"

"Uh, you're gonna put me in that water."

"Yes, and do you know why I'm going to put you in that water?"

"So when I die, I can go to heaven."

He said, "I think we need to explain."

Then Walt and Mama started talking to him as I stood there listening, first to one and then to the other, and thinking to myself, This means I can't swipe candy anymore or it will go on my record in heaven instead of Mama's.

Then the Elder said to me again, "Do you understand now?"

I nodded my head. "Uh huh."

Then we walked out into the water where he baptized me. I had looked forward to this day since I was seven. Then all the way home, shivering with a blanket wrapped around me, I was thinking to myself, Now I hadn't better do anything wrong or it will be just terrible.

The 24th of July was coming and Walt said that there was going to be a celebration in Short Crick. I jumped with excitement. "Do we get to go?"

"Oh, that would be nice to go down there and see the old place again," Mama added.

Walt was chuckling. "There's a dance there Saturday night you might want to go to."

Mom acted like she could hardly wait. "OK, Walt. You said that. Now, I'm going to take you up on it."

"When are we going to leave?" Ester asked.

"Well, I don't like driving at night so let's leave tomorrow morning early about 8 o'clock. I'll be here to load up."

"Oh, goodie." I was dancing around. Everyone was happy except Rod. He was standing by the stove looking at the floor. I asked him, "You comin' too?"

He shook his head. "No, I've seen enough of those damn hills."

Joe did have a job feeding VaNoys cattle, shoveling manure, cleaning corrals. He bought tools and a book called "Popular Mechanics" that taught him how to build and repair things along with lumber for building himself his living quarters. The little cabin was twelve by twenty feet, and an old potbelly stove kept it warm. Then he bought an old model-T Ford for fourteen dollars. He laid a blanket on the ground to overhaul the motor. Then when it was running, he would take us places. He even gave Mom enough money to buy me and Haisa new dresses.

Sarah also had jobs baby-sitting, she would buy material and make me and Haisa dresses, so when we went to Short Crick, we were dressed nice.

Morning came and the joy of contemplation was so great that I could hardly sit still for Sarah to do my hair. Then we were on our way. How I enjoyed the scenery in southern Utah. As we got towards Arizona, I kept seeing chipmunks cross the road and run in the sagebrush. It was a bright summer day.

"Can you stop? I want to catch one of those chipmunks."

"No, we got to get there and see where we are going to stay for the night."

As we arrived in Arizona, there were big red hills and mountains. Oh, I could hardly wait for Walt to stop the car.

"Can we go mountain climbing?"

"Well, if we go, we've got to go together so you don't get lost," someone said.

Walt stopped by a house where he went inside. He came out and said to Mother, "There's a little house that's empty over here they said you could stay in."

Then he drove to the house. The little house had a pot belly stove and a bedstead with coil springs, but no mattress. We had brought blankets thinking we might have to sleep on the ground. Mama made the bed for herself and us girls. Walt slept in his car.

The next day we girls went mountain climbing to our hearts' content. When we came home in the afternoon, we washed up in a pan of water so we could change to our better clothes for the dance. That night it seemed so cute to watch Mom and Walt dance. No one would ask me to dance, so I asked Mama to dance with me and she turned to Walt and said, "You dance with her, will you?" So I danced with Walt one time. But the Virginia Reel looked fun and I did not really need a partner, so I got in on that, too.

The next day they held a meeting and the celebration after the meeting. There were long tables with watermelons. Somebody said they had bought a whole truckload. There were several people cutting them as quick as kids would come and take the pieces away. I spotted Lucy. "Hey," I hollered. "There's Lucy Charlotte, Irene." I took off towards them. "Hi, you guys," I hollered out as I came bounding towards them.

"How did you get down here?" Irene asked.

"Walt brought us. How come you're here?"

"We've been staying here for a while."

"How come you don't live at home anymore?"

"Cause there's this guy there and he's really mean to us. Mama let him stay there after Daddy died."

"He would make me do all the dishes," Irene commented.

"He's not like our daddy and I don't like him," came from Lucy.

"Nobody likes him. I don't want to live in the house with him there. I think he stinks." Irene looked so serious.

"He does stink," Lucy added. "Oh, oh. There he is."

"Where?"

"Over there standing by that lady in the blue dress."

"You mean that short guy?"

"No, the one in back of him. The tall man in the white shirt."

"Oh, what's his name?"

Reed Stratton. But we call him Stinky Reed."

"How about stink bug?"

"Yeah."

We laughed as I threw my watermelon rind into the weeds. I went for another piece. I was closer to Reed and looked at him and thought, "Ugh, don't get too close to him."

I got my melon and returned.

We walked on to find Mama. Mama exclaimed with joy, "Oh, there's Charlotte, Irene and Lucy! Where's Francis"

"She's over there with Reed."

"Reed who?"

"Reed Stratton."

"Did she remarry?"

"I don't know, but I don't like him. He's not my father," Lucy cried with disgust.

The subject was soon changed as we continued to enjoy the celebration. Most of the people we had seen in meetings were down there and Mama was shaking hands and kissing and hugging women she said were Charles's other wives, Edna, Elvera and Bonnie, along with many other people Mama knew. Mama went over to talk with Francis, but I went off with my friends.

A few months later after we had returned to Murray, Francis came to visit Mama. She brought Reed with her. They talked for a while then Reed said he could get Joe a job.

"What doing?" Joe asked.

"I could get you a job nailing chests of drawers together."

"You'd like that," Mom said with excitement.

She turned to Reed. "He's a good carpenter. And he's really smart. He was able to build that little house where he has his own living space and he made these tables and benches. I think he would like that kind of work."

"Maybe I'll like it. Maybe I won't. Joe mumbled. "When do you want me to start work?"

"I don't know yet. I'll talk to the boss and let you know."

So Joe went to work within the week. But it was extremely aggravating to him when his boss gave him a check and it bounced. He paid him once a month and for three months straight, his check bounced. Joe was mad as hell.

Then Reed and Joe went to work for another boss. Joe came home and gave Mother his check to buy groceries at the store. Mama piled high two big carts full of groceries. When we went to the check stand, the man called the bank on the check and said to Mama, "I'm sorry, Lady, but this check is no good."

We walked home with our tongues nearly hanging to the ground. When Joe found out, he slammed the door and later returned with a huge bottle of beer.

Mama said, "Now, Joe. You can't drink that in this house. This is a dedicated home."

He was laughing, "Who gives a shit. The only thing keeping it together is the termites holding hands."

Mama called up Walt and Francis. Within a short time, Walt arrived with Francis and Reed. It was late afternoon. Joe was sitting in the big chair smoking one after the other in the front room. I was watching from just around the corner of the doorway from the kitchen.

Reed came in and said, "I'll handle him. Joe," Reed hollered, "you take your stuff outside.

Not budging an inch, Joe replied, "Mind your own damn business. This is my home."

Walt chipped in, "You don't have the right to desecrate this house. Now, you just get up quietly and go outside."

Reed yelled, at Joe "STRAIGHTEN UP!! OR GET OUT."

Joe came out of the chair, "FUCK YOU. You set me up at that damn place knowing the bastard would give me bum checks. Or maybe you got the money for my work!" "No, I didn't. I didn't even get paid. He owes me for seven months."

"That other son of a bitch is another fuckin crook. Maybe you got paid for my work on that job too."

Walt hollered, "Your filthy mouth isn't going to get you paid any quicker." The thing is that Francis was the secretary working for Joe's Boss Micolas, so who knows if the bad checks were on purpose.

Joe grabbed at Reed's shirt and said, "This bastard had better get my money for me or I'll kill him."

This was curious because The Brethren expected young boys to work for them for nothing, and if they were not willing, they were kicked out of the group. Like the LOST BOYS OF SHORT CRICK. Joe strutted out slamming the door which shook the whole house.

Mama said to Reed, "Golly, I'm sorry for the way he treated you. He just needs to cool off and get over this thing."

Reed hollered at Mama, "Get over it? Hell, your son's insane. He needs to be behind bars."

"I don't know," Mama said. "I've never seen him this bad before."

"Well, he's just getting older now to where you nor anyone else can handle him," Walt declared.

Reed Hollered, "He is the results of your committing adultery on the prairie. Your sin is why you have produced a child of the devil."

"I resent that. We did not commit adultery. We signed a marriage covenant."

"That is no more a marriage than a couple of cat or dogs shackin' up. GOD DOES NOT honor that!"

A few more weeks passed by. Joe, being resourceful would go pull nails, and clean old brick at sights where homes were being demolished. He had a large pile of clean bricks. But one day someone offered Mom twenty dollars for the whole pile. Mom sold them without Joe's knowledge or consent.

When He came home, he demanded "Give me the twenty bucks!"

"I bought groceries already."

Joe looked in the fridge, and yelled "Goddamn it, more of the same shit." He stormed out mad again.

But other times he would enter the house in a good mood. He would turn on the radio then him and I would dance to music like The Old Irishman Shanty song.

He taught me how to yodel, and it was so fun.

When suppertime came, Mama would holler "Supper's ready." Joe would throw open the door. We had potatoes and flour gravy, fried onions and whole wheat bread with lard spread on it, seasoned with salt and pepper.

Joe looked at the table and asked "Is there anything besides pig slop?"

Mama answered in an indignant tone, "That's not a bit cute. If you don't want to eat, you don't have to."

Joe laughed and walked off without eating, mumbling curses over the meal we had just asked God to bless.

Joe had also worked as a dish washer for Harmons Kentucky Fried chicken restaurant on State Street in Murry, so he could eat pretty good meals.

Mama sighed "I don't know what's the matter with him. He didn't used to be that way."

A few nights later Joe came home drinking beer. The police must have followed him. As Mama was out talking to the police, they said they were going to put Joe in jail for a week for stealing cigarettes. Mama cried and asked them not to but they took him away.

Later when they let him out, Reed, Francis and Walt were there when Joe came home.

Joe walked in the door and said to Mama, "Why do you let these sons of bitches come here? They're the cause of all our problems."

Reed said, "You cause your own problems, Joe."

Joe went into the kitchen, then after a while he came out with a cup of sugar. He was laughing a little bit as he went outside. I went outside and seen him. Put the sugar in Reed's gas tank. He walked away laughing.

I had no idea what that was about until about a week later a hard, rapid knock came on the door then Reed burst in with a red face seething with anger. "Where's Joe?" he demanded.

"I don't really know." Mom replied.

He stomped over to Joe's house. Banging on the door then he resorted to kicking. "I know you're in there. Damn you, come out and face me like a man,"

"What's the problem?" Mama rushed over.

Pushing Mama back, "Just stay out of this, if he can play a man's game, he can take a man's punishment," Reed continued to wham at the door with his foot.

"What on earth did he do?"

"He put sugar in my gas tank."

"Joe wouldn't do a thing like that, I don't think. Would he?"

Francis had been standing near the corner of the house, obviously not wanting to get too close. Now she came butting in, "That's what's the matter with you, Edith. You've stuck up for your damn kids come hell or high water. They never can do anything wrong in your sight."

"I didn't say he never does anything wrong. But what makes you think he did that?"

"Joe's a maniac," Reed hollered. "He knows what sugar would do. Who else would? Or did you do it?"

"No of course not. Who ever heard of such a thing?" Mama was scratching her head as though bewildered.

Walt came home from his Watkins route.

"What can I do to help the boy?" Mother asked.

"Help him?" Reed sarcastically remarked. "I'm the one who needs help." He held out his hand. "Have you got $200 to help me get a new motor?"

"Two hundred dollars?" gasped Mother.

"Yes, $200. How would you like to come up with it like I have to just because of your damn boy," Francis snarled.

"Well, I've tried to raise him right, but he just won't listen to me." Mother braced herself against an old tool box.

Reed was leaning over her, "The time you should have gained control is at six years old, and if you can't gain control over a child at that age, you've lost 'em. If

I had that boy living with me, I'd make a man out of him. Maybe you wouldn't approve of my methods, but he'd know who was boss or else."

"Well, you act just like you'd like to kill him."

"Naw. I wouldn't kill him, but he might wish he were dead a few times before I'd be through."

Walt pointed at mother, "You have to admit, Edith. It would take far more force than you could give him for him to ever straighten up."

It was getting dark and the sun was setting. Just then the door opened and Joe came out smoking a cigarette. He stood there, looking at everyone.

Mom quickly exclaimed, "I don't know where you get that nasty habit from. The priesthood doesn't teach you that."

"Who gives a shit? That's your religion, not mine." As Joe strutted by Reed. blowing smoke in his face on his way to the house.

Reed was watching like an animal getting ready to attack his prey. He followed Joe. My heart beating fast, I hid behind the piano. Reed lunged to get Joe in a choke hold. At that, Joe hit Reed, knocking him to the floor, where he spit up three bottom teeth.

Reed hollered "YOU WILL PAY FOR THIS."

I ran to the bathroom and went out the window to the chicken coop away from the house. I could hear loud voices for some time, then someone ripped the curtains down. I could hear Mama's voice yelling and I just hoped nothing would happen to hurt her.

A chair came hurdling out the window, shattering the wooden section between the windows.

"Haisa! Haisa!" I was calling for my sister. "Let's get out of here before Joe kills somebody. Come on! Let's go!" I was crying while pulling on her arm to come.

We took off without a coat or anything except the clothes on our back. Down the street we went as hard as we could go. We wanted to use the phone near a store to call the man who baptized me. But someone called the police on us. We stayed shivering in a phone booth trying to figure out how to make it work without money when a police car showed up. Cold, tried, and confused, we were huddled together near the floor to try to keep each other warm.

The policeman took us to a detention home for runaways. But back at the house, Joe was picked up by the police and charged with assault. And in his absence, Reed and Walt leaned heavy on Mother.

Reed told her "The damn kid needs to be committed in the mental institution."

And Mother said, "But he's not nuts."

Walt said "That's what you say. No normal kid would act the way he does."

Reed said "YOU BETTER MAKE UP YOUR MIND, EDITH. IT IS EITHER HIM OR US! If you want your damn boy. WE will leave and wash the dust off our feet as a testimony against you and your family. And you will be turned over to the buffetings of Satan."

"Oh no I don't ever want that to happen."

Then you had better do as we tell you. And have him committed before he kills someone."

Mother was like a person without guile. never thinking anything bad about anyone. She could not see the wolves in sheep's clothing. hovering over her. She caved and my dear brother was committed into the Prove Mental Institution. This was in 1957.

Haisa and I want into a series of foster homes, one after another, for about three months. I rather enjoyed them. At the last home we were there for approximately seven months. It was a place that had ten children. I enjoyed the company. I adjusted to the home life learning all the little chores they deemed as my share. I had no complaints. The girl Martha was my age. She thought James Garner was handsome. I liked Perry Mason but we both agreed upon the Beach Boys and we both liked to draw pictures of the different characters.

Mama came to visit one day.

Mrs. Florence called, "May, there's someone here to see you."

I came in. "Mama!" I ran to hug her.

She was laughing with tears in her eyes. "Oh, it's good to see you."

"Carol went to Mutual. She'll be home shortly."

(We had changed our names from Haisa to Carol and from Kaziah to May.)

"Could I get you something to eat, Mrs. Hancock?" Mrs. Florence asked.

"Oh, you don't need to do that," Mama paused, "unless you really want to."

"I'd be glad to."

"That's very nice of you."

Mama and I sat on the couch. "How you doing, Mom?"

"Oh, I'm just plugging away. How's my sweet, precious daughter?" Mama pulled me to her and kissed me on the forehead. I was enjoying Mama's hug.

"Just fine. Hey," I asked with excitement. "You want to come up and see all my nice clothes?" I jumped up as if to lead her to my room. "I've learned to do my hair, too."

I turned around slowly in front of her feeling proud while flipping my ponytail. Mom laughed.

Mrs. Florence came in carrying a plate. "Here you are Mrs. Hancock. I hope you like this. It's fresh from our garden."

"Whole wheat bread and fresh tomatoes? I sure do. Thank you very kindly."

"You're welcome." Mrs. Florence left the room.

"Well, it sounds like you're getting good care here anyway."

"Yeah, it's OK. I'm gonna get some of my art work I been doing." I quickly went up to my room and sorted through my stuff and took some pictures downstairs.

Mom had finished her sandwich. I moved the plate over onto the coffee table to set my art work in front of Mother.

While she was going over them, she said "I've moved to Sandy, we don't live in Murry anymore."

"Is Joe still there?"

Mama was looking at the floor. I was waiting.

"Joe has some problems he needs help with. I don't know what to do for him. Walt and Reed hold the priesthood so I had to let them make the decision. They decided it would be better to put Joe where he can get professional help."

"What did they do with him?"

"Well, we had to put him in the Provo Mental Hospital, so they can help him to get well so we can bring him out someday. I'm just home by myself now. I've gotten off that welfare. They're good when you need them, but the trouble is they want to know every cotton picken' move I was making. So I just quit 'em. I'm selling Dabit now and cleaning houses. It works really well. I just put a little Dabit on a rag and boy, ya' ought to see the dirt fly. Why, yesterday a lady let me clean her whole kitchen and I made $10. That's how I got enough money to get on the bus to come up here to see you. Two days ago I made $3 by cleaning one woman's bathroom. The Lord has been helping me to get enough work to keep my bills paid. Oh, I've got to tell you. You know that white cat with the one green eye and one blue eye? Well, last night I felt something wet down by my feet. I turned on the light and there she was with a batch of kittens. It made me so happy to think I wasn't alone." Mama was smiling with tears in her eyes.

"Oh, how cute." I was tickled, too.

Mother stayed visiting until Mr. Florence came from work and gave Mother a ride home.

Carol and I wanted to come home. We called Mrs. Herzog (our case worker). Mrs. Herzog could not see any problem with us going home so we packed our stuff and came to live with Mama. Three years had passed, and it was 1960 when we moved home.

The house in Sandy had an acre and a half, with old adobe walls. We were happy to have a bedroom of our own. Mom had her room and Walt who moved in as a boarder, slept on the couch in the front room. He would drive us to get groceries, and that was nice. But it seemed odd not to have Sarah or Ester around.

So I asked, "Where is Sarah?"

Mother replied, "She got married."

When? How come WE didn't get invited to the wedding?"

"Well The man has another wife and so it has to be kept a secret."

"Who did she marry?"

"I don't even know. But Brother Guy knows and he said she has been placed where God wants her to be."

"Well can we go visit?"

"No we cannot."

"Well shit. What about Ester?"

"Well she got married too."

"Who to?"

"Karl Dewigglie."

I found out years later that Mom let Ester go to work for Karl in his herb shop. And while there, he raped her. And because he held the priesthood she could not come home after the trauma of being raped. No, Karl went to the brethren and had her married to him, her rapist.

I thought a lot about Joe being put in the Provo Mental Hospital. Walt, Mom, Carol, and I would go visit. Sometimes they would not let us see him because they said he was extremely violent and they had to lock him in a 'no visiting' area. I sat there looking at all these people with their strange actions. One man paced the floor from corner to corner for the longest time while another threw himself down and his eyes rolled to the back of his head. He shook while he was frothing at the mouth. Even the nurses seemed a little strange. I sat quiet, looking around me, waiting until we were on our way home.

I said to myself, How horrible it would be to have to stay there. That's what happens when a person gets really mad. They lock 'em up.

All through the summer I was always looking for something that needed to be invented, because I had just finished reading a book about George Washington Carver, a man that invented many things and even had found over 100 uses for peanuts.

So I went around the yard looking at things and thinking. After looking over the entire place, I came to the conclusion, "Gee, whiz. Everything has already been invented." Little did I know!

One afternoon Uncle Walt (who was about 60 at the time) and Mom (just in her 50s), weighing approximately 180 pounds, about 5'2", and almost as broad as she was tall, joined Carol and I in a game of baseball on our front lawn. Mom really hit that ball. We had hardly ever seen her run. It was almost like watching a little ball bounce as she took a step. She was laughing all the way. Then Uncle Walt got up to bat, and I thought it was pretty neat to see him out there, a good old sport. Boy, they did give us kids a good game, one to be remembered.

One day when Mom was gone to work, I put some water in an empty Watkins deodorant bottle and squirted Carol. She got the clothes squirt bottle and squirted me with more water.

Oh yeah! So I filled up a cup of water and threw it on her. Ha. Ha.

So she filled up a bucket with water and threw it on me. "That's what you get!"

"All right!" I went and got the hose. She saw me coming as I brought it into the house. "Oh yeah! Hee-hee, ha-ha," as I squirted her royally. This was so much fun I could hardly stand it until we realized what a mess we had made. Water was all over everything and just running out of the door. We went to work before momma came home. Mom entered with a smile to see a much cleaner house.

I would chop wood to prepare for winter. When I had a big pile done, Mama paid me a little so I could buy candy for myself and dog biscuits for Turby, my little cream-colored puppy. I loved that country life. It was like a small chunk of paradise.

To get to our house just off State Street, we had to go down a lane, over a canal, then down a slight hill, so you could not see the road or other houses from our place. To look around us you could see large stretches of land. There were apple trees and pear trees on our front lawn and large cotton-less cottonwood trees lined the driveway. I made a hammock between the two pear trees and put a mattress on it. I could enjoy a rest on a hot summer day in the shade of the trees. There was a big yellow rosebush growing next to the house on the south side, and a trumpet vine on the southeast corner of the house by the edge of the lawn where hummingbirds spent many happy hours.

Large reddish orange poppies came up every year in a big patch on the east side of our house. Carol and I were old enough now to keep up the yard. We planted marigolds and 'four o'clock' by the porch. I looked at our beautiful yard one summer day and thought, Boy, this place is really nice. Even a movie star would want to live here if they knew it existed.

I sold seeds door to door for the American Seed Company, well sort of. Mother bought most of them, so I could earn a sleeping bag. Then I slept outside on the lawn in the summertime. One afternoon Mom got a phone call. She shouted with excitement, "Aunt Genevieve's coming! She's at the airport right now and she'll be here in a half hour."

Carol and I looked at each other. "Wowee. Aunt Genevieve's coming."

Did we fly through that house making beds, sweeping floors, doing dishes, etc. It was funny to think how fast we could work when we wanted to. We knew that if it were not clean enough, she would just stay at Hotel Utah. Aunt Genevieve came and took us out to eat and bought all kinds of nice things for Mom and us. It was through her generosity that we were able to see the other side of life. Mom had told us that Genevieve was a millionaire.

When I was 13 years of age, I began running around with girlfriends, listening to music, experimenting with makeup, and dying my hair. The year flew by quickly. I thought I was having fun. I dated some boys. Did some kissing. And drank beer once in a while. But beer tasted so horrible I could not see how anyone could like it. I was just drinking it to be like the other kids.

Mother came in the house after working hard all day and looked at me in my stupid condition. I was 14 then.

She said, "May, what are you going to do with your life? I have tried to teach you girls to be decent, not to cut your hair, or to wear makeup and do all these stupid things. You have no conception of what it is like to earn a living. IT IS A DOG-EAT-DOG SYSTEM OUT THERE. The world is a cold and cruel place. You are sheltered here by Walt and I who love you. But the kids you think are your friends. They don't care at all about you. I don't know what is going to happen to you if you don't straighten yourself out. That's not the way the brethren teach you to be and you know better. Why, what if Uncle Roy Johnson (He was the head of the Brethren the priesthood counsel) came to our home and seen you?"

I pretended that I did not hear. For days after that I experimented to see what swear words I could say and get by with. Also, I got hold of a pack of cigarettes and smoked them just to show my independence. I kept running around with kids my age. But I was looking for work so, when a kid I had been dating told me that he was going out with his boss to dig cacti for people who wanted to have rock gardens. And asked if I wanted to come along to earn a few dollars I jumped at the chance. And I came home with $10. Then when Sunday came and Mother asked me if I was going with her to church, she was referring to the Polygamist meetings that I found depressing with the same old tune they would preach that we the young kids needed to come to the FEET of the Priesthood counsel to be placed in marriage where God wanted us to go. Rather than find our own partner. Even when Walt and Reed would come to read from the book of Mormon to us every other Sunday, I hated that too. Because one time while Walt was reading, Reed was sitting on the couch with a newspaper in front of him but shit he had his hands shoved down his pants, fondling his privates while gawking at Carol. How in the world can I learn anything while seeing that going on?

So I said to Mother, "Frankie's boss called and said Frankie was sick but he asked if I could go dig cacti's today to fill his orders so that's what I am going to do."

Then Mother said, "You know we are not to work on Sunday's and what if today is the day when God raptures His saints, and you are left behind? And when you come home you find yourself alone?"

I had already told the boss I was willing to work that day and he was honking his horn for me, so I ran out and jumped in to his car and we took off. And all the way heading South as I stared out the window. Mother's words were weighing heavy on my mind. Then the boss drove off the highway behind a hill but there was no cacti around.

I was puzzled and said, "Where is the cacti?"

He stared at me then pulled out a ten-dollar bill between his fingers and said, "Here I will pay you if you just let me put my fingers between your legs."

"OH! HELL NO! FUCK YOU!"

So he was quick to pull out a 10-inch dagger and held it to my side then he said, "You think you are too good for me don't you.? I could kill you, dump your body for the wolfs and coyotes to shred and no one will ever find you."

With that I cranked the door handle and fell out of the car. Jumped up and ran as fast as I could up the hill to get back to Highway 89. Praying out loud "God help me save me. I will repent. I will attend the meetings I will obey the brethren. Save me God."

It was quite a hike but I made it.

And then on the highway the boss pulled up and said, "Come on get in I will take you home."

"Hell no you bastard!"

"I am sorry I truly am come on you can ride in back and hold the shot gun to the back of my head and if I make one wrong move you can blow my head off. If you can't forgive me and let me take you back home then I will kill myself right here and now."

"Well that won't be any great loss."

I thought of the great distance we had come if I were to try and walk it, or if I tried to hitch hike. Well maybe this was the better choice to make. I checked the gun it was loaded, so I got in and held it to his back all the way home. Then once I was safe back home the promises I had made to God, I knew I had to keep. That particular life changing event was in 1962.

Then I found out one girl I had as my stupid friend, started to brag about how she had lost her virtue. I was sick. I left her house, and on the way home I thought, Dear God. I don't need this crazy way of living. I just don't need it. I've got to amount to something. I felt a longing for an association with God in my life.

I had not been to "group meetings" much. Carol had been going. She soon married and left home. We never knew who she was given to, so no wedding or nothing. I found myself alone more than ever. It took a little time for me to adjust to doing things by myself all the time. But I found solitude quite pleasant. What I did not know until years later is that Karl the Dewigglie worm had struck again. And while Carol was baby-sitting for Ester, he Raped Carol too. Then he told the brethren it was consensual. And they married Carol to him also. Now I was the only chicken left in the barn yard.

I began to wonder about what Mother had said and knew that I had not learned any vocation or skills because I did not want to go to school any more. I dropped out without finishing the eighth grade because there was a dumb kid there who, without fail, would tease me in the hall about how he thought my nose was bigger than anyone else's. I got so tired of his insults. When he would see me coming down the hall, he would stop, lean backwards a little, put one hand over his mouth to laugh and point at me with the other hand. Then he would say while chuckling,

"Here comes the beak of the week." And worse than that He would holler out, "HAY MAY, HANDLE MY COCK."

He had humiliated me so many times that after a while, looking in the mirror, I said to myself, Well, my nose is a little bigger than most of the other girls, but my eyes are kinda' pretty and my mouth looks ok, I guess. I looked like a young "Jody Foster". And I thought, One thing is for sure though. I am not going to make it through this world with my looks. I'm going to have to make it with my brains.

My art work was not all that hot either, so I tried typing. My mother was an expert typist in her day, but it did not seem that any of her talent had rubbed off onto me. I began to feel odd and I wondered what I would really do with my life. My heart kept taking me back to my art work. I could imagine myself as a great artist, so I got the books from the library and studied Rembrandt and Titian.

One summer afternoon I had been doing a lot of drawing of faces, trying to get good at it when a knock came on the door. It was Reed and Francis. I had not seen them for several years. I said, "Come in. Mom's outside in the garden. She will be here in a minute. She just went out to pick some beans."

To be polite I sat down in the kitchen with them while waiting for Mother to come in. I could not help but notice Reed's appearance as he sat on the chair with the two back legs on the floor and leaning the back of the chair against the wall. His face was long like a poker player with a pointed nose. His skin was a mass of pimples and his hair was going every which direction. His eyes were somewhat bloodshot and his lips quite heavy. His clothes looked as though they had been slept in for days. They were quite soiled and the odor that came from his direction was something else. Francis had not changed much. She was quite plump with a pleasant face with little rows of pinned up curls on the top of her head and long braids wrapped in a circle, as thou it was a crown on her head. Francis' clothes were soiled but not all wrinkled. She had somewhat of a decent appearance.

I was lost for anything to say as I looked at them and they at me.

"You're Haisa?" Reed said.

"No, I'm Kaziah May. I think I'll go tell Mother you're here."

I went out to the garden. "Fran and Reed are here to see you, Mom."

"Oh, all right." She went around the back door to the kitchen and I went to the front door to my bedroom to return to my art work. Mom came to the door after about half an hour and said, "I was telling Francis and Reed that you are trying to be an artist. Would you like to show them some of your work?"

"OK." I brought out what I thought was good enough to show. They looked at my pictures.

Then Reed said, "Do you know how many artists starve to death? They die by the thousands. Even some better than Kaziah. That is your name, isn't it?"

"Yes, but most people call me May."

"OK, May. Anyway, as I was saying," Reed went on, "even if she became really good at it, there are already 30 people in line waiting for every artist's job that is available. The market is flooded with all kinds of people looking for a job."

He was apparently talking to Mother. As I sat there listening, my eyes were fixed upon the coal bucket. I felt I did not need to hear that as I was fighting an inferiority complex anyway. I looked up at the clock and said, "There is something I need to attend to. Excuse me." I quietly picked up my papers and left the room.

I heard them talking as I walked away. "May is really growing up fast, isn't she."?

"Yes, she is the only one home now. All the rest are gone."

I went back to my art work.

When Winter came, I spent much time walking down the canal bed when it was snowing and enjoyed the peaceful beauty. I built half an igloo on our lawn and laid down inside of it looking up into the sky at night with the snow falling in my face. I enjoyed smoking a cigarette I had found on the ground. I laid there thinking, wondering how I could become an artist. Mother could see some talent in me and she was kind enough to spend $10 to buy me a very small amount of oil paints and brushes. I continued to spend many hours drawing objects and experimented with the oil paints.

When Mother was going to clean the Marion Hotel one morning, I asked if I could go. I did not expect any pay. I just enjoyed being with Mom and worked with her to see what that job was like. She seemed contented just to go and fill her little niche every day, happy to have a job cleaning spittoons, scrubbing floors, making beds, emptying garbage containers. But even this type of work seemed to have a sense of dignity about it as I watched my mother. She was not the type of woman to smoke, drink, chase men or do anything to make me ashamed of her. Her character was something I felt I could be proud of. I always felt good about my mother.

CHAPTER TWO

One Saturday Reed and Francis came to visit Mother. While they were all talking in the kitchen, I preferred staying in the front room. Reed was telling Mother that the things that Joe had done to reject priesthood direction in his life, along with his hatred for Reed, were the reasons why he was still in the Provo Mental Hospital.

Reed declared with a very emphatic statement, "No one can fight against the work of the Lord or the Saints and prosper." Looking at Mother, "You might love him but you've got to let him go."

Francis chipped in, "I had to let my son Louis go because he wanted to leave the work, although it hurt me very much. He has apostatized. He has abandoned the faith and left as some of my girls have done. I couldn't hold them, Edith."

Standing next to Mother, Walt brought his finger down on Mom's shoulder while he kept poking her as he said, "You have got to decide what are you going to do. Are YOU going to obey the priesthood counsel over you? You can't worry about your kids."

Mom looked up at them, "Well, Joe would be a good boy if he could just straighten himself out. He could hold the priesthood."

Reed jumped into the conversation, "He never will amount to a hill of beans. He's a bastard child from the beginning since you and Joseph Hancock never had a priesthood marriage. You think you can go out on the prairie and commit adultery and it have no effect upon your kids. He never will allow the priesthood to guide him in anything. He has sold his soul to the devil."

"Oh, he has not. What makes you say that?" Mom asked.

"Anyone!" Reed's voice having much impact and his finger pointed at Mom. "Anyone! I don't care who they are. Whoever turns away from God joins up with the devil and his forces. There's only the two sides: God and the devil. If you're not for one, you're for the other. The only chance that boy had is if you would have handed him over to me years ago. I could have made a man out of him. But you wouldn't do it, so now it's too late. All you can do is see him go down the drain."

Mom was looking up with her finger to her mouth as if she were having difficulty coping with this announcement. I had been watching through the doorway. I figured I had heard about enough when Reed went on to say, "All your children are bastards and you've got to give them up and let them go to hell if that is what they want to do. You can't deprive them of their free agency."

I was so full of disgust at all this kind of talk. Reed turned and looked at me and my impulse was to look right at him and pretend to throw up, then I turned, walked out of the front room, and slammed the door. I thought, Boy, what an ass. Who does he think he is anyway? Calling us bastards yeah, real bastards. Boy, why does Mama even let them in our house? Most of the time when they came after that, I would go out of my way to let them know they were not wanted in our house. I would flip him the "bird" or walk out and slam the door whenever they would enter the house.

One Sunday afternoon they came over again and I told them to their faces, "I wish to hell you guys would stay home. Can't you see you're not wanted here?"

Francis said, "Well, that's too bad. Uncle Walt invites us and so does your mother. They're the head of the home. You're not," and she pushed her way into the house.

I tightened my mouth, turned on my heel and walked out, slamming the door, hopped on my bike and took off. I thought, Boy, I wished Mom would quit inviting those creeps.

As I rode away out into the country, it became rather cold since the sun was going down and I had left without even thinking of my coat. But I despised the thought of returning until I was so cold, I had to return. They had finally left. I had been gone approximately three hours. I went to sleep that night with the beginnings of a bad cold.

During the night I woke up with terrible pain in my back. Mom called Francis because Francis was supposed to be a registered nurse. Reed and Francis came out about 8 a.m. the following morning. The last people I wanted to see was them, but now I was in so much pain that it did not seem to matter who was there.

Francis said, "Well, her back's out of place. She needs to go see a chiropractor."

I was crying, "What will he do?"

Francis replied, "He'll push and pull on your back until your bones are where they belong."

"Oh, no! I couldn't stand for anyone to even touch my back," I cried.

Walt said, "Well, maybe we could take her to Uncle Roy's for a blessing."

"That sounds like a really good idea," I commented.

So I got dressed in my street clothes and Walt and Mom took me up to see Roy Johnson. I just knew in my heart I had faith to be healed, and with perfect faith in the blessing, kept saying in my mind all the time that he was praying, I know I will be healed.

When he was through praying, my arm which before had been very painful to lift, just went up on its own without the slightest pain. I didn't even lift it. It just went up in the air by itself. I stood there while they were talking then began to faint. As I was going down, someone caught me.

Uncle Walt said, "It's because you're so full of evil spirits most of the time that when they are all rebuked, you don't have anything left to hold you up."

What an embarrassing thing for him to say in front of Roy Johnson. I thanked President Roy Johnson, as we called him, then we all shook his hand and left.

All the way home I was sleeping on the side that before had been so painful. The spirit of peace prevailed and I felt very content and thanked the Lord in my heart for a blessing to get rid of all that darn pain. I thought maybe I was full of the devil.

Reed and Francis were there when we got home, but I remained calm. Reed began to tell Mother that the reason for my back pain was because of the way I had treated him. "The Lord is trying to teach her a lesson. I hold a high enough position in the Sanhedrin, both on this side and in heaven, that this girl could lose her life over her actions. I am sent by the Lord to teach this family the Gospel and if she can't accept it, she will have more than just back pain. She will be destroyed."

Mom said, "I tell May she shouldn't be like that but I don't know. Sometimes she just doesn't listen to me."

And actually, I was not very happy with the ill feelings that I had been harboring. It was not like me to really hate anybody and the strong dislike I had been developing for these people was not natural for me. I began to wonder if there might be some truth to what Reed had said, as I stood there on the other side of the door in Mom's room.

"The reason people hate me is because they can't stand to hear the truth," he hollered, "and I'm not about to lie just to make someone happy."

The talk around the group was that no one liked him but I did not know why. The only thing I knew was I did not like him. I was very confused as I listened to him ranting in the kitchen.

Did God really send them? Is something radically wrong with me? My mind was in such turmoil as I felt tears of frustration running down my face. I attempted to pray while kneeling on Mom's bed, something of which I had done very little up to this point.

"Oh, God, our Eternal Father. Hallowed be thy name. Thy kingdom come, thy will be done on earth as it is in heaven." I was weeping profusely. "Give us this day our daily bread and forgive us of our debts as we forgive our debtors," thinking very carefully of every word I spoke. "Lead us not into temptation but deliver us from evil for thine is the kingdom and the power and the glory forever, amen."

I laid there crying, just hoping that prayer somehow, some way, would do some good. I fell asleep.

That night something kept repeating, "Ephraim, Ephraim." The next morning I asked Mother, "What does Ephraim mean?" I explained my dream. She told me that perhaps that I was of the blood of Ephraim. I asked her how I would know. She told me that it tells you in your patriarchal blessing. I asked if I could have one, so she arranged it with Brother Guy Musser.

We went to his home and there in the front room he gave me a blessing. The main thing that I noticed was he did say I was of the blood of Ephraim, which is a lie, but a very common one, and had come into this world with the desire to serve the Lord. That was easy for me to believe. He said that because of my former state in the spirit world, the devil sought to destroy me that I might wander in the world and be lost and forgotten by the saints.

I thought how horrible that would be.

"Also, I should seek to come under the direction of the priesthood and to labor diligently to qualify my mind and spirit to be added upon that I would have to suffer heartache and sacrifice and that I would be called upon to go through many experiences that would require faith, patience and prayer. But if I would seek the Lord in all things, great should be my reward in the end. Along with many things. He also said that I would be blessed with children.

I felt very sober about this blessing. I felt like this was God talking to me through Brother Guy and now I must build my whole life around fulfilling this. No matter what it may lead me into, I must live so as to learn what my religion is and then live it. I wanted to go to meetings.

Walt had at that time been living in our home to help Mother with bills and to supply her transportation. So he took us every Sunday that a meeting was held.

One Sunday Brother Guy spoke. "Brothers and sisters. I feel it a privilege to meet with you here today. I feel inspired today to tell you that we need to clean up our minds and our homes. There are those amongst us who are worshipping idols. They are also devoting much time and monies with the gentiles."

My first thought was, Idols? Really? I continued to listen.

"We come here today to get the spirit of the Lord. We hear the brethren speak and we might say to ourselves, 'What a beautiful meeting I have heard today.' Then when we leave those doors, we go to our cars and upon arrival at our homes, we have put these teachings to one side while we go turn on the televisions and again, we are back to our old lifestyle we had yesterday. What good is God's truths to us if we are not willing to practice what we have learned? Do we search out the scriptures in our spare time or are we too interested in what the national harlots are doing? Are we reading about the prophets and the saints so that we may become like them, or are we watching shows where someone is breaking one or all of the Ten Commandments? What the Lord wants is a broken heart, and a contrite spirit, for you to give up Babylon. Come out of here, oh ye, my people, that you be not a partaker of her plagues."

I was writing down what he was saying as fast as I could in my little note pad.

He continued "When the Lord sends his destroying angel to take vengeance upon the earth, are we going to be found doing, thinking, and living, the same as the wicked? If we are, the angel will not know the difference."

I looked at Brother Guy with thankfulness for guidance, as a spirit of conviction ran through me.

He went on. "We are like buckets full of mud. We need to cleanse ourselves so that we can receive sweet milk."

Reflecting upon all the radio I had listened to instead of studying the scriptures, I thought, Man, I'm guilty. I loved the influence Brother Musser had over me. It made me want to forsake myself and strive to improve. A spirit of joy filled my soul.

He went on to say, "We should show love and honor to the priesthood and those who have been valiant in the work rather than worshipping movie stars just because we think they have a cute face."

My little note pad was full so I just enjoyed the rest of the meeting. We sang;

"The spirit of God like a fire is burning.
The latter-day glory begins to come forth.
The visions and blessings of old are returning
And angels are coming to visit the earth."

I sang with enthusiasm.

"We'll sing and we'll shout with the armies of heaven,
Hosanna, hosanna to God and the Lamb.
Let glory to them, in the highest be given
Hence forth and forever amen, and amen."

"The Spirit of God Like a Fire". words by William W. Phelps," Hymns, p. 213.

That Sunday night Brother Guy's sermons were having such an impact on me that when we got home from meeting, I went straight to my bedroom. I collected together the pictures of movie stars I had. With a solemn mind I could see Brother Guy was right. I picked them up and walked to the front room. I opened the door to our coal and wood stove and said goodbye forever, as I carefully put in one at a time. When that was done, I found Joe's hammer. Then I got my little radio, carried it to the front porch, swung the hammer down so as to shatter it to pieces. I picked up the pieces and put them in the garbage can. Then I returned to my room, pausing to think about what to do with my records and record player. I thought of someone who might want them. Then. I picked up the records and player and carried it over to the fourth house down the road.

I asked Carla, "Do you know of someone who would like these? I don't want them anymore. I have something more important to do with my time."

She smiled and with open arms said, "You're just giving it to me?"

"Uh huh."

"Goll, thanks."

"You're welcome."

I walked home and as I dusted off my hands, I thought, There's a little more mud taken out of my bucket. I feel better already. Then I stood again in my room. A good feeling came over me. "Oh," I exclaimed as I remembered something. I opened my top dresser drawer and took out of a round can several necklaces I had acquired over the years. I also noticed the statue on my dresser. I grabbed it, too. "I don't need you anymore either."

I made another trip to the neighbors' then on my way back I stopped at the canal to look into the water. A thought ran through my heart. If I devote myself to finding out what my religion is and then live it with all my might, who knows, I might even surprise God.

Mama and Walt had been watching me.

Walt came home one afternoon after visiting with Brother Guy. "I told Brother Musser today that you were cleaning house to get rid of the gentile influence that's been in this home for so long. He was pleased that you would do that." Walt sat in the large chair in the front room. "Can you sit down for a minute?"

I was very anxious to hear what else Brother Guy said. I sat down quickly.

"He told me that you are to be my wife."

I looked at him and instead of being calm, cool, and collected, a spirit of resentment moved in fast.

He continued to talk but my mind was blocked off. I interrupted him, shaking my head. "It isn't going to work like that. I don't even love you," I exclaimed as I brought my eyes up to meet his.

"If we both love the gospel, we can learn to love each other."

I was still shaking my head. "Marry Mama!" I shouted. "She's of the same religion. Heck pick on someone your own age. She loves ya'. I don't!"

"You need to marry who the priesthood gives you to," he snarled back.

"You wish," I said sarcastically. Jumping up off the chair then bowing before him while looking him right in the eye and raising my voice even louder, "There's no place in the scriptures that says I have to marry you, so there!" Turning on my heel, I walked out and slammed the door before he could even speak.

I marched up by the canal. I shivered to think of marrying Walt, exclaiming, "Oh, yuck. The nerve of that old man. He never gives up. I'm so sick of it." I was thinking how he tried to get Sarah and he tried to get Ester then Carol. Now me. "Shit!" I exclaimed as I spit in the water. I thought to myself, Yeah, and Mama's always behind it just because she loves him.

I sat staring into the water for a long time, thinking. Then came Mama walking down the driveway. She had just got off the bus coming home from work. I stood in front of her. "Mama, why don't you ask Walt to marry you?"

"Well, I can't give him children. So he wants to save himself for a young girl who can."

"Well SHIT. He ought to quit saving himself and pick on someone his own age."

Mama looked tired so I took the bag out of her hands. "Thank you. That gets heavy after a while."

I peeked in the bag. "Mmmm. Pickled pigs' feet. We haven't had any of that for a long time."

Upon entering the home, everyone managed to drop the marrying subject.

About a month later a strong wind had picked up the roof off the chicken coop and laid it on the ground. Reed, Francis, and Bill (Francis' nephew) came out to take the roof apart as Mom and Walt had said that they could have the lumber. I was not doing anything on this beautiful summer day anyway, so after watching them working in the sun for a while, I thought, It would be a good idea to make some lemonade and take it out to them. So I did.

As I arrived carrying a pitcher and some glasses, Reed said, "Well, thank you, May."

"You're welcome." I poured Francis a drink.

"Thank you."

"You're welcome."

Then some for Bill. "I'll just set this

here if you guys want more, OK?" As I looked at what they were doing, it looked like fun.

"Ya' got another crowbar or hammer?"

"I don't know."

"Hey, I think we got one in Joe's tool box. I'll go get it."

I hurried to the house, returned, and commenced to extract the nails from the boards that they were going to take home. The sun was high and hot. After several hours we would chitchat a little but mainly we kept working. I was getting quite hungry and my neck was red.

"I think I'll go in and make some sandwiches. Does that sound good?"

"Yes, it sure does."

I went in and made some with tuna fish and got some radishes from the garden. I returned with this platter and salt.

We were all eating. Reed said, "You're a pretty good worker, ya' know that?"

"Oh, yeah. Well, what I'd like to do is get a job."

Reed asked, "What kind of a job are you looking for?"

"Well, I don't know. I've got to be good at something." I want to be an artist to paint portraits.

Then, He snarled, "Well artists are a dime a dozen. Hell, there is a reason they are called starving artists. No one in their right mind wants to pay someone for pushing a pile of paint around on a canvas. You need to provide a product that people actually need, not just what they want. Do you want to know a million-dollar secret that will allow you to get any job you want?"

"A million-dollar secret, huh? What's that?"

"Come here and sit down." We sat on the lumber pile under the shade of the chicken coop.

"OK. What's the deal?" as I propped my arm under my chin so as to give him my undivided attention.

"I know this works because I've done this several times. Now, first of all, figure out what job you want. What do you want to be doing for the rest of your life? I don't care what the trade is. This will work. OK. Then find a place that will hire you to do janitor work or whatever for whatever wage they want to pay you just so you are there working around those who are doing the job all day long. Then you are seeing the jobs actually being accomplished. All right?" He sat there with his fingers protruding out. As he counted, he would put another finger out. "Then third, you learn what you can at home on your off hours so you can find out all the technical questions concerning the trade. OK?"

"Yes." I was taking it all in like rain falling on a desert. I was absorbing it. "Uh huh." A thrill was going through me.

"Fourth, you have got to be willing to do extra and work overtime so that when there's little things that need to be done to help out, you just get in and do it but make sure it's done right or you will be in trouble. OK?"

"Yeah." I could just visualize how this could work.

"The manager or employer of the place will appreciate what you're doing and recognize that you have the ability to take responsibility and it's the nature of people to leave work for someone else if they think they can get by with it. So you will have things left for you to do, even though it's not your job. Those whose job it is will leave it just because they know you will do it. So what will happen is the boss will walk in one day and find the janitor, which is you, busy doing all these other jobs. Then because he is so impressed you will likely be moved up the ladder. But you have to be careful of jealousy. Because when you know enough that the manager is afraid of his position, that's about the time you're liable to be fired. But by that time, you know enough to go to work for someone else."

I was confounded.

"Now, do you see how that works? You have gained practical experience, on the job training, and even if you need a degree, you could take the college course much faster because you already know most of the answers."

I sat there scratching my head. "Man, that's really smart. I'm going to write that down," I said as I jumped up.

"Oh, you're a smart girl. You'll be able to remember it."

That gave a new light on things. I was very impressed that Reed would come up with something that intelligent. I could feel some vibes radiating as I admired the excellent idea. Later I tried to remember it and wrote it down, as I felt that was a very important key.

A few months after that there was talk of construction in the area, another subdivision was being developed. So Mother sold our home near State Street and bought another home directly east four blocks. We had no sooner moved in there when I met our neighbor, Mrs. Ren, a little Italian lady. She was about 5' tall, 160 pounds, with curly hair and a jovial smile. I was invited to her house to have some crispy Italian treats, which I accepted. As I sat in her home, I looked around me. Here was a humble looking house from the outside. Oh, but the inside was a compilation of beauty and order. Everything was spotless. I felt myself having a love affair with the way this woman kept house.

I took her to our house and showed her my art work. I explained, "I'm trying to be an artist." We were looking at a pencil drawing I had done of the Mona Lisa.

"Why, young lady, that's beautiful. How long did that take?"

"Gee, I don't know. I just kept at it until it was done." I was thinking to myself, Gee, you're cuter than Mona Lisa.

She must have read my mind. She said, "Maybe someday you could do me if you would like to, OK?"

I quickly replied, "I'd like that."

For a week straight I was unpacking and cleaning. Boy, after seeing the likes of her home, I resorted to cleaning some things with a toothbrush. I was trying to have the second cleanest house in all of Sandy, hers being number one. Then when I could really feel good about our home, I would go visit her.

One day she sat still while I drew her picture. When I was done, I showed it to her.

"That's very nice. How much do I owe you?"

"Not even one penny," I smiled.

"I know, I know what you'd like. I give you." She took me to her front room. Opening a door to a chest, she brought out several pieces of intricate crochet work. She had made these doily masterpieces, a set for a couch, chair, and end tables. "Here. I would like you to have these."

"Are you sure?" I gasped.

"Yes. I've saved these for years for someone special and I know you would like them."

"Oh, I would." We hugged for a few seconds. "Thank you." As I picked them up to go home, I felt such appreciation for the elegance she had passed my way. "Thank you again. I will cherish these knowing who made them and all those hours spent."

"You have a hope chest?"

"Sorta' kinda'."

"When you get married, you can remember your neighbor, huh?"

"Yeah. I'll remember my neighbor," as I gave her another hug.

A few days later I went to visit. She was out shoveling goat manure into a wheelbarrow.

"Where are we taking it?" I asked.

"I'm spreading it on the garden spot."

"OK." I wheeled it out there and dumped it and returned. "I'll do that if you like."

"Would you? Then I'll go spade that there."

"Okey dokey." I was happily shoveling and hauling manure for my friend.

The next day I was out by the side of our house where I had planted marigolds and chrysanthemums that were facing the rose bushes next to the fence. I had put my chair right there so I could read the "Journal of Discourses", while basking in the sun and was enjoying our beautiful yard.

Mrs. Ren walked by, "Hi. How are you?"

"Fine."

"What're reading?"

"I'm just trying to expand my mind. What's ya' doing?"

"Oh, I'm dis'ta' going to the store."

"Can I come with?"

"If you'd like."

I hopped up, "Just a hairy minute. I'll just put this book in the house."

She laughed, "What is a hairy minute?"

"Well, see it's one that might actually be longer than 60 seconds 'cause it's growing." I flashed a big smile.

"You's funny."

We walked off talking about many things under the sun. Then she said, "My grandson is coming to see me in a few weeks. He's such a fine young man and very handsome, too. I would like for you to meet him. He has just bought himself a brand-new red Fiat. It's a sports car with a convertible top. He's just the sweetest boy. I love him so much."

I was thinking to myself, Oh boy. I'd better be careful because I've got to find out who God wants me to marry and this might be tempting. With a quick reply, "I have a boyfriend already."

"You do?"

"Yes, he comes to see me once in a while."

"Oh."

Actually the boy I had referred to was just a friend, not a sweetheart, but it seemed to be a good excuse, then I changed the subject.

"Do you think that maybe someday you could teach me how to make some of those tasty little crispy things that you gave me the other day?"

"I'd love to," she said as we went on.

It seemed like everyone had ideas of whom I should marry. The next Sunday in meeting as I took a seat waiting for the meeting to begin, I felt a soul satisfaction to be numbered amongst the saints. I looked around me casually at the caliber of virtue and dignity of the women present: their faces with little or no makeup, their long hair well cared for, their dress modestly below their knees while their sleeves were wrist length. I felt contented to be dressed in like manner and was thankful this day that my hair had grown out and the trace of black was nearly gone. My mind went back to a year and a half ago, my condition and frame of mind then as compared to now. I was glad I had not done anything at that time that I could not repent of. A smile settled on my countenance and my heart quivered with joy as these words went through me: "I have come home to stay. These are my people." My eyes were wet. I was prepared to hear the word of the Lord.

President Marion Hamon arose. "We'll sing as our opening song, "We Thank Thee, Oh God, For A Prophet." Then as the meeting was conducted, there were many valuable principles discussed. But my attention seemed to be focused upon President Dale Timpson's sermon. When he got on this subject, I put my pencil to the pad I had been holding.

"You young people here today are blessed. Many of you are children of the covenant, were chosen from the other side to come down through your parents to carry on this special priesthood work and calling. Some of you young ladies are quick to run about trying to find a husband. Or you young men run without being sent to find a wife. With little or no thought of preserving your birthright amongst the saints and the covenants you have made in the preexistence. The Lord would have you at this time seek to bring yourselves to the feet of the priesthood, that the mind and will of the Lord may be made known as to whom you have made covenants with on the other side."

In the spirit of obedience, I could appreciate his sermon, for truly we should seek God's will on something of such importance.

After a while he sat down and President Roy Johnson spoke. "Brothers and Sisters, I would like you to ask yourselves: How much do we truly appreciate having a prophet, seer and revelator to lead this people?" He paused then continued, "There is something I would like to bring to your attention. If you will turn to" The Doctrine and Covenants, Section 132, verse 7.

7: And verily I say unto you, that the conditions of this law are these: All covenants, contracts, bonds, obligations, oaths, vows, performances, connections, associations, or expectations, that are not made and entered into and sealed by the Holy Spirit of promise, of him who is anointed, both as well for time and for all eternity, and that too most holy, by revelation and commandment through the medium of mine anointed, whom I have appointed on the earth to hold this power (and I have appointed unto my servant Joseph to hold this power in the last days, and there is never but one on the earth at a time on whom this power and the keys of this priesthood are conferred), are of no efficacy, virtue, or force in and after the resurrection from the dead; for all contracts that are not made unto this end have an end when men are dead.

Section 132, verse 7, The Doctrine and Covenants.

(THIS DOCTRINE is how they keep the members, kids are afraid to death to leave, the brainwashing continues.)

Then he stopped to appeal to the congregation.

"Here is the man (pointing to President Roy Johnson) who the Lord has blessed and preserved that we might be left without excuse. Will we follow him as though the Prophet Joseph were here with us today? Or will we be found treating lightly those things that God has revealed to us through him? What type of rewards do we expect to have in this life or the hereafter unless we can sustain him in all things as our prophet, seer and revelator."

I felt grateful that the Lord had preserved President Johnson who was well into his 80s.

Then he continued to read until he had completed verse 11:

10: Or will I receive at your hands that which I have not appointed?

11: And will I appoint unto you, saith the Lord, except it be by law, even as I and my Father ordained unto you, before the world was?

Section 132, verses 10-11," The Doctrine and Covenants

This type of talk is very intimidating to tender minds.

"Can you, young people expect to marry without appointment and have the Lord's blessing upon that union? These things we must think about very carefully, brothers and sisters. When a marriage is sealed by the Lord's anointed, there are angels commissioned to watch over and bless that man and his wife or wives, so long as they remain true and faithful."

He continued to talk but my mind was rehearsing what had already been said, like a sponge can only absorb so much and my mind was full.

When Brother Guy arose, he said, "We would like to ask these young men to sing for us at this time 'Glorious Things Are Sung of Zion' to the melody of 'Israel, Israel, God Is Calling.'"

Glorious things are sung of Zion,
Enoch's city seen of old.
Where the righteous, being perfect,
Walked with God in streets of gold.
Love and virtue, faith, and wisdom,
Grace and gifts were all combined;
As himself each loved his neighbor;
All were one in heart and mind.
As himself each loved his neighbor;
All were one in heart and mind.
There they shunned the power of Satan
And observed celestial laws;
For in Adamondi Ahman
Zion rose where Eden was.
When beyond the power of evil,
So that none could covet wealth,
One continual feat of blessings

Crowned their days with peace and health.
One continual feast of blessings
Crowned their days with peace and health.

Then the towers of Zion glittered
Like the sun in yonder skies,
And the wicked stood and trembled,
Filled with wonder and surprise.
Then their faith and works were perfect.
Lo, they followed their great Head!
So the city went to heaven,
And the world was, "Zion's fled!"
So the city went to heaven,
And the world said, "Zion's fled!"
When the Lord returns with Zion,
And we hear the watchman cry,
Then we'll surely be united,
And we'll all see eye to eye.
then we'll mingle with the angels,
And the Lord will bless his own.
Then the earth will be as Eden,
And we'll know as we are known.
Then the earth will be as Eden,
And we'll know as we are known.
"Glorious Things Are Sung of Zion," words by William W. Phelps, music by Joseph J. Daynes," Hymns, p. 243.

How I loved the thought of there really being a people or place like Zion. The meeting closed and I went to the car. Mom and Walt were talking, but I was in a little world of my own. That city will return, I thought to myself. I must be careful what I am doing or what I say 'cause there might be angels around. If I can stop swearing when I get mad or hurt myself, boy, that would be neat.

When Winter came, Reed and Francis came to visit one snowy night. When I answered the door, Reed had a box in his arms. "We brought you guys some meat."

"Come on in." I took the box. "We were about to have supper. Are you guys hungry?" I asked.

"We haven't eaten," Reed answered.

"OK. I'll make you guys a plate, too, then."

"Ya' ought to put that stuff in the freezer," Francis commented. "There's some steaks and hamburger."

"Hey, I could fry up some hamburger with onions to go with this." I had fixed macaroni cheese, and salad. I pulled out the table to add another leaf in the middle then when it was ready, I called, "Would everyone like to come 'n eat?"

When we were just finishing up the meal, Reed commented, "We delivered over 700 pounds of meat around to the different homes today and that's just today. We have been able to load up that much about twice a week."

"How do you get all this stuff?" Mama asked.

"Ya' know that Mr. Meat on 33rd South just off State? He lets us clean out the lockers of the people who don't keep up their fees."

"Well, golly. Doesn't he charge for it?"

"Well, we're paying him three cents a pound. That's what he could sell it to By Products for. It was about $20 for today's load."

Francis interrupted, "Nearly all of Bill's check from working at the Capitol Theater goes to support this work of helping the saints."

Reed was looking at the bowl of macaroni so I passed it to him.

"Well, that's really nice of you guys to do something like that. We sure appreciate it."

"This is why the Lord has brought us together for the benefit of the saints. They work hard to support their big families, but sometimes they need extra help to make ends meet," Reed said.

I thought, Now, there's a man who thinks about someone besides himself. That's refreshing.

"If it wasn't for the good Francis and I do to help out this priesthood work, she wouldn't have been justified in leaving Elmer" (the man she married after Charles died) "But according to the laws of God, a woman can leave her husband I don't care who he is if she is going to a better man, so that she can elevate herself in the Lord's work. Most men won't require the service and sacrifice out of their women that it would take for them to earn their exaltation."

I began to clear the table but was still listening.

Reed continued, "A man might ask his wife to do something and maybe she does it, maybe she don't, but if it were my wife, I'd see to it that it was done. That's the only way to really make something out of her in the long run. I wouldn't put up with the damn rebellion that most men put up with. Everyone I have ever taken under my supervision to train I made something out of them."

Everyone at the table seemed to believe Reed so why shouldn't I.

Francis said, "It's true. He trained Alfred to where he's now the manager of the R. C. Cola Company. Reed was offered a job at Sperry Univac. They had a test that 500 men took but only eight passed it. Reed was one of them, but he turned it down," Francis said.

"Because that's not what the Lord wanted me to do. I need to be free and independent. I can't be tied down to a steady 8-hour job. When Brother Guy asks me to do something, I've got to be able to go do it right now."

"That's why I like selling Watkins products," Walt added. "So I'm not so tied down all the time."

This conversation was somewhat confusing to me but at the same time very interesting.

Bill got up and imitating the Yogi Bear voice, said, "That's why they call us the Three Mouse Catters. Yoyo yoyoyoyoyo hoho de do."

I snickered with a little laugh. "You guys like some Jell-O? Yabba dabba do."

"I would," said Bill. "How about you?" He was still imitating Yogi Bear.

I could not see where these people were as bad as I once had supposed or they would not be doing all these good things. The bars of resistance I once had held high had now slipped pretty low, as I found myself talking to them as free as I would anyone else. The next time Reed came over, I got him off alone. I thought to myself, If he's so smart, I'd like to ask him something.

I began, "How do I go about finding the man I made covenants with? Do I just make an appointment with Brother Guy and ask him or what?"

"Oh, you could. That would be one way."

"Yeah, but I'm so darn bashful. I don't know if I've got the nerve yet, and besides" giving way to a little nervous laughter, "what I've been thinking is Brother Guy's the only man I know that I might not mind marrying. Ya' see what I mean. How do I approach that?"

"Yeah, I kinda' do." He paused for a while then said with a red face, "I hope I don't hurt your feelings, but I'd like to run something by you. Brother Guy is in such a high position that he can take his pick from the cream of the crop, the prettiest women with the best birthright and such. I don't know how much of a chance you'd stand so you might want to prepare yourself for a disappointing answer. But you could ask."

Boy, somehow that short statement had a way of knocking my props out from under me. I sat looking stupid for a while, trying to sort things out in my mind.

"I could ask for you if you'd like me to."

"Huh?"

"I said I could ask for you if you want. I go up to see him all the time."

"That might be a good idea 'cause Walt's got some crazy notion I'm supposed to marry him, and if there's something cooking like that, I don't even want to hear it."

"I think Brother Guy's out of town today and tomorrow but he should be back Tuesday. So I'll make an appointment then and get back with you. OK?"

"OK."

Three days later Reed and Francis came over. I was alone. I invited them in, anxious to know what was said. We sat down in the front room.

"Well, are you ready for this?" Reed asked.

"What did he say?" I was bracing my feelings to be prepared to hear whatever.

"Well, it was as big of a shock to me as it probably will be to you. But he told me that you are to become my wife."

My mouth fell down as I gasped for air.

He went on to say, "Brother Guy has asked me to look over this family for years, but I didn't know why. Then today he told me right out, point blank, that you made a covenant with me on the other side."

I felt like something heavy was crushing me. I rested my head in my hands with my eyes closed while trying to form a picture of Brother Guy telling them this. I had prayed all day for priesthood direction, now this heavy weight was upon me. Will I follow it? Where's my devotion? Where's my guts? I asked myself. Can I bring myself to do the will of the Lord?

Reed put his arm around me. "You could learn to love me in time if you let yourself. If I can get you to keep your bars down so I can get a word in edgeways, you'll be alright. I do love you even when you were swearing at me and flipping me the finger. I tried not to hate you for it. The work of the Lord is more important than love." He was patting my shoulders.

Francis commented, "We need you in our family. I think that's why the Lord wants you to come this way so you can help us in the business so Bill won't have to work so hard." (They had been washing a few glass gallon jugs and selling them for a little money.)

Francis seemed nice enough about the whole situation.

"Uh, well, I've got to think about it for a while. OK?"

"That's OK," Reed said. "Take your time, but if you wouldn't mind, maybe you could help us once in a while when we get a lot of orders so Francis isn't up so late."

"Yes, I wouldn't mind helping you once in a while, but I have this house to keep up 'cause Mama's been working pretty steady."

"Well, that will work out OK. How many days do you think you could help?"

"Oh, maybe two or three."

"OK. We'll come pick you up."

After they left, I thought to myself, Don't you dare get bitter or resentful. There must be some reasoning behind it or the Lord wouldn't ask me to do it, even if I don't see the reason right now. (But keep in mind how Carl Dewigglie raped both Ester and Carol, then went to the brethren and told them that they had consensual sex, so both sisters were told they had to marry Carl or they would go to hell. But I did not know that at this point in time, I wanted to throw up every time I thought about it.)

Maybe I can learn from him though because we both believe in the Gospel. He does know the scriptures more than I do. And that's something. And if he didn't love the work of the Lord and the truth, why would he study all the good books or be helping the saints? I looked at the set of "Journals" (approximately 21 volumes), as I scratched my head. Reed's read all of those books. Maybe he could guide me.

A few days went by and Reed had called me to see if I was ready to help him yet, but I had preferred housework until one certain afternoon. Mama came in tired as usual. I had steamed some broccoli. We sat there eating it with bread and butter.

"Ya' know what!" I said. "Reed and Francis went to Brother Guy to ask where I belong and you know what?"

"What?"

"Well, they said that Brother Guy told them I belong to Reed."

"Oh, really!" Mama exclaimed.

"Yeah. They told me Tuesday when you weren't here. They want me to help them in their little business whenever I can."

"Yeah. I've been over there a few times helping them burn their empty boxes. So you're going to marry Reed. Is that it?"

"I don't know. But I thought maybe at least helping them once in a while would be better than no job at all, ya' know."

"Yeah, I know. Believe me, 50 cents a day is better than nothing."

"They haven't discussed pay or anything, but I guess it don't matter."

Mama retired to bed. I came in with a wet washcloth for her forehead and rubbed some lotion on her feet as usual. Then I remembered some art work I had been doing.

"Hey, I have something to show you." I returned carrying two pictures. I held the one in front of Mama.

"Oh, that's our house. Did you do that just today?"

"Yeah."

"Yes, sir. You just keep going. I think you'll make it someday."

"I've got this one here," showing her the other one I just started. "It's supposed to be a spot like the Sacred Grove where Joseph Smith's vision took place."

"Uh huh. You're making headway all right."

I bent over and kissed Mama on the cheek. "Good night, Mama."

"Good night, sweetheart."

I left the room closing the door carefully, thankful for Mom's encouragement for me to become an artist. In another six months, I would be 16 years old and would soon have to make decisions about the direction of my life.

When Walt came home that night, he brought in three bags of groceries. As I was putting them away, he said, "Have you given it anymore thought about becoming my wife?"

Just then a bottle of prune juice slipped from out of my hands. Bang! It shattered on the floor. "Oh, man! What a mess!" I exclaimed. I began picking up the pieces of glass very quickly. "Ouch." I had cut myself. I finished cleaning up the glass and mopped up the juice. I could just feel myself brooding over the answer to his question.

"Have you thought about what I said?"

My mouth was tight, just about ready to blow.

"I'd be a better husband than half the guys you ran around with years ago."

"So who gives a hairy rat about what happened years ago," I hollered. "I wouldn't marry them and I'm not marrying you either. Can you get that through your thick skull?"

"Well, you're not obeying priesthood direction then."

"I don't believe that that came from Brother Guy. I think you made it up."

"I never made that up."

"Oh, yeah? You'd tell the same thing to every girl in the world if you thought they was stupid enough to believe it."

Walt pointed into the air and in a loud voice shouted, "You'll go to hell then."

"Fine. Then I'll marry the devil while I'm down there. But I am NOT MARRYING YOU!" I stormed into my bedroom and slammed the door.

"Walt shouted, "Then I am not bringing anymore groceries in this house then, You can just starve."

I told Mom in the morning I was going to work with Reed and Francis, because this house is not big enough to hold both Walt and I.

"That will be alright then if that's what you want to do. They do help the priesthood a lot." I called Reed and told him to come and get me. I was ready for work.

The first thing I noticed is the structure they were using for their bottle washing shop was Joe's little house. Joe, being put away in the mental hospital, Mom must have given it to them, perhaps to pay for the motor, that Joe wrecked.

After I spent the day at Reclaim Bottle gluing new jug boxes together, we grabbed a hot dog and malt then went to their apartment uptown. The front room was dark, the only light being from the doorway of the kitchen, and the walls had brown wallpaper with little yellow flowers. While I sat on a chair, Reed set on the bed in front of me. While he was talking, I was looking at the boxes of stuff of who knows what in piles around the room and the debris on the floors. I thought, Well, I guess they're so busy working they don't have time to clean it up.

All of a sudden Reed caught my attention,

"The children that are born to my women will be given to Francis."

The way that came across somehow was the last straw. I already felt like a time bomb waiting to explode and he had just lighted my fuse.

"What? What did you say?"

"Francis being the first wife is in the position that all the children will be given to her."

I got up and thought, What the hell am I doing here anyway? I don't even want to marry this damn man anyway, let alone have my children given to another woman.

"Forget you" were my last words as I walked out and slammed the door.

It was 10:30 p.m. and it was pitch black outside. There were no street lights. A creepy feeling came over me as I walked fast away from there with fury running through me. As I walked, I realized my condition. I was without a coat or a dime in my pocket and Mother was living in Sandy. I thought, Now, let's see. How far away is that? I guess about 25, maybe 30 miles. I had paused to figure this then I thought, Well, Reed and Francis brought me here. Damn it. They can take me home. So I turned on my heel and headed back. They had calmed down somewhat and so had I. I came in, looked at them in that dreary room.

"You guys brought me here. You can take me home," I stated.

"We have been praying that you would have a change of heart and come back. I think you got a misunderstanding of what I was trying to say," Reed said. "What I was getting at is that children would need to show respect to Francis just as much as they would their mother and it wouldn't hurt for the child to have two mothers."

Well that sounded much better and I surely was tired. They made a bed for me in the kitchen and I slept there with Francis. Reed and Bill slept in the front room. Within a few days I asked if they would take me to see Brother Guy and they agreed to do that.

Reed said on the way up there, "Even though Brother Musser told me that you are to be my wife, they are likely to try to give you to someone else."

"Why in the world would they do that?"

"They want to give you your free agency even though you are meant for me. It's because my mission is so important, they won't give you to me unless that's what you want. Women are a dime a dozen, but good ones are darn hard to find."

"I don't understand."

"Well, look, if a woman can't follow priesthood direction, then she isn't worth her salt."

"Well, maybe so, but I need to know what God wants me to do so I can start out right and hopefully end up right."

"Well, be prepared because they might even try to turn you against me."

"Why do you think so?"

He whispered, "I'll tell you a little secret. It's my mission to correct the priesthood counsel when they are out of line and they don't like being corrected."

Well, we arrived and Brother Guy said to me, "Who would you like to marry? You can have your pick."

He named five different men: Walt, Bill, Wayne, John, and Carl. But he never mentioned Reed.

I thought, I don't like any of the choices. So I said, "I'd rather wait to know who God wants me to marry, even if I have to wait 100 years, rather than marry the wrong man tomorrow."

Brother Guy seemed somewhat surprised at my answer and said, "Well, that's all right, then. What are you doing and where are you staying now?"

"Well, I'm just staying with Francis and Reed right now because they need help in their business. I left home because of Walt having some crazy ideas that I am supposed to marry him."

"That's OK then. Just go back and stay with them until the Lord reveals something in your behalf."

I thanked him and we left. Reed was excited. "See. See what did I tell you? He told you to come and stay with me. He knows that's where God wants you. But he didn't tell you that until he could see that you couldn't just be pushed around. You have passed the test. You have passed the test!" He looked up in the air and clapped his hands.

I felt so confused I hardly knew what was up or down.

About a week later Reed and Francis needed to go south to Short Crick so I went with them. On the way I started saying, "I sure would like to marry Brother Guy, you guys to tell me the things you know concerning the gospel and getting a real job."

"Well, but if you marry Brother Guy, he isn't going to treat you very good because he has so many wives of a higher birthright, and if you marry him, I won't be able to counsel you on anything because you will have to listen to whatever he tells you."

"Oh, come on." I bumped his shoulder with my shoulder. "You're not going to get away from me that easy."

I said that because he claimed to hold authority like Joseph Smith, and that was supposed to be the same authority as what Jesus held. I knew I had no special authority, knowledge, or anything, But I was eager to learn all I could, from any one that could teach me about anything. I craved intelligence, and it seemed as thou he did have a few good ideas.

Francis looked at Reed, "That's a proposal, isn't it?"

"Yes, it is. May proposed to me," he exclaimed with excitement.

I did not think I did. "I was thinking you might be able to answer some questions once in a while."

But Reed carried on, "I told the Lord that if this was for sure right, to have May propose to me, and you have done it." Then Reed said to me, "There are very few women who can qualify to live the higher laws, the reason being they can't deny themselves of their own mind and will enough. Christ said, 'Father, thy will be done, not mine.' He is the example of the world and He is who we have to follow if we ever expect to see our father in heaven. Ever since the church was first organized, the saints have had to deny themselves. The road to godliness is a tough row to hoe and not many are willing to sacrifice their all to follow the Lord."

As I heard these words, some of it made sense.

He continued, "A religion that does not require the sacrifice of all things, does not have the power within it sufficient to lay hold of eternal life. Most religions of the day are busy trying to give people their own mind and will. That's how they become so popular."

Somehow during the course of this conversation, I had managed to rip off all my fingernails as I commented, "I don't know if I can sacrifice everything or not. But I hope I can."

"You can. I have confidence in you and I know that you have above average intelligence because if you didn't, you couldn't stand to hear the truth without becoming angry."

"Well, the thought has occurred to me that those who have it easy in this life, in my opinion, don't really ever prove themselves and their loyalty to God."

"That's one thing about the principle of plural marriage. It was designed to uproot all the evil and selfishness from one's character for them to stand to live it," Reed stated.

"Can we stop and get some root beer?" I asked.

"Reed, you ought to stop and get her some." Said Francis.

"Yeah, I will in a minute. I'm looking for a service station so I can go to the bathroom."

We stayed at the Crick (Short Crick, Arizona) for just one day then we came back to work doing bottles. After a day's work was done in the little bottle shack, I was sweeping the floor. Reed braced himself against the rinse tub with his arms folded, watching my every move.

"All the things that I tell you about the gospel are for you to keep secret. They're for your benefit that you might understand how important this work is."

I stopped and was leaning on the broom while the orange rays of late afternoon sun came through the doorway.

"My mission is so extremely secretive," Reed continued, "that when I was given a patriarchal blessing, it could not even be written."

I thought, Hmmm. That's really something.

"Where and by whom did you receive the priesthood?" I asked.

Seeming somewhat shocked at my question, "My priesthood? That is to be held in confidence, but I will tell you this that my priesthood and mission is like unto the Prophet Joseph wherein God told him that whatever he would bless, God would bless, and whatever he would curse, God would curse. I have been given that same blessing. Also, that before God would let me go very far wrong, he has promised me he would take me on the other side. I have already earned that right."

I resorted to a seat on a coke box while leaning my back against the wall. "Well, why have the brethren thrown you out of meeting in Short Crick then?"

Reed took a jug box down and put it in front of me where he sat. He began expressing himself with his hands going up and down. "They don't even comprehend my mission and calling. They are to guide the people in the group, but when they step out of line or preach wrong doctrine, then I'm fast for making an appointment with them to tell them wherein they have erred. Do you think they like being corrected?"

"Well, I don't know. What have you had to correct them on?"

"For one thing, there has been several women that were meant to come into my family. I told them, and also I told the girls, but they have married those women to other men. Because they have done this, I told them that they will forfeit some of their wives to go in my family in the hereafter. Turnabout is fair play. And if you don't think that makes them mad, then just think again. Uncle Roy told me that I was either an extremely righteous man or he said, 'You're a devil.' I told him that it was for him to take it to the Lord to find out which. Roy is responsible for marrying Rebecca to a Catholic rather than give her to me. If you don't think he will pay for that! But if her husband dies or she gets a divorce, I'll still try to pick her up." Reed's eyes were bloodshot.

I got up to turn on the light. "Here comes Bill and Francis with a small load of jugs," I said as they backed up the truck. "That's good!" I hollered to them.

After Bill and Francis came in and some general chitchat took place, Reed said, "Sit down you guys. I was talking to May before you came in. I was telling her about how the priesthood council will be accountable to God for what they have done to me. Just the same with some of the others in the group. Like when I took the truck over to Lar Ricks. He cheated me out of $20 by putting in a used part when he charged me for a new one. And you know what happened? Three days later his whole shop went up in flames."

Francis said, "That's true. That really happened."

Then Bill said, "Did you tell her about that girl, Charlotte, who was supposed to become your wife and the priesthood married her to someone else?"

Reed took over the conversation, "Yes, and the girl's mother committed suicide because she knew where her daughter belonged. In fact, I don't know of even one incident where anyone has done wrong against me where God did not step in and punish them extremely for their wrongs." He kept waving his hand around in the air to swat some flies that seemed to be having delight in teasing him by landing on his sweaty forehead.

"See once a person has swallowed the Joseph Smith story. they are open to believe anything."

What Reed said could not be proven. But then neither could Smiths story be proven either.

But Jesus said that in heaven men and women are not married or given in marriage. But single as the Angels.

But I had not read the Bible to know that.

Francis said, "Tell her about your father."

"My father used to beat me all the time when I was young and not let me go anywhere, or if I had anything, he would take it from me. I couldn't even have a car when I was 17 until I left home. But before he died, the doctors couldn't find anything wrong with him, but he was starving to death on a full stomach." Reed was bawling. "I went to see him on his deathbed. He was just skin and bones. Then for the first time in my life, he said, 'I'm sorry, Reed. I have not done right with you.' Two days later he died. That's deathbed repentance and God doesn't honor it."

Francis said, "Can you guys get this truck unloaded? I'm starving to death."

As I stood in the doorway scratching my head, I thought, I hope nothing happens to me 'cause of my big mouth.

Bill got on the truck and began to throw the boxes of jugs to me as I threw them to Reed for him to stack. We unloaded the truck.

While traveling down the road, I began to reason things out in my mind. I can see why those women might not want to marry Reed, but if I have to marry him in the next life, would it not be better to learn how to cope with the situation here rather than to prolong the inevitable, if it's God's will?

I glanced over the horizon. The dark purple in the night sky was streaked with radiant orange and pink, as though it were exploding in the mountains, portraying the glory of God's art work.

After finishing work, we went to the Farmer's Daughter, a cafe. We went in and Reed asked, "What would you like?"

"Well, I don't know. What would you like to buy for me?" Looking over the menu, "All this stuff looks kinda' expensive."

"It doesn't matter. Order what you like. You're worth it."

I smiled. "Well, I've never had shrimp, but its $3.25."

"Fine. Order shrimp then."

"OK. Thank you." Then while we were eating, my eyes focused on Reed with gravy on his chin. He ate like someone would take it away if he did not shovel it in fast enough.

My natural feelings would go on the altar of sacrifice, if I must make myself obey him, I said to myself. You don't have to love someone in order to obey them. All I want to do is serve God. There's no law that says I ever even have to kiss him. But I can obey if I force myself. If I can earn my exaltation, then it will be worth whatever I go through.

That night I dreamed I was being horribly abused by a wicked man who had Reed's face with the freakiest expression. I woke up very offended in my innermost feelings. This dream shook me up so bad that for days I was trying to remove it from my memory. But after several weeks, I thought Well, maybe that was from the devil and he's trying to stop me from going where God wants me to go.

Francis and Reed were able to resume possession of Francis' old home on 5th East as Mr. Pine's lease had expired. So we moved from the old apartment to this large, decrepit house. If I had not known better, I would have thought it was haunted, but it did not worry me because this was Charles Zittings old home.

They brought all those boxes of who knows what and piled them in the large front room. After the move was completed, no one seemed to care about anything, but where they would sleep. Looking at the filth that they were accustomed to, I figured Well crud, I know how to clean up any darn mess in this whole blooming place. So fine. Once I get this filth taken care of, it won't be such a hell of a mess. So I took to cleaning up one mess at a time every chance I got to where the place began to look half civilized. All this was around 1963, the same year JFK was shot.

CHAPTER THREE

I had only lived with Reed and Francis for three months when Francis was hit by a car and taken to a hospital. She could no longer wash bottles. We were sitting at the kitchen table. Reed looked at me, "Can I count on you to carry on the responsibility of the business? You're the only one that can do the job now."

"Well, I'll do my best."

"We've got some past bills to pay. We've got to come up with $140 for gasoline we've charged, and $72 at Keith's for truck repair that hasn't been paid yet. But if we don't come up with some money to pay on the taxes on this place, we're going to lose it. They haven't been paid for the last three years."

"Well, sounds like I'd better get in gear. I think I know enough of everything that's been going on out there to pretty much be able to handle the orders. Do you want me to start up a batch right now? Or did you want to go see Francis at the hospital?"

"Well, let's start up a batch and do about 70 for Bestline Janitorial, then we'll go see Francis this afternoon."

"OK. Oh, hey! I just remembered Mama gave me the $18 that the government sends her for my support. I've still got it. Would that help you?"

"Yes, it will. How often do you get that?"

"Just once a month." I handed it to him.

"Thanks, May. Women are supposed to give their husbands all their monies, but there's sure a lot of women too stubborn to do it. Is this all you got?"

"Yeah, that's it."

"OK. Thank you."

I filled the vat with boiling water and the caustic soap Reed put the jugs in. I got on my apron and gloves and looked at the clock. OK. Fine. I washed off the outsides then threw them on the rack to drain, rinsed and put them on a rotary brush to clean the insides, inspected, then boxed them. I raced for an hour as fast as I could go, then stopped to look at the stack: Eighteen cases, four jugs to a case. Hmmm, I looked at the clock. I ought to be able to make it an even 20 cases an hour. I looked over at Reed.

"Are you ready to race? It's five after. Let's get these hummers humming." said Reed.

Determined to get the lead out, I took a deep breath, grabbed the jugs, and concentrated on every move to make it count to pick up lost time. Reed was running to put jugs in the vat then take off the clean jugs to stack.

"Hadn't you better slow down? You're working the crap out of me." said Reed.

"Oh no. We don't even want to slow down. Let's get this hummer revved up into third gear. I'll take them off the end. You just throw the clean case on. OK?"

We continued until five after. I stopped to count again. Eighteen with me taking off the end. Hmmm. It would take about five hours to do one hundred cases, I thought.

But after six hours, we were finished.

"Boy," I exclaimed while taking off my apron. "It would be neat if someone else could take them off the end."

"Well, I'm not going to. When you're full of piss and vinegar, there's no one who could keep up."

"Ah, come on. I was teasing."

"Maybe when I was younger, but not anymore. But you're young and it don't hurt you one bit. In fact, it's good for you."

I had my hand on the light switch. "Are we ready to go?" I asked.

"I guess so but when we get back, you need to clean all these cases. And if you've got any extra time, you could go to taking the rings and lids off the ones we are going to do tomorrow right here."

"Well, can't you just do that when you go to put them in the vat?"

"Yes, I could, but it'd make it a lot easier for me to just grab them and stick them in."

We left to visit Francis. That night when we returned, I fixed us some potatoes. At the table I asked Reed, "Do you want to help? You could take rings off if you want."

"I would if I could but I'm just too tired."

"Well, what'cha got to do any better?"

He jumped back sharply, "It's not for me to account to you for what I do or don't do. It's for you to concern yourself with what I give you to do. I dictate your jobs. You don't dictate mine."

I snapped back, "Well if that's the way you feel, just don't help me. I don't care." I could not get to the shop fast enough.

As I was cleaning cases, I felt somewhat confounded as I went over the day again. What did I do to get him going? Oh well, put it on the shelf. It's no big deal, I thought.

I worked until ten o'clock cleaning cases and removing rings and lids. Then Reed came out. Looking over what I had done, he commented, "That's enough. You can quit for the night. But you need to start getting up at five o'clock."

I sat on a case, "Why so early?" (I had been getting up at 6:30 a.m.)

He stood in front of me looking down. "It's like this. If you get up early, you will find that you will be able to think more clearly and be able to organize your work far better."

I was trying to make my tired brain hear him out.

"What it is, is that in the morning hours, the Lord has appointed four angels to be here to help you and if you're not there at five o'clock to meet them, they will just leave and let you work out your own problems."

I was staring into the night. "Well, how do I know when they are helping and when they're not?"

"How many times have you had a problem and the answer just comes to you and the answer is such a good one you just knew it would work? That's when these angels are talking to you."

Boy, I was thinking of several times that had happened.

"Now, wouldn't you much rather have their help than not?"

"Oh, for sure!"

"Well, OK. That's why you need to start getting up early."

"All right. I'll set my alarm. Are you going to get up too so we can start up a batch first thing?"

"No. But you can finish taking off the rings and lids and I'll get up as soon as I can. But nearly every night for hours while you're sleeping, I'm communicating with the other side to find out the mind and will of the Lord on different issues. That's the only reason I can't get up early or I would. There's many times I don't even get an hour's rest, but you don't know it."

I said nothing more but retired to bed. I got up early to work in the shop, but was eating my breakfast when Reed came in.

"Hi" I said, "Ya' want me to fix you some breakfast?"

He looked in my bowl.

"This is just oats with water and honey. Actually, it tastes better than it looks. But don't worry about this. I can fix you some 'taters and eggs."

"Naw. Don't bother. I'll get something at the hospital. I'm going to see Francis."

"Should I come too?"

"No, you got work to do here."

"Okey dokey."

Then approximately two or three hours later, I was cleaning up one of the bedrooms. I had swept the floor, made the bed and was dusting off the dresser when I looked over towards the window which was open. Reed was there. All I could see was his head looking in. It startled me.

Then he said, "So that's how you spend your time playing around. I wanted to know what you were doing when I'm not around."

What a strange gesture, feeling kind of shaky, to be put on the carpet for questioning. I answered, "Well, I made the bed and swept the floor and was dusting off the dresser is all."

"If that's all you've got done this morning, that's not enough. Francis could have had all the beds made and all the floors swept in that amount of time."

"Well, I did the dishes too and had some breakfast."

"Ya' better get out here and get a batch of jugs started."

"OK."

The days flew by.

The hospital was ready to release Francis to come home, so Reed and I went to pick her up. She had to walk with crutches. We helped her into the car and out of it upon arriving home. I was under one arm and Reed under the other. Taking our time, we finally made it to her bedroom. Turning so Francis could sit on her bed, we helped her take her coat off.

"Oh. Be careful. That hip is so dang sore. It's still got a water blister on it as big as your fist."

"Is there anything you'd like me to help you with?"

"Untie my shoes and take off my stockings."

"OK." I kneeled down, removed her shoes and was taking off her stockings.

"Now, take it easy. There's a blood clot right there." (She was pointing to her shin bone halfway up from her ankle.) "Don't touch that right there."

I stretched out the stocking so as to pass the sore place without touching it, then finished removing it.

Reed came back in the room chewing on a stick of celery. He plopped himself down in the chair next to her bed. Shaking the stick of celery at me, he began, "For as long as Francis needs help, you're to be her nurse to see to it that whatever she needs you to do, you do it. Do you understand?"

It came across that I needed to be commanded or something. My intelligence was offended. "Well, I don't mind taking care of her. It's OK."

"What I'm getting at is when you get up, you come see what she needs before you eat or anything. And when you come in at noon, I want you to see to it that Francis has something to eat before you sit down to eat. And when you come in at night, you come and see whatever she needs before you go to bed. Do you know what I mean?"

"Yes, but I don't know what all she needs. She'll need to tell me."

"I'll tell you what I need" said Francis "But you've got to be real careful. There's some liniment in the bathroom on the medicine shelf in a white bottle. I'd like that rubbed on my hip."

"OK."

After a week I knew what my duties entailed. In the morning I helped her into the tub so I could give her a bath. I brushed her false teeth, then helped her dress and put her shoes and stockings on. Then after work I helped her undress, massaged liniment on her sore spots, then took a wet washcloth to wipe her feet, after which I would massage her feet and back with regular hand lotion. But she liked a lot of massaging on her back and fell asleep while I was massaging. Then when I was through, I would ask, "Is there anything else you need before I go?"

"You haven't massaged my feet yet."

"Yes, I did. You were asleep."

"No, I wasn't. You're just trying to get out of it."

"I can do it again." So I did. I would do it three times rather than argue. Then I would cover her up.

"May I go now?" The clock said I had been there for nearly an hour and a half.

"I guess," she said with a huff.

Then I left for bed. I came to expect two hours of my day would go to Francis, so I just planned to have it so.

After several months she got well enough to walk without crutches, but she still wanted all the attention I had been giving her.

Reed and I were just finishing up a batch of bottles and I asked, "How many new cases did you say I needed to make up for Utah Fruit?"

"Well, their truck holds 210."

"So that's how many we make then, huh?"

"Yeah."

"OK."

Reed changed the subject. "I've been visiting a girl in Riverton for a couple of weeks now, and I think she might come this direction. Francis and I are going out there right now to see her. Her name is Zella Holts. Her great grandfather lived the principle so she's from good lineage. I told her Francis was my sister, so she thinks I'm single. We're going to see if we can talk her into going to meeting with us next Sunday to see what she thinks of the principle. What do you think about it?"

"Well, I don't know. What does she look like? What is her character like?"

"Oh, she's not bad looking, but she's got one eye that looks off over to Joneses when she's talking. That's about all."

"Well, what does she act like?"

"I haven't really seen her do much, except her grandfather asked her to iron him a shirt, and she went to plug in the iron and it sparked. So she started sassing her grandfather telling him to do it himself. But I wouldn't put up with that kinda' noise. I'd straighten her out in one hell uv'a hurry."

"Hmmm," I grunted. "I think I'll go fix something to eat and do this later."

They left, so I thought, I'll go out into the field and get me some watercress and enjoy the sunshine for a minute. I picked a handful of watercress and washed it in the water from the flowing well. I was thinking about what Reed said, and I felt a little numb. I thought, I don't know how many women he will bring in. God said that is the law. I guess it really doesn't matter 'cause whether I fail or succeed, it only depends upon my efforts. I sat down under a tree watching some wild geese fly overhead. I thought, oh, you beauties, as a thrill of joy went through me. I'm so glad I love animals and birds 'cause when Reed gets thirty wives or more, I can always find happiness without having to have him by my side all the time. I looked over the tall green grass and wild herbs. Laying my head back against the tree, I closed my eyes for a moment. I'm such a tiny thing in the scope of God's creation, but I'm glad God invented all these other little things. As I was staring into a wild rose bush next to me where a little rose near the ground was almost hidden from sight. I reached out and held it in my hand without picking it. As my mind drifted, I remembered something I had heard in meeting of how all God's creations know that God is their master and they strive to serve him to the best of their ability. This little rose has a spirit. I smiled. Here it is. It is growing to its fullest beauty, knowing that no one may ever see it except God. As a tear came to my eye, I looked to the heavens. I had never before supposed the love and nobleness of a rose. I cried a little as I said to myself, If God recognizes a rose, then he must see me, too. Thankfulness settled in my heart as I kissed the rose and said, "You sweet little things. The Lord sees you and I have seen you. You've made both of us happy."

I hurried back to make cases so Reed would not wonder what I had been doing. I was getting used to the idea of having to account for my time. I got by that day alright. But the next day when they came home from the cafe after having breakfast, Reed asked, "What have you been doing while we were gone?"

This was such a daily routine that I knew he was going to ask that. I made it a point to not only make good use of my time, but to remember what I had done. Being fully ready for this question, I would let them have it with both "barrels," like I was answering to a sergeant. "Well, first I got the washer going to wash the first batch of clothes, then while they were washing, I done the dishes and cleaned off the table and the stove. Then I went in and took out the first batch and rinsed them, put another batch in, then hung out the first batch. Then I came in and swept the two bedrooms, front room, and the bathroom and kitchen. Then I went and rinsed the second batch and got another batch started. Then I hung out the second batch and I just got through mopping the kitchen floor. Now, I've got to tend to the third batch of clothes."

"That's pretty good," Reed commented. "Now when you're finished with that batch of clothes, go start up a batch of bottles."

"Well, I just need to do the rugs next then I'll be done with the washing."

"All right. Then come and get me and I'll put the bottles in the sink."

That day passed quickly.

It was a Sunday. I had put on my best dress and hurried downstairs to the bathroom where I stood washing my face. Reed came up from behind and asked, "Here, will you wash these?"

I opened an eye and looking down saw his outstretched hand holding his false teeth that looked and smelled like they had not been cleaned for three months. I shut my eyes quickly. The thought of obedience ran through me as I said, "Uh, just a minute." I dried my face then held out my hand. Clink. Clink. Yuck. They dropped from his hand into mine. I thought, Oh well. It's no worse than baby poop., I guess. I could feel my face pulling every which direction. I opened part of one eye to barely see the tap where I held them for water to wash off all it would, then I sprinkled Ajax cleanser on them so I could finish the job. I handed them back to him.

"Thank you."

"It's OK."

We went on our way to meeting.

One of the brethren got up to speak. What he said was permanently imprinted upon my mind. "Those who are out in the world that have not had a chance to know the truth are yet in a natural territory. But when a person is brought to the feet of this order of the priesthood to where they are taught the fullness of the Gospel, must gain a testimony. Once they have a testimony of the truth, then they must make a choice to either embrace it with all their heart, might, mind and, strength or deny the truth and join the adversary and his forces. Those who turn against this work become darkened in their minds until they fall into the category that the Lord spoke of where-in they have ears that do not hear, eyes that do not see and a mind that cannot comprehend."

My mind reflected upon the demons who had persecuted the saints in the early days of Mormon history—the murderous mobs that were led by apostates. The realization of this sermon left me as sober as a judge. My soul was full of vibrations as I joined with the congregation to offer up my favorite song:

"How firm a foundation, ye Saints of the Lord,
Is laid for your faith in his excellent word! What more can he say than to you he hath said,
You who unto Jesus, you who unto Jesus,
You who unto Jesus for refuge have fled.

In every condition, in sickness, in health,
In poverty's vale or abounding in wealth,
At home or abroad, on the land or the sea,
As they days may demand, as they days may demand,
As they days may demand, so they succor shall be.

Then singing loudly, as I thought the Lord would enjoy hearing the last verse:

The soul that on Jesus hath leaned for repose
I will not, I cannot, desert to his foes;
That soul, though all hell should endeavor to shake,
I'll never, no never, no never forsake!

Taken from the hymn, "How Firm a Foundation," by Kirkham, Hymns, p. 66.

Two weeks later Reed had Zella living in the home with us. He told her she was to keep the house up, but she seemed to have a different idea. Anyway, the house needed more attention than it was getting. But all this accounting that I would do continually made me extremely sensitive of how each moment of my time was spent.

Some months passed and we picked up a few more bottle accounts. One day Reed came home from breakfast. He had asked me before he had left to start up a batch and work by myself until he returned. But knowing that the bottles would go twice as fast with his help, I thought it would be a better opportunity to clean out the fridge and mop the kitchen floor. When he walked in the door and saw me there wiping off the kitchen table, he said, "Why aren't you out there washing bottles?"

"Well, this is such a mess. It needs to be done anyway so I thought I would get this done first."

"How am I supposed to pay the bills if you're going to play around in the house all day?" Slamming his fist down on the table, he said "I don't care about this house, how filthy or how clean it is, it isn't going to keep the family and pay the debts. A business will support a family and a house, but a house and a family doesn't support anything. Now, if I have to keep you out of this house entirely to get the work done in the business, then I'll do it."

"Yeah, but how can we live if things get too damn filthy in here?"

"That's not your problem. If Zella doesn't clean up the place and we live in a pig pen, I don't care. But I want you to spend your time strictly on Reclaim Bottle. As long as there is one bottle to be washed that we can gain an extra five cents, that's where I want you spending your time."

From the tone of his voice, I was for getting out of there and getting a batch started up immediately.

So I tried to do all that I needed to in the business and still clean the house in the evenings. A week later, about seven o'clock at night, Reed came home from the café and I was in the house doing the dishes. As he opened the door and saw me standing there by the sink, his voice raised to a horrible pitch.

"I told you to stop doing this damn housework. And I mean it! If you can't be obedient," raising his hand in the air, "I promise you in the name of the Lord that you are going into dissolution. Now, let this house go and get out there and unload that truck."

There was no way that I had one word of defense. I scrambled to the door as fast as I could and ran out to the truck to unload.

Reed followed me out to the shop with his railings continuing, "What good is a clean house if we starve to death? It's your duty to support my family and I can't afford for you to play around doing Zella's work." He continued even more emphatically, "I'm putting you in the position of being the support of my family. This is the mission that the Lord has for you at this time. This is the most important thing that you can concern yourself with."

"Well, are you going to help me?"

"It's not for you to worry whether I help you or not. If I help you, fine. If I am doing more important things, then that's my business. I'm out trying to bring other women into the family. That's more important than putting bottles in the sink."

He was standing in my way. "Excuse me. I've got to put the cases right there."

We were taught in meetings almost every other Sunday that the man is the lawgiver to his family. Saying no more, I continued working as fast as I could. Reed helped me for a while then returned to the house.

I contemplated over what had just been said. I thought, Well, if this is what God wants me to do, then God will help me. He'll send angels if he has to. I know he will. I asked myself, Are you a quitter? No, I'm not a quitter. I'll do it, even if I fall over dead.

So in time I became very efficient in the duties of the bottle business. I came in the house one afternoon and looked at the filth. Zella had locked herself in her room and had been there for hours, which was common. I felt like screaming to release some of the anger. Having to live in such filth was a real trial!

A longing to communicate with Mrs. Ren was overwhelming as I went to a corner in the front room and sat down to make a little card for Mrs. Ren. It was 7:30 p.m. I had not seen Mrs. Ren in nearly two years. I folded a piece of paper and looking at one of Francis' plates, I drew a rose on the front and put a little message inside.

When Reed and Francis came home, Reed asked what I had been doing so I showed them the card. He hollered,

"So that's what you do when we're not here. You can't be trusted alone. You waste your time and neglect your work."

I was shocked that they would be so provoked over what I thought was such a trivial thing. And it was not as if I had done nothing all day.

Francis started in on me, "You could have had all this ironing done in that amount of time."

Reed butted in, "No, she could have had that truck unloaded and all the rings and lids taken off."

"Well, hell. If she has time to play around with drawing pictures, she could have done the ironing."

"She hadn't better try it again," Reed yelled while grabbing the note from out of my hand. "Oh, look at this, how nice what she's wrote," as he began to read it in a mocking fashion. "'Howdy neighbor.' She's not your neighbor anymore," he added with a gruff voice. Then he continued, "'How's that sweet little lady doing today? I miss you a bunch. I think about the times we went for a walk or was working in the garden.' Oh, pooh, pooh, pee doo," he adds, "'It was fun even when we was shoveling goat manure, just to be around your smiling face. I'm sorry I couldn't see you on your birthday or get you something, but I hope you enjoy this rose and when I'll see you, nobody knows. Love ya', Mazie."

Francis blurted out, "She'd rather shovel goat manure for Mrs. Ren than she would do anything for me."

Reed added, "All these damnable traditions she's got to get rid of. She thinks she's got to do something for someone just because she likes them, even if it's some old Catholic." In a commanding voice he shouted at me, "You must forget everything you learned before you came here and believe nothing or say nothing that does not conform with what I teach you. Anything or anyone that you knew or loved, you give 'em up. Do you understand? You're to love only those of my family. Why don't you tell Francis you love her instead of this old woman?"

"Well can't I ever see her again?"

"You might see her at a distance, but the sooner you cut yourself off from her, the better off you're going to be. You can love me or Francis. Even Zella would like you to show her a little love." Then he ripped up the card. "Now get out there and get that truck unloaded before you're up until midnight getting the work done. He continued "Put this in the garbage, so you're not tempted to waste your time anymore."

So I picked up my box of oil paints and pencils and set them in the garbage can. I dared not say anything. The contention was so thick in the house that you could cut it with a knife. I hurried from the front room past the kitchen table and hitting my hip bone on a cast iron frying pan handle, "Owww." Then I pushed it out of my way. I could not get outside fast enough. As I unloaded the truck, I was thinking to myself about Reed's saying I was to give up every friend I used to have. I thought I had not called anyone or gone to see any of my old friends and they had just quit trying to make contact with me a long time ago. So, now Mrs. Ren would probably forget me too because they forbid me from even phoning her. As a last resort to communication, I said in my mind, I love you, Mrs. Ren, and I hope you know it. I didn't forget you just because I moved away. When you're sitting in your big chair crocheting, I hope you remember me. I wiped a tear from my eye and hoped that somehow, she would get my message.

I kept working in the shop until after 11 o'clock so I could bring myself to try to forget the whole mess and start over. Then I finally had guts enough to go back into the house. I took care of Francis and retired for the evening.

That night I found myself caught up in a dream or nightmare. It was like I had a job to do in the basement of that old house. It was dark and dingy with cobwebs hanging from the bare floor joists. With the cobwebs and it being so dark, I could hardly make out anything as I walked very carefully back to the coal room about 25 feet away where I would load up my arms with something and carry it back to the bottom of the stairs. I tried not to disturb in the slightest, any of those hanging cobwebs that went every which direction. As I made these trips back and forth, I noticed several huge black widow spiders as large as both fists. They were watching every move I made as though waiting for their chance to spring upon me with their deadly fate. I moved so slowly I scarcely dared breathe until I woke in a sweat.

I got up and turned on the light but the nightmare was so clear, it would not leave my mind. I knelt to pray, "Dear Father in heaven. Please remove that horrible nightmare and let peace take its place. I pray in the name of Jesus Christ, amen." I tried to concentrate on something nice until I went back to sleep. This identical nightmare would plague my nights to the extent of reoccurring two or three times a week.

One day while I was working in the bottle barn, Bill came out and said that he had won a radio.

"Can I have your old one?" I asked very excitedly.

"Well, I guess so."

"All right! Thank you."

I plugged it in so I could have a little music. I whistled and tried to keep step while washing bottles to the tune of "The Orange Blossom Special."

Reed said, "Man, are you fast! I'm going to get Zella to help me keep up."

I had developed a little bounce to each step for a kind of an exercise for my legs so that I would not get varicose veins or whatever I might get from being on my feet all day. The radio was a definite improvement.

CHAPTER FOUR

For two weeks every time I went in the house, Francis would bring up that card I had made for Mrs. Ren and start harping on it. I had sent all my art supplies to the dump already and I had said I was sorry several times. So I could not understand why she kept up her railing. By the tone of her voice and repetition of her complaints, one would have thought I had committed some grand crime. I looked at her after I had endured it for two weeks straight and said, "You're trying to drive me crazy, aren't ya'? Like, that's been two weeks ago and you're acting like I can't be forgiven and start over. What the hell is the matter with you anyway? Are you jealous or something?"

"Jealous, huh! Hell, I'm not jealous," she ranted on. "You're such a baby, no wonder they always called you 'Baby May' all your life. You've never grown up yet. Now I've got the damn job of trying to make a woman out of you."

"Well, what do you want me to do that I'm not doing? Huh? Come on. Tell me. There's something aggravating you, so what do you want me to do?"

"Go mildew," was her reply as she turned on her heel and left the room. I did not think that was very cute but it ended the argument. I started some ironing while Francis sat down at the sewing machine. Reed came in and turned a chair around with his back to the wall and was reading a little.

Then he put the book down and stated, "Francis has done enough work when she lived with Uncle Charles that she has earned the right to a celestial glory if she never touched another stitch of work again as long as she lives. I promised her from the day of our marriage that when I got other women that they would wait on her and treat her with the respect she deserves. That's why I won't put up with any one of you calling her a liar or showing any other disrespect. If I did, I would have to answer to Uncle Charles, her first husband, who was a member of the priesthood council. I have to see to it that she is treated right. Not just any woman can have that place. Francis was born of a royal birthright to start with, and that entitles a woman to a position in a man's family right there. Just like Rebecca, Charles' daughter. When she comes into my family, if she ever does, she will be over Zella and May just because of her birthright. Even Zella is over May because her father did marry her mother by the laws of the land. Also, Zella's grandfather lived the principle."

"Well" I asked, "What about where it says that a person is not responsible for the crimes of their father or mother but for their own?"

"That's fine. I'm not saying you're condemned. I'm just saying that you never will hold a high place in my family because of it. If you were a chosen spirit on the other side, God would have sent you down here through a chosen lineage."

He was trying to make me feel like green slime on the floor because Mother and Father did not have a priesthood marriage. I remained quiet for quite some time. Then I got up courage to say, "Well, all I can do is all that I'm able to do. I can only do so much and I guess it really doesn't matter who dictates my jobs to me. If I can do the job honorably, God will judge me and say where I go in the end. I'm not going to worry about it."

It took all the courage I could muster to stick up for myself, feeling somewhat shaky. I was crying a little bit inside but, would not let on that I was offended. I made an excuse to go outside and was excused. I went to the bottom of the barn and hid myself in a dark corner and plead my heart out to God:

"Oh, Father. What am I? Who am I? Am I a freak? Am I a malfunction?" As I gritted my teeth and wept bitter tears, I remained in silence for some time. As I was searching my mind and my soul, then I uttered, "Anyway, I do love You and I love the brethren and I love the truth." As I knelt there sobbing, I felt as though I had received deep puncture wounds in my soul that left me bleeding and no way to stop my loss of blood, as I weakened and fell to the floor with such sorrow to think that I might never be on the right hand of God with the Saints. As I lay there after a while, a peace came over me that seemed to erase the memory of any sting or pain as the thought came to me, Why should I cry? It is my nature to be a servant and God will give me knowledge and strength. Why should I care if I serve all I can with all my strength and see to it that I do my best, whatever the job is, until I am dead? I'm not afraid of dying. Then God will judge and do what He wants with me. He made me so whatever my position is, it is OK."

With this thought repeating itself in my mind, I gradually gained strength. Then I heard footsteps upstairs and quickly got up and dusted the dirt off my clothes. Wiping my eyes, I ran over to the boiler and blew off the steam so that it would sound like I had a reason for being down there. When I came up to the top of the barn, Reed was standing there. The goat that Francis and Bill got from the auction was bawling wanting Francis to milk it.

I looked at it and said, "I wonder if I should learn to milk the goat. It's been bawling there for about two hours. I'm going to ask Francis if it is all right. Is that OK with you?"

"I don't care." said Reed.

I hurried to the house, "Francis, is it all right with you if I learn to milk the goat?"

"I don't care. Go ahead."

"Fine, I will" as I grabbed the milk bucket and went back to the nanny. "OK, Gretel, it's OK. I come to take care of you," as I stroked her fur and knelt down to give her a hug. "I get to milk you. Isn't that neat? OK. Now, hold still. I'm just new at this," as I began to make the milk flow. Tears again filled my eyes. "God made you and I'm doing you some good and you like me, don't you?" She looked at me and I hugged her again. "I'm so glad we got you," I said. Then I put the bucket of milk on the fence and scooped out a can full of chicken feed. I gave Gretel a handful then called, "Here, chick, chick," as the chickens ran toward me and I showered grain over the ground. "You, cute little things. I'm so glad we got you too. Come on Gertrude," I called to a little pet hen who was running as fast as she could to get in on all these goodies. Then I looked up into the apple tree. Since it was dark, my little pet pigeon was not noticing that there was grain on the ground. I shook the branch a little, "Come on baby. You've got to get in on this deal too." She opened her eyes and flew down to eat with the chickens. "Thank you, God, for all my little friends." I stood there watching them as it got darker and darker.

Then the door opened at the house. A hard, demanding call was made, "May, get in here."

I swallowed and stood there with a blank stare on my face as I made my feet walk toward the house. Oh dear, what now? As I entered the kitchen, there was Francis with her hands on her hips and her frown obvious, and Reed looking like he was ready for battle.

Reed snarled, "You used the phone today without permission. Who did you call?"

"Uh, well, I didn't call anybody. Mom called. I just answered the phone. She was telling me that Walt was really sick and she didn't know if he was going to die or not."

"Is that all?"

"Yes."

"Well, Francis, why didn't you just ask May? She'd have just told you if you didn't know who she was talking to."

"I'd rather you ask her yourself if you want to know. I don't care who she talks to. I just know she was on the phone and she didn't ask me if she could use it. That's all I know."

"Well, why don't you call Edith and see how Walt is. Maybe we ought to go see him tonight."

I spoke up, "Yeah, maybe we ought to. Maybe we can help him or take him to the hospital or something."

"Yeah, Francis. Let's go see him," Reed said. "Call Edith and let her know that we're coming."

Francis called and we went there. Walt was dying. I do not know what they were talking about in the kitchen—Reed, Francis, and Mother. I was in the front room rubbing some pan oil Watkins liniment on Walt's back. I made him some orange juice and helped him drink it.

Anyway, Reed and Francis did not take Walt to the hospital and two days later Walt died. Francis made the arrangements to have him buried. Three days after the funeral, Reed and Francis and I went over to see Mother

"You know, Edith," Reed said, "if you'd turn the equity you have in this house over to us, you could just come and stay in our house and work in the business, then you wouldn't have to worry about paying the bills and living alone."

"I don't like living alone. You know. That just might be an idea. So I'd just come and work there with you guys and then it would be like a life estate, huh? Like, instead of having a life estate here, I would have one over there. I think I like that idea. I could work there with May. Yes, let's do it."

So, a few days later, Francis got the papers together and Mama signed her property over to them. Then she came to live with us. I liked the idea, too. Mom was given the job of putting the jugs in the vat to help me wash bottles. But Mother told Reed that she had no intention of ever marrying him. She just wanted to live there and help in his family.

I turned 18 in 1965, shortly after Mother came to live with us. Reed told Francis to set up an appointment with Brother Guy Musser to marry me to Reed. He had taken Zella to wife just two weeks before, then he said, "Today's the day. Get yourself ready."

I knew it was the day but I did not know what time the appointment was for. I had been working in the bottles.

There was no joy, no anticipation or anything to look forward to. Unlike other people, I had no desire to kiss him or sing love songs or anything of the type. How can I describe anything so dreary. But I loved the thought of being obedient to priesthood counsel. I thought by obedience I might earn the right to be numbered with the saints. My life did not mean much to me, only for the good I could do to help in the priesthood work. By that time Reed and Francis had managed to convince me that this was Brother Musser's counsel. I felt that Brother Musser's counsel was the word of the Lord to me.

I went upstairs and put on my white blouse with fancy lace in front and my green suit I had found at the Magna dump and had sent to the cleaners and shined my shoes and combed my hair with waves in front and a braided bun in back. Then I went downstairs with a feeling of sacrifice. To do God's will, not mine, I thought. Christ didn't want to be nailed to the cross, but God's will was more important. A cold shiver went down my backbone as I said, "I'm ready."

Then all during the ceremony that took place in Brother Musser's living room, I was saying to God in my mind, Please give me strength and guidance. Then Brother Musser looked at me when it was all said and done. I did not even kiss Reed then.

I said to Musser, "I hope I can endure," with a very sober expression.

He laughed, "What a funny thing for someone to say who's just gotten married."

I failed to see the humor as I was dead serious.

CHAPTER FIVE

Two weeks later Reed began to spend much of his time doing what he called "his job" to keep everyone in line. He sat in the kitchen with his chair standing on its two back legs, with his back against the wall, with the Journal of Discourses in his hands. Zella was doing the dishes and I was folding the clothes I had brought in from the line.

Looking at Reed one would notice his one hand down inside the front of his pants, apparently fondling his privates as he often would do. His complexion was naturally red most of the time. He began to read on page 99, Volume 25:

Why should we need further proof that Joseph Smith was a prophet or that his predictions are being fulfilled? Why should it be necessary to prove that the word of God has come to the world through him and that the world is indispensable?

The Journal of Discourses, p. 99.

He paused there from reading and declared, "My mission is like unto the Prophet's. The Lord has given me a promise that whatever I will bless, he will bless. And whatever I will curse, he will curse. Every time I have told anyone what the Lord wanted them to do and they did not follow that command, they have lived to regret it. I can name hundreds of instances where people just refused to do the mind and will of God and they will reap damnation for it."

I came over by his side while he would find something else and read it. I was looking at the words so as to follow him and I noticed that he would say a different word than that which was in the book. Noticing it happening quite often, I opened my mouth, "Well, that's not what it says at all. You're pretending like you're reading it, but you ain't."

"Never mind. I know the way to read this book and I don't need you to correct me either. Just shut up and sit down. You might learn something."

"Well, why can't you just read it the way the Prophet spoke it? Heck, we'd like to know what they said."

"I put the words in there the way they need to be, to put over a point, so you get the correction you need. You don't get what was pertaining to someone else a hundred years ago." He went on. "Even when you go to meeting, it's for you to come home and come to me and I'll give you a correct interpretation of what was said so you don't get some screwy idea from something you heard in church. My family treats lightly what I tell them. That's why everyone here has so many accidents. Bill with his arm, Zella with her leg, Francis being hit by a car, and May's hand being scalded, just because you're all disobedient and you treat lightly the things of God." Whirling his fist in the air with a loud declaration of speech, "The whole church was brought under condemnation for the same damn crime: treating lightly the things of God, and the Lord is not pleased with it. I keep telling you over and over again. Now, what will it take to make you straighten up? Will someone have to lose their life over it?"

Similar sessions would go on regularly. We heard this doctrine so often, we all had it memorized. But I do not recall even one time when I had any type of accident a cut, a burn, stepping on a nail, or whatever that he did not remind me of some little thing that he had told me to do that I had not done to perfection, and that was the reason for my accident.

I feared being disobedient, to say the least because I heard this so many, many times. I would shake when he would even come towards me not knowing what would happen next.

I had been with the family for over two years giving all my labor without pay while all the monies were counted on Francis', Reed's and Bill's income taxes and Social Security, like Mom and I didn't even exist.

Reed was still preaching. "If anyone here desires to leave for any reason, they will walk out of here with only the shirt on their back." "But what about if they turned over land or a house like Mama. Then what?" I asked.

"I don't care. It's the same whether they put in $50,000 or five cents. It makes no difference. I'm not going to reward someone if they choose to apostatize. I'd just tell the brethren that they had turned traitor to the work."

I looked at Reed, "It's time to milk my goats. Can I leave?"

"Well, hurry. I'm not through."

Quickly leaving the room, I ran through the yard to get my milk bucket and scrambled toward the pasture. His pasture consisted of five acres of trees, several ponds fed by flowing wells, grass, herbs and wild flowers everywhere. Stopping to take a pinch of fresh watercress by a flowing well, I noticed a friendly little frog sitting proudly on the bank. "Hi. How ya' doin', little feller?" I felt such joy to be in the field far away from the house where the sun was shining and my goatees were getting fat from the abundance of feed. "Ah," I sighed, as I looked to the heavens. "What a beautiful day." As I walked with a little bounce to my step towards my milk goat, "How ya' doin'?" as I stroked her fur. "Everything OK out here?" As I sat on my foot behind me, the milk was hitting the inside of my bucket. She turned and licked me behind my ear. "OK. OK. I know you love me." And springing to my feet, "Thank you." whistling a tune on my way to my other little friends.

When all the goats were milked (I had five), I was on my way back to the house and noticed a mother hen that I knew had seven babies. I watched her teaching them to find little things to eat as I smiled and counted them again. There were only six! "Did you lose one of your babies?" Feeling sorry when I was passing an old lumber pile, I heard a "Peep, peep." I put down my bucket and climbed the fence. I followed the little "peep" and thought, He's right here. So I began carefully to remove one board at a time. I think the noise scared him because I seemed to move over half the pile before I caught him. "There you are you cute little thing. Let's take you back to your mommy. She's been wondering about you."

Then I returned to the house. Reed sat there still full of fire, "What the hell takes you so long to milk a few goats?"

"One of the little chickens was lost under the woodpile. I had to find him."

"Well, you should be here hearing something that will help you to get your exaltation, if you will just follow it. The only reason the Lord has been blessing us as a family at all is because of my prayers. I petition the Lord, day and night to forgive you for treating lightly what I have been telling you, but I don't know how much longer I can hold back the wrath of God from coming on this family. The prophets since time began have been treated with impunity while they alone held the keys and the powers of heaven over their dispensation."

I thought on that statement and sure enough, that's the truth. And the people didn't like the prophets either. I thought, But they should have been obedient anyway so that God would have spared them from destruction.

Reed went on preaching while I sat there silently, then I blurted out what was on my mind, "Well, what if your leader teaches you something and you follow him and it's wrong and you're doing it 'cause you don't know it's wrong?"

"Huh," he grunted. "You can't judge your leaders. God put them over you, not under you. Can the lesser judge the higher? What kind of order would God have if everyone was doing their own damn will instead of God's? It's for you to follow your leaders and God will hold them accountable. Even though you may be learning and steadily going up the ladder, your leaders are learning also and they are going up ahead of you still, so that you never can catch up. Where I am now, you may be 20 years from now, but I will be just that much higher. Now if everyone were allowed to just do their own will, heaven would be made into a hell in a hurry, wouldn't it. The order of heaven always has been and always will be: God speaks to the head of the house and then man speaks to the tail. God doesn't ever come directly to the tail. You get it? If I were to lead you wrong and you followed me, you would go into heaven for obedience, and the fault if any, would be on my head. What you need to worry about is being obedient. You never will be able to judge me. Never," his eyes seeming to drill a hole through me.

Then he started hollering, "Now because Edith has come to live with us, I want everyone here to know that just because she is older than Francis, that doesn't make her on the same level," turning to Mother with his finger pointing at her. "Don't you try to boss anyone when it's not your place."

"Well, Reed. I don't try to boss anyone. I just do my own job and that's it."

Francis blurted in, "Yes you do. You try to boss Zella when I'm not here. And you always get May to do your work for you. I'm the boss over these women, not you. You get out of my position and stay out."

Reed stared at me, "I want you to quit obeying your mother. You are to obey Francis, not Edith. For the adultery she has committed on the prairie to have her children, she doesn't deserve any praise. She needs to be recognized for what she is. She never had any more of a marriage than a dog or a cat, and she thinks God will accept it?" shouting at Mother as he slammed his fist down on the sideboard. "HE WON'T! He won't accept nonesuch." He turned to look at me, "I want you to call Francis 'mother.' She is worthy of the name. But this old bitch is not. Do you understand?"

The impact of his voice almost nailed me to the wall. I stood there with my mind blank and did not know what to say. I always had wished Daddy would have grabbed Mother and taken her to the priesthood to get married. I had wished that all my life, but I had never thought of Mother as a bitch. A quivering, sickening feeling came over me as I had to listen to everything that he had to say about Mom.

As he continued to rail on, "You call her 'Edith.' That's a good enough name for this old slut. That's what the Lord would call her. She can go on lying that God will accept her marriage just because she done it in sincerity. Why even the devils in hell are sincere. You know it?"

"Well, Reed, we tried to live honorably. But it was hard to know where the priesthood keys were. Joseph was studying to try and find that out. Our intentions were good."

"Hell is full of devils that had good intentions like you. God doesn't honor it in the least degree. May never will be free from your sin until she can put you down and recognize what you are, but as long as she thinks you're a somebody, she can't advance herself. The first step to perfection is to repent of your sins. Now how are you going to repent of a sin if you can't even recognize it? You first have to recognize it then you've got to be sorry then admit it and then forsake it, and never pick up that sin again."

Reed looked directly at me, "You have got to first recognize what your mother is. She is an adulterous woman. Then you must feel sorry over it. If you don't, you should. If you had any idea how your exaltation is hanging by a thread of whether you can recognize these things, you would feel damn sorry. Then you need to admit it. Quit telling yourself that you love her."

Then with his fist slamming down again on the sideboard, "THEN FORSAKE HER!" He pulled out The Bible and began reading where if a branch is dead, you cut it off lest the whole tree go into the fire. "If you don't cut yourself off, you will go to hell with her."

"Well, uh, what about the part where a child should honor their father and mother?" I asked.

"That is referring to a mother worthy of honoring, like Francis. Her children can call her mother all day long, and that's just fine, but Edith is not a fit mother because she has denied the priesthood by taking authority to herself to marry herself to that old boy she had affairs with on the prairie (meaning my father)."

Mom tightened both her fists and stamped her foot on the floor, "I have not denied the priesthood, Reed. You lie when you say I have. I have always loved them and tried to do what they say. I wanted the priesthood to marry Joseph and me, but he couldn't figure out if they had the authority or not." Mom's voice dropped quite low, almost a mumble. "I don't know. Maybe he was kinda' stupid in that respect. If he had just taken me, we could have had things right and it would have saved us a lot of problems." She boldly declared then, "But he studied the priesthood's teachings and he told me before he died for me not to surrender so much as my little finger to anything except the teachings of Joseph White Musser, and I haven't. So there! Now, if you'll move yourself, I'll get the pig bucket. I've got to feed the pigs."

Reed stood up and moved his chair. Mom took the bucket and went outdoors.

"All of you, with the exception of Francis, are outcasts from the priesthood work. I'm trying to redeem you, even if the priesthood council has given up.

Brother Guy has told me many times 'if anyone can do anything for them, meaning you people, you can.'" Reed was twiddling his thumbs while his hands were resting upon his belly with his chair leaned against the wall. Out of the corner of his eyes, he looked at Bill as he said, "The priesthood had given up on Bill because of the trouble Bill stirred up with several women in Short Crick. They were ready to kick him out of town. And if I had not taken him in, he'd most likely have apostatized."

Bill said nothing. The room was somewhat quiet for a time, then Reed, looking at Zella, said, "No one would want Zella. It's plain to see she's not all there."

Zella had a frown on her face a mile long. "Gee, thanks. Thanks for letting me know what you think," as tears formed in her eyes.

"Well, it's true. I didn't say that I didn't love you," rubbing his hand across his bald head. "But I can't lie just to make you happy. If you weren't half cracked, you'd get in and do something in a day rather than sit around sulking. You'd also take a bath once in a while instead of being so damn filthy. But I'm glad you're here. I just know that no one else would put up with you. You'd probably end up in the nut house."

At that Zella flared up and barked back, "Why should I do anything? If I do something, Francis says its wrong and if I don't, she's mad. Hell, Reed. How would you feel if you were getting beat all the time?"

"That shouldn't stop you from doing your work if you wanted to."

The door knob turned. Mama came in from feeding the pigs. Holding her hands out away from her dress, she said, "Excuse me," as she walked in front of Reed. "My hands stink."

He looked at the muck on her hands and arms from the chore. A smirk crossed his face as he said, "That's a good job for you. It's one pig feeding another."

"You just pipe down. That's not a bit cute," Mom said while washing her hands.

Bill got up. "Francis and I are going to a dance. There's a couple of girls there I been watching pretty close. Maybe the one girl will become my wife or both. They seem to like me."

Reed leaned forward as the two front legs of his chair hit the floor. "Well, if they come towards this direction, you'd better let me meet them before you get your heart set. Because you're better looking than I am, it would work well for you to get the fish on the line and then let me see if I want them or not."

"I don't know if they're that far along. I haven't said much about religion."

"Well, take your time with them. Get them to fall in love with you first or you'll be dead in the water."

This went on until after 11 o'clock. I left the room thinking, What IS right? I know Mom has taught me to uphold the priesthood all my life. She has preached to me time and again how valuable they are to us. I tried to put it from my mind, placing it on the shelf and asking God for understanding that I might know what truth is in time, as I sure can't change the past.

About this time I had been married approximately three months. One day after all the work was done, I needed to sew a rip in one of my skirts and had settled down in a recliner in the front room. It was 9:30 and I felt the need for more rest. Reed approached me with a gruff voice, "Are you ready to go to bed?"

"Actually, I'd rather sleep by myself. There are enough beds in this house. I'd really rather not sleep with you tonight. Is that all right?"

"Oh. You don't want to sleep with me, huh? Well, you'd better get something in your head, the sooner the better." His breath was beating down upon me in such a way as I would never forget. "You WILL sleep with me and anytime you get to where you don't want to, I will put you down as the LOWEST person in my family and you will be made to feel it. You will be put down lower than a concubine."

I was already put down lower than anyone except Mama. He considered her to be a concubine. In my understanding that meant that anyone could beat me that wanted to and I would be deprived of food, anything that was good, and I would be made to clean up all the filthy jobs (like when Reed would mess his underwear). Also, I would be made to do the heavy lifting like carrying the water out of the basement in buckets just because he wanted it done like that because that was just the way he treated Mother on account of her refusing to marry him.

I said nothing while picking up my sewing and making my way upstairs to the attic to his bedroom. Totally shocked at his answer, heartsick and confounded, I laid myself down in the bed.

Then Reed snuggled up to me and in a low voice, as if attempting to apologize, "Just don't ever defy me, honey. I'll be good to you. I'll let you have a little more rest. OK? You can go to sleep now, but I want to wake you up later. Is that alright?"

Reed would demand that I take care of him sexually three to five times per night. He would sleep during the day while I worked. So at four in the morning, after he became somewhat satisfied, he turned to me, "Well, you'd better get up and get the cases cleaned."

It was my job to go through the boxes to clean them up before we put clean jugs in them. I lay there in silence. How nice it would be to get a little more rest.

His voice became sharper, "Get up. Come on. Get out there and get your work done." Then pausing a moment he added, "I'll get you up." Coming across with a much quieter tone accompanied by a hideous giggle, he swung his legs up so as to place his feet in the center of my back and applied steady pressure, and as I was pushed from the bed, I caught myself from falling. There was no use. I did need to clean the cases.

So I got dressed quickly and scrambled downstairs to meet the day. As my face was embraced by the fresh morning air, I breathed deeply. The joy of leaving the jobs of the night and beginning a new day put a slight smile on my face, as I hurried to the bottle barn to get every necessary thing ready for cleaning jugs.

When Reed came down to the shop approximately four hours later, I had started a batch of bottles. Mother had gotten up and was putting them in the vat for me. I was wondering but I did not know if I dared ask. After a while I turned to Reed, "You know, sometimes I wonder why you treat me the way you do."

Sensing what I was referring to, he replied, "Well, any man that had you would treat you exactly the same way I do."

"You think so?"

"I know so. Women are a dime a dozen. The only thing that makes them of any value is if they can be obedient."

I stopped washing jugs to pay attention to what he was saying.

"If a man never required anything of his women, he would be held responsible for their being worthless. No real saint ever did have an easy life. So, do you think you are going to go to heaven without ever earning the privilege of being there? You're not. The early pioneers went through more than anything you've been asked to go through, and if you're not obedient enough, I can't take you where the saints are. Take Edith over there. She is so damned disobedient. She's as worthless as teats on a boar pig. She isn't even worth her salt."

He walked towards Mother then grabbed her by her hair on the top of her head and gave it a few yanks, just enough to make her holler, then let her go. While staring at Mom with his beady eyes, "I'd be just as far along if I didn't have her."

"Now, Reed. You just keep your hands to yourself," Mom said as she threw her hands up to stop him. "I'm trying to help May anyway."

"Yes, and a very damned little bit of help at that."

After a while I interrupted throwing a word in edgeways, "Reed, before we came here you didn't used to treat us the way you do now. So how come it's different?"

Reed began to laugh, "Ha, ha, ha, ha, ha! That's a good one. Let me answer you in this way. Have you ever heard of a man trying to catch a fish that he has already caught? He uses the bait for those who are yet swimming around, doesn't he. Ha, ha, ha. What a silly question."

I pondered on that a moment then said, "Yeah, I guess that's true." Mom and I stopped talking so maybe he would leave, and he did.

As the day's temperatures increased, Mom and I had been working over the boiling water for nearly five hours and were nearly finished with a batch. The bottle barn had all the windows boarded up. There was an inspecting light we could see by and also the double doors were open. It still seemed somewhat dark in the shop, but straight ahead about 10 feet of the rinse tubs was a large solid picture window. Nearly delirious from the heat and fatigue, I glanced up and looked through this window that was facing the street (5th East). A young man was riding his bicycle with his swimming paraphernalia across his shoulders, casually going by, eating an ice cream cone. I stopped working to watch him pass. I stood there with sweat running from every pore of my body. Staring as though I had been hit in the face with a steel frying pan, a feeling of hopelessness took over as I found myself caught up in a daydream. Then a lump began forming in my throat as I began to cry inside, while the thought came across my mind, someday, someday, I will be considered valuable, like a prize, and I will be paid a decent wage for my efforts, too.

Mother, noticing I had just been standing for some time, said in a sweet voice, "Come on, May. Let's finish."

"Yeah. Let's get this over with."

We went in the house for a bite to eat. Mother and I were sitting at the table eating a bowl of Zella's fresh rice pudding, hot from the oven. Francis was sitting in the front room on the couch crocheting a doily. Reed asked, "Did you get all those through?"

"Yeah, we did," I answered. "Bill can deliver that load anytime. The truck is all loaded ready to go."

"How many is there?"

"One hundred and five."

"That's pretty good. I wished everyone was as obedient as May. Boy, I'd really get somewhere."

Mom spoke up, "Well, what about me? Don't you appreciate what I've done?"

"Ah, hell. You're not much help."

I jumped in, "Well I betcha what. She saves me one third of my time anyway."

"Well, hell. If she amounted to something, the system would go twice as fast, but she doesn't."

"Well, I appreciate her anyway. I'll tell you that."

"Yeah. Just because she's your mother, you stick up for this lazy old bitch."

I had heard enough. It seemed as though Reed would delight in railing on Mother's adultery until it was just the most obnoxious thing. I left the house. Pester, my cat, met me in the driveway, rubbing her body against my legs. "Hello, you sweet thing," as I bent over to pick her up. I carried her to the goat shed stroking her fur while I sat on a bale of hay brushing my face against hers. "I sure do like you, Pester. You know that? You're a darling little kitty spirit." I closed my eyes for a moment while I leaned against the haystack as I went into a daydream. It was late afternoon and the sun was setting.

I was remembering a dream where I had heard beautiful music. I wanted to sing something so I started singing a hymn,

There's surely somewhere a lowly place,
In earth's harvest fields so wide,
Where I may labor through life's short day
For Jesus, the crucified;
So trusting my all to thy tender care
And knowing thou lovest me,
I'll do thy will with a heart sincere;
I'll be what you want me to be.
I'll go where you want me to go, dear Lord,
Over mountain, or plain, or sea.
I'll say what you want me to say, dear Lord;
I'll be what you want me to be."

"I'll Go Where You Want Me to Go."
Text by Mary Brown, music by Carrie E. Rounsefell, Hymns, p. 75.

I hugged my little friend, "Thank heavens for kittens. I sure do like you," I repeated, while setting her down so I could give the goat some hay. Then I picked her up again while I whistled the music to that song on my way back to the house.

Over the days and weeks the contention was continual. One morning Mother and I were in the front room. I had combed her hair and was braiding it. Reed came in and saw us. Being quick to rebuke me for showing any kindness to Mother, he yelled at me with fire in his eyes, "What are you doing her hair for when I've told you not to be doing anything for this woman?" He walked up to me and slapped my arm, knocking my hand off Mom's braid. "You let her do her own hair. You shouldn't want to do anything for her or even touch her any more than you would want to do it for the devil in hell."

My heart was going like crazy. Mother's hair was finished. I backed against the wall. The force of his word was so loud, it just about knocked me over. He was hovering over Mother, the saliva flying from his mouth making Mom blink her eyes, while her upper lip was pulled down tight toward her chin. As he continued his railing, "You're just as bad as Lucifer, and that's what I'll call you. I don't want anyone in my home thinking you're a saint or patterning their life after you. And I don't want you talking to my women, teaching them to be a devil like yourself, Miss Lucifer."

"Now, Reed. You just pipe down. I don't go around calling you names. You act just like I go around making trouble. I don't."

"Well, I want you recognized for what you are so you don't go around deceiving anyone by your pretty face." He grabbed her by the cheek shaking her head.

Mom's hand went up against his in an attempt to get his hand away. "You don't need to touch me. I don't want you to touch me."

"I'll do anything I feel like to you. And so will anyone else, you old devil."

"You act just like you don't have anything better to do than to rail on me and I'm sick of hearing all this."

Reed's voice heavy in rebuke, "It will be shouted from the housetops before you're through, and everyone will know what you are, Miss Lucifer."

"Why do you keep calling me a devil? I'm not the devil. I don't want a thing to do with him. Just get him away from me as far as you can."

"You have betrayed God the same way the devil did. If a person does the same thing as the devil, doesn't that put them in the same category? It does. God's no respecter of persons and you're not one bit better for your wrongs than he is for his. Until you can hate your wrongs enough to where you can atone for them, you never can be forgiven. You have got to recognize the sin you have committed on the prairie, that God had nothing to do with it. That it was just you and the old boy you shacked up with out there having a screwing good time. And that's all it was in the sight of God."

"Well, we had children, and I raised them the best I could anyway."

"Oh, pooh, pooh. That's nothing that any dog or cat couldn't do. So where are you any better? You have got to atone for your crime before you can ever be forgiven." He was still hovering over her and hollering with such impact that he almost lost his false teeth a couple of times. "And for you to atone, you would have to take your son, Joe, who you love so much, and put his head on a chopping block. And you, Edith, whether you like it or not, would have to swing the axe. Then after you had done that, you never would go around telling anybody that what you done out there had anything to do with God. And until you can bring yourself to do that, all your words of how you've repented is just a lot of hot air. It doesn't mean a thing. If God allowed you to walk into heaven without atoning for your damnable crimes, he would be showing partiality. Why not just let the devil walk in scot-free. He just as well as let you in."

I said, "Can I go? I got work to do."

"NO! You need to hear it as well as she does so you don't go treating her like some kinda' saint instead of the devil she is. If you don't quit it, you will carry the same curse on your head as she has on hers."

This type of preaching ran rampant. Every spare moment that Mom was not helping me, he would park himself in front of her and begin the same old thing again. Whether Mom was sleeping or eating or whether she was helping me, to say anything or do anything against his frame of mind would prove outright defiance.

I felt there was some truth to what he was saying but how much, I could not say. He claimed to have read all the Journals, the truth books, Joseph Musser's teachings, The Doctrine and Covenants, and The Book of Mormon. He said that he knew the laws of God forwards and backwards and that God had chosen him because he was not afraid to tell the truth like it is without beating around the bush. I knew I was unlearned, but I could sure see why Mom would not want to chop Joe's head off. I was fighting to keep down my resentment towards Reed's horrible attitude. I told myself, I must not hate. If I ever do, it will destroy me.

I had found within myself an outburst like Joe had had. I did not want to ever have that type of character, for if I ever lost control, I could see myself maybe killing someone, which I never wanted to happen, no matter what.

I worked on my feelings to try to keep calm and level headed. "Uh, can I go now? I think I've heard enough."

"All right. You can be excused."

Thank God, I said to myself, as I fled out the door. I could hardly stand it another second. I went straight to the bottle barn where I found a quiet corner and began to pour my heart out to God.

"Oh, Father in heaven. Please help me to control my feelings. I must have your help. Oh, please help me to remove this evil influence I have. I mind Reed and I know I have to do it, but I can hardly stand this tension. Please bless Mom if you can, 'cause I'm glad I was born. I hope I don't have a curse on me. I pray for help in all things, in the name of Jesus Christ, our Redeemer, amen."

I got to calling my mother Edith to make Reed happy, but when I was to refer to Francis as "Mother," I could not seem to make the words come out.

Mother had given them her home to come and help me from being worked to death. Many time I wished she still had her home and independence even though I enjoyed her company and appreciated her help.

CHAPTER SIX

A few weeks later one beautiful summer morning, I stepped outside of the house and breathed deeply some of that good country air. I walked over to where the apple trees were to see if I could find a nice one that the little worms had not polished off. I found a couple of good ones. While sitting on an old log next to a small pond near the house, I began to daydream, looking at the mud around the edge of the water. I had been thinking for about a month how it was a shame that all the clean jugs that I washed that had flaws in them. Why could they not just be broken, crushed and re-melted, saving the glass? As I pondered over the idea, I thought, Well, heck it would probably cost more for the gas to get the temperature high enough than it would be worth.

Francis and Reed had said that the ground around there was clay. I was thinking about how I had seen a show on the Indians making pottery with clay. I wondered, Is this the kind of soil? So I bent over and took a handful of the thicker mud and formed it into the shape of a bowl, then wet the surface so it was slick and finished, then I placed it on an old board.

Reed came out just then and walked over to me, he asked, "What are you doing?"

"Well, I was just wondering if this clay is the kind they use for pottery."

"Ha, ha, ha," he went on, "You've never grown up. You're still making mud pies. Do you still play with paper dolls, too? Ha, ha, ha."

I went in to wash my hands and Francis said, "Mr. Mullen called. He needs your help at Old Mill Packing (a local food packing plant) today."

"All right," I shouted with glee and jumped for joy. I ran in to change into my better clothes. "I'm ready to go," I exclaimed.

"Well, Micron Chemical wants thirty cases delivered tomorrow so you'll have to do them when you get home if you want to work over there."

"Ok, no problem."

So after working at Old Mill, screwing lids on quart bottles of salad dressing then stacking them until 5 p.m., I came in the house. Francis was standing there with a pious expression and in a commanding tone, started saying, "Bestline Janitorial needs fifty cases first thing in the morning. So you have got to get eighty done tonight."

"Well, are you sure they can't wait until the afternoon or Friday?"

"NO, THEY CAN'T!" she screamed.

Then Reed chipped in, "The bottle orders come first. You're the one who wanted to work at Old Mill, now you can do this too."

I was looking at Francis and had a feeling, I really wouldn't put it past her to not even ask the company if they could wait a day, but it wasn't worth the argument. Besides, if they got mad, they would likely not let me work over there anymore, even though I was giving them all my earnings of one dollar an hour, but shit I just loved being away from the damn contention.

"Well, Ok, if that's what I need to do, I will. But who's going to put them in the vat for me?"

"Berniece (Bill's wife) can help you when you get started up until about nine o'clock then Edith can help and maybe Bill will. We'll see."

Reed had been sleeping during the daytime as usual. Being fully refreshed and strengthened, he came out when Mother was helping me. Looking at me, Reed referred to my mother and asked, "Is this old devil doing her job?"

I was silent as I continued to work. While Reed would rail, it just seemed the best way to handle the situation would be to let him carry on without any contradictions, in hopes he would become bored and eventually leave or maybe I could change the subject. But Mother quite often would bear all she could then she would give him a piece of her mind which would prolong his being there.

"You're slower than cold tar in January," Reed pushed Mom. "Move over, I'll put them in. You take them off the end." (That meant stacking the clean jugs.)

"Well, that's all right, if you think you can do better than I can."

"I know I can do anything better than you can. Don't compare me with yourself. I'm not on your level, Miss Lucifer. I'll show you how it's done. You never do keep up with May. She always ends up doing half your work for you 'cause you're so damn slow."

"Well, I try anyway."

"The devil could try, too, and he'd be about as good maybe even faster than you are."

"Well, I'm not the devil and I resent you calling me that nasty name. I just resent it." Mom stood there with her fist doubled up with her arms by her side and slightly stomping her feet as she expressed herself.

"You're in the same category, you live the same life as the devil. So that makes you one, too."

Mom started interrupting, "Well, in Joseph's patriarchal blessing, it said he would accomplish much with his own two hands, so we would get by with the marriage we had until we could do something better. We were trying to learn about these things."

"That's just your justifying devil talking trying to justify your damn devil-mentary. You thinking you're so great just because of a patriarchal blessing. God won't have anything to do with it." Reed raised his hand in the air in an attempt to put his hand to the square, "And I promise you that in the name of the Lord, Jesus Christ."

Oh dear, I looked out into the blackness of the night. The workings of Mom and Reed had stopped. All this kind of talk was sapping my strength. Mom was standing there braced against the end table leaning over backwards while looking up at Reed. He was hovering over her with his hand still to the square with hell fire written all over his face.

"I can't help what you say. I'm here, and I'm trying to do the best that I can under the circumstances."

Then Reed grabbed a handful of Mother's hair on the top of her head and was shaking her head back and forth, "Well, your trying isn't good enough, Miss Lucifer," as he spit in her face.

Mother's hands flew up against him, "Ouch, get away from me you filthy thing doing such a dirty trick, spitting on me." Mother started crying as she went for the water to wash it off.

Ugh, a creepy feeling that sent cold chills running down my spine. I turned and attempted to make peace, "We have a job to do. If you don't want to help us, why don't you just go back to bed. I don't mind taking the cases off the end. It'll be faster than we're going, whether she's a devil, I'm a devil, or who's a devil. It isn't going to get the work done if we don't get busy."

"She'd better get it in her head and not tell me how it is. I know how it is. I don't need this old devil to correct me."

"Reed, if you don't get out of here, I'm quitting. And you two can stay here and argue all night, but I'm tired."

He turned to me, "I'll tell you when you can quit and when you can't. I'm the boss here. You're not. And you'd better quit sticking up for your damned old mother."

I paused, "Look, Reed, are we getting anything done?"

"It's up to me whether we get anything done or if we stand here all night. I'm the priesthood over this home."

We stood there looking at each other, then in a gentle voice I said, "Well, that's fine, but would you please leave us two devils alone so we can get this job done. You're probably tired and we can do it. Ok?"

Then Reed softened somewhat and said, "Well, if you're going to be so damn nice about it, then Ok." He left.

I sighed with relief. Talking it over with Mom, I said, "You know what?"

"What?"

"If you could just stand to listen to him without saying anything back, he might feel like he's talking to himself and leave quicker because it would be boring for him."

"Yeah, I know, May. But I just can't stand the way he treats me." She shook all over. "He needs to be told."

"True, but you ain't goin' to change his mind. He'll have his way anyway."

"I know it."

I was such a coward. And I wondered for years after, why I didn't break a gallon jug over his head and kill him. But then I fought every day to try to control my anger, for I asked God to help me to get thru this life without killing anyone. But My precious Mother was never given any respect or appreciation, for having turned over the monies from the sale of her home to them.

The next day I went with Francis and Reed to make the delivery and the first thing out of the manager's mouth when he saw us walk in the door was, "Oh, gee, that was really quick. I didn't expect it so soon."

My heart sunk and I thought, as I looked over at Francis out of the corner of my eye, This lady appears to be so sweet, but why would she do that to me? Is there any logic?

Then I asked the manager, "Oh, I thought you needed them in a hurry."

"Oh, tomorrow would have been fine, but it's Ok. Let's unload them over here."

A feeling of sorrow filled my heart. I could not imagine why she would want me to work into the night until two o'clock in the morning when it was not necessary.

Several months passed and I went to work at Old Mill again. I was hurrying in my usual rush at the factory. There was a little wad of mayonnaise base on the cement floor. I stepped on it and my right leg slipped sideways at the knee. As I came down, those working around me noticed the accident and came to help me. "Owe! Owe! Owe!"

"What happened?" everyone asked with excitement.

"I slipped. Owe. Owe."

They could see my leg was out sideways. I was suffering excruciating pain.

One asked, "Should we take you to the clinic just down the road?"

I nodded, with tears flowing down my face. They took me down there as fast as they could. I was waited on and the knee was put into place, wrapped up nicely, and the doctor told me to stay off my leg and apply ice packs. Then a fellow employee took me home.

When Reed and Francis found out that I had gone to a clinic instead of coming home, even though an insurance company was paying the bill, they became furious. "You should have had them bring you home," Reed yelled at me. "Francis could take care of you. You had no right going to someone else for your care."

In an attempt to defend myself, I stated, "They took me there. I couldn't say where I should go. I was too busy screaming and crying, trying to stand the pain. Heck, I didn't know where I was going."

"Well, if it ever happens again, you'd better call home. Do you hear me?"

I sat there with a bleak feeling, then murmured, "Well, I'm kinda' glad they took me there so the doctor could put it in place."

"Francis could put it in just as good as any doctor. She's a registered nurse and THIS is where you belong. The only reason this happened is because of your sticking up for your damned old mother. You need to learn obedience, or I don't know what God is going to do to you."

I was sitting there in pain and all he could think was that it was my fault that I got hurt. Not one ounce of kindness or even pity did he offer. I was so confused that I was sick to my stomach. I said, "Can I please lay down?" And because I could not get up the stairs, I went in the other room and laid on Bill's bed, since he was gone.

I could hear Reed telling Zella from the bathroom where the washing machine was, that she was to wash all Mom's clothes, even her temple garments, in the last batch after everyone else's clothes were through. With the old-time washer we had, the wash water was used many times before being dumped. A feeling came over me that was rather scary. I was remembering the priesthood brethren's teachings in meeting that the garment was not to even touch the floor, if possible. Now they are going to be washed in mop water, just because Reed said Mom was a devil and her garments were null and void in God's sight.

I lay there thinking about the crime of adultery and how important marriage was. My mind was in a turmoil, as I began to petition heaven,

"Kind and good Father who is in heaven. I'm told to despise my Mother, but I don't feel good about it, and I know that Mom is not perfect, but she could have been lots worse than what she is, and I'm thankful for her, that she is my Mother and I'm thankful she's here with us. I also ask for Your blessings to be upon the priesthood over this home that they will be inspired to know what thy mind and will is concerning us and that they will be able to guide us according to correct principle. This I humbly ask in the name of Jesus Christ, amen."

Three days later I was still hobbling around on crutches. I could not do a whole lot of work anyway, so I was resting on an old chair by the side of the house enjoying the sun. I heard a lot of yelling going on in the house but, I enjoyed the thought of not getting involved. After it seemed to have died down, I came in the house. I could see Mother in the bathroom crying, bent over the sink, washing her face. I hobbled in there and she turned towards me as I came closer. The whole left side of her face was black and blue. Her left eye was totally blood shot.

"Awh! What happened?" I exclaimed.

"I was just sitting on the toilet when Reed came in and kicked me just as hard as he could to the side of my head."

"What the hell for?"

"He said he didn't want me talking to Zella," she continued to cry.

"Oh, how sick."

I went to find Reed. He was in the kitchen harping at Zella while she was frying hamburger for supper. The table was cluttered and messy. His chair leaned against the wall as usual while he held The Journal of Discourses in his hand. "I am your Lord," he shouted at Zella. "If you think you will ever get to God by bypassing me, you're crazy. You have to go through me to even get to God. He recognizes the head of the home, not the tail."

"Reed," I rudely interrupted. "Why did you kick Edith?"

"I've told her a thousand times to quit talking to my family," he said, getting off his chair. I moved to one side to get out of his way. He was going toward the bathroom.

"And here she is in there having a gab session with Zella." We were now in the bathroom standing next to Mom. "AND I WANT IT STOPPED," he yelled to Mother at the top of his voice. Then he slammed his book on the top of her head.

Mother screamed, "Oh shit."

I yelled, "Give me that." Then I reached for the book and my crutch fell on the floor as I hopped toward him. Now yelling at the top of my voice, "WHAT IF SHE DIES FROM THAT DAMN INJURY? A BLOW LIKE THAT COULD KILL HER."

"Well, it would be her own damn fault for her disobedience, not mine."

"Well, for God's sake, will you just quit."

"I'll never quit until she gets it in her head. I'm the boss around here, she's not."

"Well, can you just get the hell out of here. She is in the bathroom! She ought to at least have some respect and some privacy." I pushed him to get him out of there.

"Well, you quit sticking up for Miss Lucifer."

I locked the door and holding onto the washing machine, I hopped over to Mother and wrung the cold water from a towel and placed it gently against her face. She was still crying. I felt so sick I nearly threw up.

"Mom," I said quietly, "just don't even talk to him. It ain't worth it."

Mom's broken voice replied, "I was just asking Zella if maybe she could help me carry some of the buckets of water out of the basement. It's really hard for me to lift those buckets, May. But Reed said it was my job and I shouldn't be trying to get Zella to do my work."

Sympathizing, I said, "I know. The whole damn thing of carrying that stupid water out of the basement is all for nothing anyway. It will just be back there tomorrow." I hobbled out of the bathroom.

Reed had gone to the shop. I went out there, looked at Reed with fury still running through me, "Why can't we just have someone come out and unplug the drain in the basement? That's all that's the matter."

In an insinuating tone, "Have you got seventy dollars or one hundred dollars? That's about what they charge, I don't," like it was all my fault when we didn't have money. "And even if someone did clean it out, it would be plugged up again with roots in about three months."

Yet they, Reed and Francis, would take all that Mother and I earned and eat out at expensive restaurants.

The memory of that horrible abuse of an elderly person haunted me for years. I have lived with a guilty conscience asking myself Why did I not kill him??? I was a coward, plain and simple. But then I might have spent the rest of my life in prison. But even then, Mother never turned against Reed or the brethren. She was and still is the most saintly person I have ever known.

I left the shop confounded and hobbled out to the fence by the pasture, leaned against a post, and looked at the threatening gray sky. It seemed that no matter how much I earned, no matter how hard I worked, it was always the same. I was trying for all I was worth to suppress my feelings, to keep my cool. When I would get to the stage where I was about ready to blow, my body would quiver with emotion begging to be released but then I would remember Joe again. I would tell myself, Cool it. Just cool it.

Bang! The thunder rumbled through the sky, and lightning flashed. I stood with rain drenching me, my mouth clenched tight. I repeated in my mind, I must never lose control. Never. Never. Never!

After a while, I hobbled back to the shop. Reed was sitting on a stool looking out the window and waiting for the rain to stop. I stood there like a drowned rat.

"Ya know, Reed, just because ya have the priesthood and stuff, that don't mean ya can commit murder to any of us and get away with it. Ya got to know in your own mind it ain't right to kick an old lady in the head. How would you like it if someone done that to your mom?"

He glared at me, "I've told you, but you are like those who have ears that don't hear, and eyes that don't see, and a mind which doesn't comprehend." As he came up off the stool, he hollered at me with real violence in his voice, "That's nothing to what God is going to do to the old devil when she gets up there. He's going to destroy her. If the blow killed her, it would just be blood atonement. she would be paying for her sins. And if you stand up for her, God will destroy you, too."

I said no more. If I would have read the Bible I would have known, Jesus died for the sins of all who love him and repent. They are totally forgiven.

Some time lapsed. My leg had healed, and I had resumed work as before. One evening I went in and asked Francis if she was ready to go to bed. She answered, "In a few minutes."

Fine, if it was just going to be a few minutes I thought I would lay on her bed and wait. I fell asleep. Then, obviously, she went upstairs and told Reed that I had refused to wake up and put her to bed. When I woke up, I was screaming. Reed had hold of the front of my blouse and had just slapped me across the face as hard as he could. I was shaking, screaming as he was hollering at me, "You wake up and put Francis to bed."

"What? What the heck is the matter?"

"She said she tried to wake you, but you would not wake up."

After a while I quit shaking and calmed down. Even though it had been years since her hip accident she insisted on being pampered. So I did my job. And any JOB was better than the JOB of having to have sex with Reed.

The next night I was leery, to say the least. I purposely told Francis, "I'll just lay on your bed until you're ready to be put to bed. OK?"

"OK."

Then I laid there pretending I was asleep with my eyes shut just enough so as to deceive her. She tiptoed to the door, barely peeked in, saw that I was, what she thought, asleep, went upstairs and Reed came running down just as fast as he could. He turned around the corner, and I sprung upright instantly.

"What's the matter?" I asked.

"You wake up and put Francis to bed."

"I'm not asleep. And I'm here to tell you Francis did not even ask."

"Is that right, Francis?"

"No. She's lying. I did try to wake her."

"Reed, I'm perfectly willing to take care of her the best I can but I can't see for the life of me what in the world she gets out of seeing me get my head knocked off."

Everyone was still for a few moments. "Well, Francis, you'd better let her put you to bed."

Not wanting to prolong the contention, I went about doing my work.

One Saturday night Reed was going with Bill to priesthood meeting and had left his instructions for me to follow. I came in the house and was eating a bowl of Zella's delicious chili.

"Ummm, Zella. This is yummy. You know it?"

Francis sitting next to me said in a very sweet tone of voice, "May, could you help clean up the kitchen? The fridge needs to be defrosted and the floor needs to be mopped."

I looked at her, pausing for the moment and thinking of all the things Reed had told me to do in the shop, and yet here is Francis being so nice. I knew if I didn't, she would get really mad and liking to be on the good side of her if possible, I replied, "Well, ok. If I hurry 'cause I got all this other stuff that I've got to do, too."

So I hustled and emptied the fridge out quick and got it to defrosting while I swept the house and mopped the kitchen floor, all except where the fridge and sink were, while

Francis was in the front room sewing and singing a beautiful hymn, something about how the wheat and tares together grow and how the Lord "Shouts the harvest home."

How I loved that song. She seemed so happy and contented. So fine, I finished the fridge and then cleaned the rest of the floor.

Then I went to the shop. Reed came home and as he walked into the shop, he said, "Well, are you ready to come to bed?"

"Well, I don't know. Do you think I need to finish this tonight?"

"What in the heck is taking so long?"

"Well, Francis needed a little help."

"With what?"

"Oh, just a few things in the house. But I can still do this, too, if I need to."

"You helped her with what?"

"Well, the place needed cleaning up a little bit."

He began to holler again, "What the hell's she got you in there doing Zella's work for? I've told you to stay out of the house a hundred times and tend to the business."

I said quickly, "Well, it ain't that big of a deal. I can still do this just fine. OK?"

"No, it's not OK. I want you to come to bed right now. Now I find out you've been playing around in the house again. I'm going to have this out. You get in here right now. "

My heart was beating fast as I followed him. We went in and Reed blew up again at Francis and said, "What have you got May in the house doing work when I had her in the shop?"

She gave me a look as if to say, "Damn you. You shouldn't have told him." Francis quickly answered, "She came in and started cleaning the house. I don't know what she was doing."

You could have knocked me over with a feather. I looked at her like, "Am I hearing right?" Reed turned to me for an explanation, I said, "Uh, no. That's not so. I was sitting here, and Francis asked me very nicely if I would help her, so I did. I figured fine, it needs to be done anyway. I can hardly stand the mess myself."

Francis turned to me with her voiced deep and convincing, "You're a liar."

At this gesture I bristled, "You're the liar and you know it."

Reed was quick to correct me, "Don't you call Francis a liar."

"Even if she is one?"

"You're not to correct her." He raised his hand as if he were going to swing it. "Do you understand?"

"Well, hell, Reed. Do you think I would just volunteer to do this work and mine too if it wouldn't make someone happy? Just think about it."

The argument became one big shouting match that lasted until two thirty Sunday morning. Francis was crying a little while hollering at Reed. "You told me that when you got wives, they would serve me."

"Yes, and they will, too." Reed turned to me and declared, "You better forgive and repent right now, or you will carry all of Francis's sins upon your head."

I thought, Francis's sins upon my head? Heaven forbid. She ain't worth me going to hell over.

Reed repeated, "You apologize to Francis."

"For what? For her lying?"

"Don't you say that again, damn it. I'll knock you so hard you won't know what hit ya. Now you say you're sorry."

I was reflecting upon Zella's battered face. I stood still, looking at the situation. "What am I saying I'm sorry for?"

"Because you lied to get Francis in trouble. Now, admit it."

So very politely like a soldier answering to a sergeant, I said, "I'm sorry."

"What are you sorry for?"

"For calling Francis a liar."

"Why?"

"Because I'm the one who lied."

"OK. You kiss her now."

I gave her a peck on the cheek. Well, that was enough, and the session broke up. I never could see getting my face remodeled over someone who would never change their mind anyway, but I thought to myself, Strange, I wonder if there is any truth to that about my taking Francis' sins if I don't forgive her. Boy, I would forgive anything rather than have all her hell on my head. So maybe I'd better get over being so stiff necked about it."

As my feelings settled down, I began pondering some of the priesthood brethren's teachings I had heard in meeting. They said, "Blessed is he that is persecuted for righteousness," and I was crying inside as I thought to myself, I sure don't feel very blessed.

I continued having two bosses until one day Francis was chastising me for something and after listening to her for about two hours, I figured she was trying to drive me crazy again. She would follow me around while I was working, just continually yelling at me. I was doing the washing with our old Maytag, so I began to whistle. I often whistled as I worked.

Then Francis became furious. She started in on me, "Don't you whistle while I'm talking to you." She grabbed some dirty socks that were floating on the water and quickly crammed them into my mouth. I pried her hand down and went to find Reed.

Reed told Francis that if she kept up that kind of thing, he would have to move me out from under her direction.

With Bill's wife Berniece, the amount of groceries brought into the house was limited—just so much of this, and so much of that. Reed and Francis seemed to have little concern for what we had at home to fix in the way of food because Francis claimed she needed a cup of coffee to kill the pain twice a day after her accident.

Reed said, "Well, it's not good to bring coffee into the home, so I'll take her to the café for a cup." And while he was there, he would flirt with all the waitresses, trying to bring more women into the house. Some men may have a bucket list, things they want to accomplish before they die. Well Reed had a fuck it list—how many women could he screw.

While they were there, they would both order delicious meals. While Bill was on the bottle route picking up gallon jugs from the cafes, he had money to buy the jugs so he would get whatever food he wanted also. My mother, Zella, Berniece, and I had no way to go buy anything to bring it home. So we were dependent upon Francis and Reed. We got very tired of bread, bottled fruit and milk.

The meat goods had not been given to them for a long time now. We asked if we could have some hamburger this one day and they brought home some coarse ground meat they said they got a really good deal on because it was coarse ground, and said, "See how you like it."

So I fried some up and made some hamburgers and I got deathly sick. Three days later I fixed some in some Spanish rice and again I got sick. Then when we went to Glen's on Forty-Fifth South to deliver him empty jug boxes, as I passed by the meat counter, I recognized these patties, and it said, "Dog Patties."

I went out by the truck and said, "Damn it, Reed, you guys bring home dog food and expect us to eat that kinda' shit. No wonder I got sick."

"Well, Glen said it was really good meat. That's all I know. Because government regulations won't allow anything but real good meat to be used for animals."

I shook my head and thought, Oh hell, I've heard of everything.

Because I was raising goats for milk, I also raised baby goats for three months for some Italians to barbecue, but they only wanted to pay me five dollars tops and I had to talk like a Dutch uncle to get that out of them. They would always try to get them for three dollars. In the meantime, we girls were really wishing we had some meat, so one time I thought, Heck. I'm not going to sell that thing for five bucks. Why in the world can't I kill it so we can eat it?

I told Reed of my plans and he said, "I don't care."

So I thought, Fine. I'm going to do it.

I had never done anything like this before. The only knife I had was from saving bubble gum wrappers as a child. That's how I got a knife from the Bazooka Bubble Gum Company. I sharpened it on a hot wheel the best I could, and then caught the little goat and tied a rope around its back legs and pulled the rope up over a beam in the basement of the bottle barn, which used to be an old cow barn, so that the blood or whatever could go in the trough in the floor. I blocked the door open so I could have more light down there, then I said a prayer as I was trying to brace myself for what I was contemplating. "Please forgive me for killing this little goat." Then I grabbed hold of its head and took a deep breath and stabbed it in the jugular vein. Oh dear. That thing let out a scream that made my blood curdle. Oh, I sawed and sawed on its neck as fast as I could. Golly, this thing was bellowing and struggling and getting loose and I would keep losing my exact place and I was so nervous, and it seemed like this knife was too darn dull. I kept working at it until I finally succeeded in killing it.

Dear me, I stood there with blood all over. I was coated from head to foot and my heart was going ninety miles an hour. Shaking like a leaf, I sighed and leaned against the wall. If I never went through another experience like that again in all eternity, it would be just too soon.

Then I took another deep breath and commenced to skin it. When I was all through, I took an old meat saw and cut the goat into pieces. I put the pieces in plastic bags and put them in the freezer, all except one piece, which I cooked. All the time the meat was steaming, those bloody screams were running rampant through my brain. I suffered hours and hours of mental torment. Then when the meal was cooked, we all sat down.

Mother said, "Oh, this is really good."

"Well, I'm glad you like it. You can have mine."

"Are you sure?"

"Yeah, I'm positive." I ate my asparagus and bread and butter and a glass of milk and sought some quiet place where I knelt down. With my broken plea, I asked, "Oh Father, please forgive me. I am so sorry. I can't even say how sorry. I don't even care if I eat nothing but vegetables for the rest of my life. Please take the screaming cries out of my head." I stayed there crying and ended it "in the name of Jesus Christ, amen."

CHAPTER SEVEN

The arguments continued to get worse and I struggled to discover ways to please everyone just to avoid the tension and bickering. There was no way to stop the arguments, but somehow, if I could just be left out of them, how happy I would be. On a particular Sunday morning, I got myself ready to go to meeting, then wet Reed's hair and combed it so he would look half civilized. Feeling anxious to hear the brethren, I hurried to the car. While we were on our way, I was thinking of different questions that I hoped the brethren would answer for me. We arrived and I took a seat on Reed's left side. A sweet spirit prevailed and the meeting began.

One brother talked about wives following their husbands and the husband following the priesthood, and the priesthood council following God. "If you women want to be treated like a queen, you have got to treat your husband like a king."

What a beautiful concept. Then they began to read from The Bible on charity. I had heard it before, but I loved hearing it again. As I listened, I was consumed by a desire, oh, how I would love to acquire that attribute. The thought was going through my mind, that is the spirit of God. That's what we came to this earth to learn, I'm sure. Joy was radiating through me like small volts of electricity.

The meeting closed and we returned home. I was so happy for the Gospel I had heard. Later, when I could be unnoticed, I went to a little spot in my closet where I could not easily be found and poured my heart out to my Father in heaven.

"Oh, Father," I began with tears streaming down my face. "I'm so thankful for the teachings in meeting this day. I pray that I, too, may acquire the attribute of charity wherein it suffers long, is kind, is not easily provoked, and seeketh not her own. If I have nothing else, may I leave this world with that in my character. Help me to overcome myself." I was thinking as I paused in my prayer, I must renew this plea and continue to strive for this goal that it may guide me through every hour of my life. "Thank you, Father, for the gospel that has been preserved down through the ages for our benefit. I pray that you will help me to overcome my imperfections. I want to live to serve you God, and your Son Jesus, for your honor, for you to have all glory, I just want to be worthy to be amongst the little chickens that are under your wings of protection. Reed is always telling me I am going to go to hell. But God if I can have this special gift of charity, then in the end when

Satan tries to grab me Jesus will say oh no you don't, she is mine. I pray, in the name of Jesus Christ, amen."

As I brushed the tears from my face, I thought, I must remember these things no matter what happens. I got up and walked into the hall.

Francis shouted, "We've been looking for you to get in here and help me. Zella's baby is ready to come."

We hurried into Zella's room. She was having labor pains. Sure enough, in about ten minutes, the head appeared.

"Come on, push," Francis shouted. "Push! Each time you have pain, push with it."

Zella was crying, "It hurts!"

"Quick, get me a bowl of water!" Francis told me.

I took off to get the water. When I returned with some. Francis said, "Hand me that string."

I felt really good watching Francis sweat. She was very diligent in her efforts to deliver the baby.

"Give me the scissors, I need another pad, now that piece of material." She was trying to stop Zella's bleeding. "Gim'me those safety pins, now hand me some cotton balls, and the olive oil." She was holding a black-haired little girl. "Now the baby blanket and a diaper."

I smiled looking at this tiny little baby. Everyone was so excited and happy over this little addition to the family.

The discussions of a name went around, and Reed said, "I think we ought to call her Francis."

Francis said, "Well, we could call her another name, too. What do you think about Kathleen?"

"Yeah, that sounds good. Let's think about it and if we don't come up with a better name, then that's her name."

Reed and Billy left the room. I left shortly after. Reed was talking in the hall to Billy, and I overheard them on my way into the kitchen. Reed was speaking, "I would like to see you take this little girl for your wife when she becomes of marriageable age."

I thought to myself, Did I hear right? Yeah, I did, I heard right. I went out in the hall to stand and listen to all this. I commented, "Well, goll, how do you know who she wants to marry? Heck, she's just barely arrived on the scene."

"Oh, she'll want to marry Billy, if he treats her right." Billy had a somewhat pleased expression on his face. Reed continued, "Bill is a good man, as good as she could find anywhere else. So, what is wrong with it?"

I could not say what I thought was wrong with it. But I figured, who knows, that's a good many years down the line.

A few days had passed by since Kathleen's birth when I walked in the house from the shop. Here were Francis and Reed hollering at Zella and Zella not able to get out of bed yet. Reed was giving this baby of Zella's to Francis over some crazy excuse they used of why Zella was not a fit mother. I looked at Zella, her face was all red from bawling.

Francis declared, "You're so filthy and slothful, the baby would die anyway. You don't even have enough brains to care for yourself properly, let alone a baby."

Zella's hollered at Francis, "Well, hell, Francis I haven't even been given a chance. You just want to steal my baby."

Reed chipped in, "Well, we don't want the child growing up to think a mental retard is its mother."

"Well, damn! Do you think that Francis is any better?"

"Yes, I think Francis is a whole lot smarter than you ever thought of being, or ever will be."

Reed walked over to Zella and grabbed hold of the hair on her head, shaking her head a little then throwing it back as he let go.

Zella's face was twisted in agony. "WELL, I'M GOING TO TURN YOU GUYS INTO THE LAW FOR TAKING MY BABY."

Francis laughed, "It's not your baby. It's Reed's baby. You're just like a Coke machine. A man puts in a dime and the Coke comes out. Would you say that the machine owned the pop? Or the man who put in the dime?"

"Well, it's my baby too. Hell, Francis, do you think it's easy having a baby?"

"I know what it is, I've had ten." (Francis had had ten children with Charles, her first husband.) "If you report this to the law, we'll just send you off to the Provo Mental Institution. You're nutty enough they'd take you right in."

"Well, what about yourself. You think you're so damn smart? You're not."

"Yes, I think I'm smart and if you say anything, I'll just tell them it's my baby with Reed."

This argument lasted for hours. During the course of this conversation, I had managed to bite off all my fingernails. Several nails were torn off into the quick. I imagined how it would be if I were in Zella's shoes. I had heard enough. As I walked away a creepy feeling accompanied me as I sought tape for my bleeding finger. I told myself what Reed had pumped into my head a thousand times, it ain't my place to try and judge those who are over me. I'd better keep my nose in my own corral.

It was obvious that Zella lost after four days of arguing. Along with the insults Reed had put some black and blue marks on her face. The child was registered on the birth certificate as Francis' and Reed's.

That night when I retired for the evening after taking care of Francis, I found myself wrapped in the midst of a nightmare. It was like I was confined in a room. It was so dark I could hardly see anything around me. There was the light of just one small candle. I was hovering around the candle which seemed to be my only hope for light. There was a small breeze coming from several different directions that would continually threaten to blow out this candle. So, I cupped my hands around it to protect it the best I could. The thought of this little light going out was very heavy on my heart as I felt if I ever lost this tiny thing, I would be left groping around in utter darkness, as in the blackness of hell, and there would be no way to light the candle again. This nightmare seemed to last for hours, teasing, and tormenting my soul to where I sweat so bad and the agony was enough to wake me. I turned on the light.

Reed said, "What's the matter."

"I just want to sleep with the light on."

"Why? It just wastes electricity."

"I can't help it. I just hate being in the dark."

"Whatever."

I laid down and tried to put it from my mind. I was so glad to see the morning come, so everywhere there was light around me. As I looked at and inspected the light in the bottle barn while washing jugs that day, a good feeling came over me. How happy I was to have a nice light to look at all day.

While thinking about trying to improve our miserable surroundings, it occurred to me that I had been there approximately four and a half years. All the things that were working in the house when we moved in were broken down or worn out and neither Reed, nor Bill would make even the slightest attempt to fix anything. The bathtub drain was plugged. And we had to scoop the water out and throw it down the toilet each time anyone took a bath. The kitchen sink was also plugged. And we had to bail the water out and throw it over the fence. Then the water heater in the house went on the blink and we had to carry hot water from the shop over three hundred feet away for all the needs, dishes, laundry, bathing, etc. I did not have the slightest idea of how to use a pipe wrench, but I decided to attack the plumbing under the tub in the bathroom to see if I could unplug it. How could I wreck anything if it did not already work?

So, I thought about it for a while then took a pipe wrench down in the basement and studied the plumbing under the tub. While standing on an old orange crate I held a bucket under the goose neck of the drain with one hand so that hopefully whatever was in the pipe would not go all over me, and the wrench was in the other hand, I tried to undo the pipe. When I got both sides of the fitting loose, it started to drain into the bucket. While I was continuing to loosen it by hand, the fitting, being full of dirt, suddenly landed in the already heavy bucket. The sudden jar caused me to lose my balance. I kept the bucket from spilling but the drain water from above went all over my shoulder and down the front of me. Hell, there I stood with this black, smelly crap all over me. I went upstairs and walked outside to the hose by the house and washed myself off, clothes and all. The water was cold, so I washed off just the worst.

Ok, now I needed a hanger. I got one and undid it so I could stick it down the pipe. I went back downstairs and felt thankful the sewer water did not go on my head instead of my shoulder. Then I commenced trying to stick this hanger down the line. The thought occurred to me if I just had a hose and ran water down there, that it might do the trick. So, I went for the hose and told Zella, "Ok, now, when I holler, turn on the water. OK?"

"OK."

I wrapped an old rag around the hose that I had stuck into the pipe as tight as I could. Then I said, "OK, turn it on."

She turned it on. It was all I could do to hold it in there until water was running down both arms. I was hoping the clog would break lose and it did. "Whoopee!"

It was a triumph that would save us girls from all that darn work. Then I cleaned out the goose neck and put it all back together. But I had cracked one nut and both rubber gaskets were shot. So, I told Reed what I needed to fix it.

"You're always messing around with something," he said. "You should have used a crescent wrench on the fitting, not a pipe wrench. That's why you cracked it."

"But, can't we just get another one? I got the drain cleaned out. It runs good." I stood there looking like a proud, drenched rat. "It'll work just like a charm when we get this fitting and two gaskets."

"Yeah, but that's such an old style that we just might have to buy the whole goose neck and that's going to be some money."

"It wouldn't cost that much, would it?"

"You bet. They don't give those things away."

So the project was left unfinished because he did not even try to find the parts. I found an old baby enema bottle I shoved up the pipe in the basement so that we could use the tub as we had before.

I got cleaned up and Reed said, "Come on. We're going to make a delivery to Plastiform Company."

I always tried to keep myself clean and decent looking. My clothes were nothing to brag about but at least my body was covered. I was always wearing either a long-sleeved blouse or sweater with a vest and a skirt which came below my knees and stockings one could not see through. I generally wore shoes I had got at Deseret Industries or found at the dump (mostly they looked like something one would see on a boy) or my bottle boots. Such was the appearance of "Mazie." Oh well, anyway, when we got to Plastiform, a really nice lady (I don't know if she felt sorry for me or what), but she told Francis and Reed to follow her to her house that night.

So we waited for her to get off work. Then when we got to her house, she gave us a whole bunch of really nice clothes. She said they would fit me, that her daughter had grown out of them. I thanked her very much and was really happy going home.

When we got the clothes in the house, Reed said, "Ok. Francis you decide where they go."

I stood there hoping I might get a few things anyway. But I knew Zella and Berniece needed clothes also, so I was glad to see them get some, too.

While Francis was deciding on each piece, my mind wandered back to when Zella and Berniece came into the family. Reed said that because we believe in the United Order, I was to share what I had in my closet with them. And I had said, "Fine, I will."

So both girls came up stairs and I stood back while each one went through my clothes and took what they wanted, Zella took my Sunday blouse and best sweater. Berniece took my green Sunday suit that this same lady had given me before in a box of clothes. It had shiny, fancy designs, much nicer than my other green suit.

I smiled as they said, "Thank you."

"You're welcome." I really did not care except that Berniece never did wear the suit and Zella wore the blouse and sweater for working every day and they were both wrecked in no time. Well, that's alright. I had never been a selfish person anyway.

I sat there on a chair in the kitchen, watching Francis, and halfway falling asleep while she was making up her mind. Then she put three blouses and two skirts on my lap. By the time she had distributed all the clothes, I took what I got and wanted to save them for best, which I did.

Two weeks later when we went to Plastiform again, this lady looked at me. I was actually wearing the same old clothes I had worn the last time I was there. Her face had an expression of hurt, wonderment, or disappointment. I could not tell which. I was lost for words and did not know what to say. So I busily unloaded the truck and then went and sat down in the cab feeling quite stupid. I was too timid to even tell her thanks again and that I really appreciated what she had given us, but they were all too good to wear for bottle clothes.

As I sat there, I wished that I had the courage to explain my feelings and my appreciation; somehow, I could not bring myself to say anything.

I had been in the family now for approximately five years. One day Reed and I were upstairs in the bedroom and I brought up the subject of when it will be my turn to have children.

Reed said, "Well, I'm praying continually for other women to come into the family so that they can take over the work that you're doing. Also, I need to have a woman to take care of my sexual needs so that you can have your children. When the Lord wants you to have your children, he will send those women that belong in my family."

The thought crossed my mind, it's kinda' hard to imagine how a woman would ever come into a family like this unless they had no idea of what they were coming into. It surely was not how I had supposed it would be.

Now I did not mind working so that Zella could have children and my supplying an income to keep the family fed, but the thought of another woman doing that for me boy, I could hardly believe that that would be the case.

I pondered this for a while, then I asked, "Well, what if women don't come into the family?"

"Oh, they will. Francis and I are working on a couple of girls right now, but I don't know how long it will take them even after they come into the family before they can do your job. I might let the 'fillies' have a little time running with the reins before hooking them up to the plow."

I contemplated on that statement for a while. Then again, I said, "Well, what if they don't?"

He threw an answer back as though to chastise me, "It's up to God when women come in the family so that you can have children."

"Yeah, but who knows how many years that would take."

"Look, if God wanted you pregnant, you'd be pregnant already."

"How could I be when you won't let it come off inside?"

"That's ok, you'd be pregnant with just the seed that's on the tip of 'Johnny'."

I said no more and decided to put the question on the shelf until the Lord might give me a better understanding. Not that I wanted his babies. But I thought it would stop the sex abuse. And I do love children.

As the months went by, I became quite used to my role of supporting the family and felt that I had been given an important responsibility. It made me happy to see the family and enjoy the fruits of my labors. I felt glad that Francis, Zella, Bill, Berniece, Mom and the babies were there.

I thought, wouldn't it be terrible if it was just Reed and I?

I had Mom's help and Bill would make the pickups and deliveries most of the time until he got a job working for Fred and Kelly's, an eating house, as a cook. I would work as long as necessary to accomplish as much as I could because it might make the difference of whether we ate chicken or feathers.

On one occasion I had a dentist appointment to have an infected wisdom tooth pulled and told Reed it was for 11:00 a.m. Tuesday. They went away and were not back, so by 11:15 I was beside myself. The dentist might make me wait all day now. Not having a driver's license but impatient to go, I drove the truck over there. While I was being waited on, an hour and a half later, Reed, Francis and Bill showed up. One would think I had committed the crime of the century and here came the forces to take me away. Good grief, I thought when I got outside the dentist's office.

Francis and Reed both started in on me at once. "What the hell do you think you are doing stealing the truck? Reed could have you thrown in jail."

I smiled, "That's kinda' a pleasant thought actually."

"You have no business taking off." Reed said, "I could have you reported to the priesthood. Now, you leave these trucks alone. Do you hear me? Don't you ever, ever do that again."

"Well you promised to be back in time to take me and you weren't, so that's why I had to do it."

"I don't care if you're late or not for anything. You'd better not leave the yard." His bloodshot eyes seemed to drill a hole through me.

"Here's the prescription for pain pills."

"Forget it. Just get in the car." He opened the door and shoved me in, and I fell into the seat.

They left there without getting any pain pills for me. I could not figure if it was 'cause he just was mad or tight 'cause they cost $3.

When we got home, Reed snarled, "Are you going to wash any more bottles today?"

"I don't know. My head hurts so bad. I feel like I've been stabbed in the side of the head with a knife. I'd like to rest."

"Well, alright, if you have to."

The pain was pulsating with each beat of my heart. I needed the medicine to kill infection, but I used salt packed in the hole instead. I tried to rest for about an hour. It seemed hopeless so I got up and went down to work and to try to concentrate on something constructive.

I started repairing the end table for holding clean jugs. I was thinking to myself, Heck, it's only three stupid dollars. Big damn deal. Maybe they would have bought it if I hadn't made them so mad. I don't know. But if they don't give a hairy rat what I suffer, then fine. They can just keep the cockeyed money. I hope they enjoy it. I was hammering to drive nails in the old wood with tears of pain and frustration. The nails were too big and the 2"x6" board split. I should have known better. Everything just seemed crazy.

Shortly after that day came a change. The workload demand increased immensely. Francis and Reed contacted a company, Mount Olympus Distilled Water, that wanted 200 cases washed two or three times a week. That would bring in $32 per day at four cents per bottle whenever we worked for them. That sounded pretty good to us, but it meant extra work on top of handling our regular accounts. I had been washing, with Mom's help, 100 to 120 cases of easy to clean jugs and making about $20 to $25 per day at five cents per bottle. This would be a good opportunity to get some bills paid. We could do 200 cases for this company in a day because all we needed to do was to remove the lid and label, run them through the water, rinse them and box them, removing any heavy dirt, as they intended to run them through their bottle wash again.

Reed said that I could handle the account by switching around my sleeping hours. He said if I would work six hours, then sleep for two, then work another six hours, then sleep another two, on and on, I could go 'round the clock that way.

So, we agreed to handle this account.

But it took seven hours to run the batch. Then by the time I would eat and rest for two hours, then work for another six to eight hours and have two hours rest...

Different ones of the family took turns to help me to run during the night hours. In the morning I would load the truck ready for delivery. When we arrived at Mount Olympus, I would throw the cases to the back end of the truck to one of their employees. He would stack them then after the 200 were unloaded, he would put their returns on the truck, which I would stack.

When we got home, I would unload the truck, rest for two hours then get up and start up the batch. Somehow between putting Francis to bed at night, doing whatever I had to do for Reed sexually, for the months of that summer, I was averaging four to five and a half hours of rest per day.

My arms were not used to doing that much handling of the cases. When I would lay down, they would sting and burn, and I would cry from pain that was so bad. I tried laying on my arms, holding them up in the air, putting them in a bucket of cold water, anything. The only thing that would stop the pain was for me to go back to work.

I was so extremely tired and delirious from the heat in the building, fatigue, and long hours, I would continually feel myself falling asleep with my eyes wide open standing there working, although I was moving in as fast a momentum as I could. But the constant fear of the cement floor in back of me and the boiling water in front of me would keep me awake until the job was done. When I had loaded the truck, I would no sooner sit down in the cab after telling them that everything was ready, than I would fall asleep in less than a minute.

One morning I told them the load was ready and I sat in the truck to go. I woke up when Reed began hollering and shaking me as he said, "You've got something radically the matter with you. Why can't you stay awake? Every time you sit down anywhere you fall asleep. Whatever it is you've got, it's bad. Brigham Young prophesied that the people in the last days would have a sleeping sickness come over them." He grabbed my arm and was shaking me. "Wake up and listen to me!"

"I am awake."

"Yeah, but are ya' listening? For every crime there is, there is an evil spirit that enters into one's body and takes over. And what you have got to do is rebuke it. It's a sleeping devil that's got a hold of you." He was still shaking me. "Do you understand? I have prayed in your behalf but you're the one that needs to plead with God to get rid of this evil spirit."

As the weeks and months went by, I fought and struggled with myself, praying, "Oh, Father in heaven, please help me overcome this sleeping spirit."

When I went to meeting sometimes, I would wake up, with my head bowed, only to notice I had been drooling on my hymn book. I would quickly wipe it up with my hankie. What a low cut. I could just feel myself blush. But the next thing I knew I was asleep again.

This problem was seven days a week for four months, May through August. I fought with myself to try everything and anything I could think of to make myself stay awake throwing cold water on my face, slapping myself, or singing out loud. But the moment I stopped, zonk... I would be out like a light.

One day as I sat in the truck ready to go on another delivery, Reed woke me up again, shaking me, "Wake up. Are you awake? Now listen to me. Are you listening?"

"Uh huh."

"There are all kinds of devils. There are laughing devils, crying devils like Zella has, justifying devils like your mother has. For every crime there is, there is an evil spirit, and you've got this one awfully bad. It's so damn bad I can't even wake you up at night. It's like you're dead. I shake you, kick you, pinch you, and it scares me. You just act like a dead person and I don't know what to do about it if you don't control yourself."

I did not ever want him to know that this was my plan for escape. I would work myself to death and be free from all the hell. Many nights I would think to myself, this is it my last day on planet earth. I am ready to meet God. But then I would have dreams of walking in heavenly gardens all night and wake up amazed at how beautiful Heaven was.

Well, Reed continued to rail on, "I'll tell you one thing, you can be glad that you're not living in the days of Brigham Young. If you lived in those days and you fell asleep when he gave you something to do, he'd do with you like he did with one man that fell asleep on his horse while he was on guard duty. Brigham Young came along, slapped the horse on the ass driving the horse out of camp and the guy was never seen or heard of again."

"Well, I'm so tired I could fall over on my face even while I'm working and, I've even thrown cold water on my face, but it doesn't help."

"Well, you've been getting four to five hours of sleep. You should be able, if you're any good at all, to go on two or three hours per night, and you're getting twice that, so you should be fine."

"But I read in a magazine a long time ago that the average person needs from six to seven hours of sleep to be well rested." I looked up at Reed as his eyes were beating upon me.

"Well, they're talking about lazy bums. That's just what people want to get, not what they actually need."

With every day being so heavy with such a dredge of work upon my head, I became somewhat delirious. It was as if I could not even remember a time when I was not exceedingly tired. And I made a comment to Reed, with a sincere desire to know the answer to this question, "Why did God make us to come down here and to suffer so?" Every day I believed that it was right for me to push myself so that I could not be blamed for neglect of my duties. I really could not see the purpose of life.

"Well, some people don't get their rewards in this life," Reed commented.

But in my mind, I could not imagine how even in the next life the Lord would let me off the hook. With all there was to be done and so few people willing to devote themselves enough to do it. I just figured at least when I get on the other side, I will have the joy of knowing that I am building God's kingdom and maybe He might allow a little bit of sun to shine on my corner of heaven.

Two nights later when I laid my body to rest, I found myself wrapped up in a dream. I was in a canyon-like environment. The autumn colors were in the trees and the temperature was pleasant. There were many different types of beautiful plants amongst the trees. A meadow with flowers, not many rocks but green stretched out before me, landscaped as if by God Himself. I noticed a canal with the water very clean and clear it was approximately eight feet wide and four feet deep. As I slipped in for a swim, I saw exotic fish pass by me every now and then. Then I swam to where a few ducks were. I was laughing and just loving it. I swam around with the ducks as though we were friends or something. Then I came to a flat landing that looked something like a golf course with flat stretches of green grass, and an occasional tree here and there. I stepped out of the water to explore this environment. I walked in the grass for a little ways then went towards a grove of trees. On the left-hand side of the trees and bushes I turned as my attention was captured. I had never beheld such beauty. I gasped at the view which nearly took my breath away. I had stumbled onto a flower garden surrounded by a slight mist, each flower in its radiant glory portraying beauty to its fullest potential. I was standing on a path that led through this garden. Oh! My attention was captured by a lovely white flower, with blossoms about five inches across. I touched the petals which were almost as soft as the dew. It was like some type of rose bush standing five feet tall. There were some plants that stood four feet here and there and they were spaced so as to have other flowers growing between them according to color, size, and height. Surrounded by such splendor, I just stood there in awe. They were all coordinated together so as to create a masterpiece. Oh, you sweet things, as my eyes focused upon glory after glory of the flowers, giving me a spiritual uplift like I had never known before. The joy was vibrating through my body to such an extent that I woke up with a thankfulness that I had seen a glimpse of heaven. With tears in my eyes, I whispered a prayer, "Oh thank you, God. Now I understand the reason for living that we might someday be worthy of dwelling in your kingdom."

I could look upon the duties placed before me in a different light now, with a more firm determination to strive to deny myself anything that God did not want me to have.

One night after the day's work was done, Reed was talking to his family in the front room. "I fell in love with a girl when I was seventeen. This was Caroline, she had beautiful red hair and a lovely body. I took the matter before the Lord and I was told to leave her alone, to let the Lord have time to work with her. Then she would be given to me. I was in such a hurry. Instead of waiting upon the Lord, I went to see her again after I was told to leave her alone. I read her the 132nd Section of the Doctrine and Covenants and told her I intended to live that principle. His head dropped into his hands as he stared at the floor. Then in a whimper like a child, he cried, "I kept going over to see her. She wouldn't even answer the door. I wanted her so bad. Three days later my papers came to ship me off to the Army."

I listened as compassion was taking over. Reed looked at me and said, "I'll never love any woman like I did her. I love you 'cause you love the Gospel, but not like I loved that woman. I've learned obedience by the things I've suffered. When God speaks, I obey. I could have lost all the women I have in this life and in heaven just over that."

I bent over and put my arm around him while he continued to sob. I had pity and felt so sorry for him.

After a while he gained control of his emotions and said, "She will be amongst my women in heaven."

"How many wives do you have in heaven?" I asked.

"There are approximately 500."

"What do you mean approximately 500? Don't you know how many you have?" I gave way to a little laughter.

"Well, some of them get tired of waiting for me to return. They leave to marry other men, but that's how many I had the last time I was there about six years ago."

I sat down by the vanity somewhat confounded. "Now say that again. You went to heaven and what now? Did you say 500?"

"Yes. I have 500 women over there."

"How in the world did you get 500 wives?"

"There are thousands of good women over there whose husbands are not worthy of them. There's seven women being born to every one man right now. But all men are not worthy to take them, so what few good men there are have to, according to God's laws, take more than one. I could have more than that if I wanted them, but 500 is about all I can handle. They do the work, but my job is to organize them along with teaching them the Gospel and keeping them in line. But they mainly keep themselves in line. It's a big job for me just having affairs with all the ones who want to get pregnant. I only visit them once every seven years. They continually plead to the Lord for me to come over there. Just as soon as my mission here is done, I'll be gone. That's why I keep trying to train you to take over the responsibility here. If I can get it to where you are doing it all, then you won't miss me when I'm gone."

I sat in silence then asked, "Can I be excused? I think I left the light on in the basement of the barn."

He glanced out the window and seeing it was on said, "Alright, go on."

I stepped outside into the cool evening air. As I slowly walked to the barn in a daze, trying to sort out my thoughts. I stopped to rest on a bale of hay near the stack. I leaned over one so as to relax and closed my eyes. As I was trying to visualize all these women, something was saying, "You're just a number with no more significance than a speck of dust."

Then the spirit within me struck back as I sat up, tearing into the darkness, as I shook my head and said out loud, "Oh, no! I'm not just a number. I've got a brain." With feelings running rampant through me, "I'll do the work so that their suffering will not be upon my head of why he is not with them." I was thinking of what the brethren said in meeting, of living so that the blood and sins of this generation are not upon our heads that I might stand blameless before the Lord at the day of judgment.

A strength filled my body as a spirit of conviction entered in. I will do my part, all that is asked of me for I know God will help me. How do I know that? I just do. And if Reed does not have long to live then maybe I won't have to die young to be free of him. My life I have dedicated to God, to ask what He will of me. The Lord will judge all. This is where I want to be found in that day.

Half an hour passed quickly while I renewed my covenants with God, and contemplating what had been said in the meetings that if a woman lives worthy, the day will come when she can pick the husband of her choice. I got up and turned off the lights. Then on my way back to the house, I was singing,

I think of his hands pierced and bleeding to pay the debt,
Such mercy, such love, and devotion can I forget?
No, no, I will praise and adore at the mercy seat,
Until at the glorified throne I kneel at his feet.

Then with tears in my eyes,

Oh, it is wonderful that he should care for me,
Enough to die for me!
Oh, it is wonderful, wonderful to me!

I Stand All Amazed," music and words by Charles H. Gabriel," Hymns, page 80.

Renewing my covenants with God to do his will and forsake my own, I looked forward to hearing the brethren more so than before.

When meeting time came Sunday afternoon, I took a notepad with me. When the brethren spoke, I would jot down everything that I felt was pertaining to me so that I might not forget it. I appreciated the sweet attitude from one of the speakers who said, "Jesus set the example that we must do good, even for those that would do evil towards us."

As I heard these words, my whole soul was consumed with joy. I could see why God would love Christ for He truly did do that. Then they spoke upon the principle of forgiveness. They said that we must learn how to forgive seventy times seventy. As I jotted that down in my little pad, I thought How well fed my soul has been fed this day, As we sang the song,

God Be With You 'Til We Meet Again.

Words by J. E. Rankin, music by W. G. Tomer, Hymns, page. 47.

During the following week, everything that anyone would say to me that would tend to rile my nature, I would go off by myself as soon as I could and seek for strength to overcome my rebellion. I thought about this principle of forgiving "seventy times seventy," and it occurred to me let's see, seventy times seventy how much would that be? That goes up into the thousands, doesn't it? Heck, who could ever keep track of all that. Then the thought struck me, Well, maybe that's the point. You're supposed to forgive and forgive and forgive until you don't know anything else but how to forgive. I bet that's what he's getting at. Ok, fine.

I remembered what someone had said a long time ago. They said if you want to like a person, then what you do is keep repeating in your mind every good thing that person has ever done, but all the stupid things you have seen them do, don't even think about that, and try to forget it. Then after a while, you could begin to like that person. I thought to myself, Heck, I gotta' work with them anyway. If I can just be a friend somehow.

Just then Billy backed in the load of jugs and started walking towards the house.

"Hey, how about giving me a hand?" I said.

He started clapping his hands.

"Very funny," I said.

He turned to keep walking.

"Darn your potato hide. Get back here," I hollered.

"In the morning," as he waved his hand to say goodbye. "It's 5:30 p.m. and I'm tired."

I stood there looking stupid. Oh, just like that, I thought to myself, Well, what has tired got to do with the price of rice in China? We need to unload them tonight just in case it rains so the cases won't be ruined.

He shut the door. But I thought, Well, that's alright. I'm not going to be judged according to what Billy does, so I'd better get over my hang-up as fast as I can.

I seemed to have some kind of crazy drive in my mind. It was like I felt anything I can possibly do today I'd better get it done 'cause God will have tomorrow's work for me to do tomorrow. I felt myself on a time schedule that was very pressing. It was so demanding but I could not explain why, even though I had worked through the night. I told myself a little trick like, OK, May, now just pretend, just think you're waking up now. Ok? This is the start of a new day, right? Now, get busy.

Seeing the family get by on what little bit I could earn, I felt very deficient in what I was able to bring in for their support. I always thought, there's gotta' be a better way. Heaven help me and we're goin'ta find it. I worked to unload the truck by myself as I thought, it really doesn't matter, 'cause I'm going to do all I can whether he helps or not. It's just that we would get more done and I'd feel better towards Bill if he would get off his 'tuther end.

Feeling like a rag, I went to bed and fell into another dream. I found myself in a mansion next to a park. In this lovely room I felt so natural standing there in a lovely white gown. Beauty, order, and cleanliness surrounded me. The wood furniture had a deep walnut stain. The carpet was a cream color with a slight purple cast, that seemed to be a simple touch of elegance. Delicate white lace curtains graced the window. The walls were covered with a white wallpaper with light silver designs. I was standing alone in this bedroom feeling very content as I glanced out the window, I could see the tops of the trees because the building was three stories high. There was a lawn, so rich and green. The grass was not like it had been mowed but more like each blade knew how high it needed to grow and then had stopped growing at about three inches. I could appreciate an occasional little white flower here and there amongst the grass. It seemed very fresh outside like a rain had just cleansed the air. The sky was a light gray blue. There were no clouds in the sky but no sun shining either. The peaceful stillness that prevailed left a permanent impression in my memory.

As the morning came and my dream was over, I left the bedroom, taking with me peace in my heart. I stepped into the hallway of the attic and could see all the junk that Francis had saved for years—an old trunk with broken leather straps, a bunch of old chairs with the backs broken off, her old quilting frames with a half-finished quilt still on it, some old bedsteads and a dresser with the mirror broken up, and boxes of all sizes with old clothes, and raw material pieces. Then a couple of old carpets, one with a big ragged spot on one side. Oh dear, this is a fair description of Francis' precious junk coated with layers of dust and cobwebs.

Reed had said that 'cause of the filth in that area, it was a comfortable home for evil spirits to dwell. As I looked at the mess for a moment and then hurried past it, how thankful I was, indeed, that I could comprehend a more blessed realm than what I was living around.

As I entered the kitchen, everyone was talking around me, but I was wrapped up with the thoughts of my own mind. All I could hear were sounds. A feeling came over me that even though there were all these people around, I am alone. Then as I began frying some eggs, Reed distracted my attention by singing, "It Is No Secret What the Devil Can Do' to the tune of "It Is No Secret What God Can Do."

"What he's done for others, he can do for you."

Singing to Mom with both arms flying up, whirling around in the air while Mom was sitting there looking up at him.

"With arms wide open, he'll pardon you."

He stopped there and shouted, "The devil's the only one that's going to pardon you."

I thought to myself, here we go again, I've just gotta get out of here. I'm so tired of all that crap and I've heard it so damn many times. Just let it go in one ear and out the other. I ate my breakfast and went to work.

Reed always claimed to have a bad back and said the doctor told him that he was to get more rest and quit working, or the work would kill him. Billy had brought back a 50-pound box of staples on the truck that needed to be moved into the shop. Reed told me to carry it in. I tried then dropping it back down, I said, "I can't. It's too heavy."

"Can't is a coward too lazy to try," he commented.

So although I only weighed 110 pounds myself, I picked it up and moved it in. Reed, being large in stature, approximately six feet tall and weighing two hundred and thirty pounds, did not even offer to help. His attitude was obvious.

I thought to myself, fine, if ya' don't want to help, don't." I already had a hernia and serious back problems.

With the demand for jugs for our regular bottle accounts for root beer stands and fountain syrup, along with Mount Olympus, I knew that it would not lighten up through the two remaining summer months until August. We had handled that account for two years, but there was soon to come a drastic change. The Mount Olympus Distilled Water Company decided to use plastic bottles to replace the glass for over half of their orders. So, Mount Olympus no longer needed us to recondition their jugs. During the same time period the Coca Cola Company switched from a glass gallon jug to a gallon carton, like a milk carton. I was not bothered anymore by supposed "sleeping devils." I was able to relax to the extent of getting six to eight hours rest.

Because of the scarcity of jugs due to what the Coca Cola Company had done, we picked up other accounts—more root beer stands who had jugs returned to them to be cleaned. Those jugs were somewhat unpredictable and could not be run through at the fast pace of a regular syrup jug. Many of them were dusty from sitting in someone's garage or basement, and most of them had large water rings and lime deposits.

The method that Francis had showed me for cleaning water deposits was to pour a little hydrochloric acid in each bottle, then dump it back out into a little cup, put a little rinse water in there, and a piece of 3M pad, then insert a long wooden stick, shaped in a V, at the bottom so as to fit the bottle. By chasing the pad around the bottom of the jug while applying pressure with the stick, this is how we removed water rings. Then I removed the pad and put the jug on a rotating brush hooked up to an electric motor that had bristles fastened into a metal shaft by a thin wire. The most I could clean by working all day was thirty cases, that being only 130 jugs. I looked at the situation and at that time we had gone down to where I was only making $7 a day to support the family. I thought to myself, Boy, this is sick. I could do better than that at Old Mill.

My mind was constantly striving to come up with a better way. Then I got an idea, I had thought this over in my mind pretty carefully as to the things I would need to make an improvement. I found almost everything by searching through the debris at the dump. I found a 71-gallon plastic acid container and sawed the one side off with a skill saw, then I drilled holes in it near the top so as to fasten some 2"x4"x4' board legs to make this little vat waist high. Then I took some old angle iron from the basement of the barn and with a dull hacksaw blade and dull drill bits, I made a rack and bolted it together so it would hold six jugs in the draining position. I lined it with wood so the jugs would not break and fastened a plastic skirt around the bottom of the rack so as to avoid any acid splashing on me.

Then I directed the skirt into a half of a 55-gallon plastic container to catch the acid for recycling purposes.

I experimented as to how much I could dilute the acid and still have it clean the jugs. Then I had also found some old plywood at the dump and brought it home, too. I cut it up into pieces approximately 3'x5' to stack jugs on. I was ready to try my experiment of rolling the jugs into this acid solution, rinsing a little bit around the inside, then placing them on this rack as fast as I could move. I was doing this one afternoon when Bob and Bev came to the door of the shop. They were some friends of the family.

Bob said, "Boy, is this Speedy Gonzalez or what! I've never seen anyone work like that woman, but I'll tell you Reed, if she doesn't slow down, she's going to have a burn out."

I was sure happy that I had made this improvement because now the jugs could sit overnight, soften the dust and dirt, remove the water ring, and I could run them through in the morning just as fast as I could go. I also thought of using a plastic stick instead of wood, so we got a one-inch plastic rod 17 inches long, it would last longer. I fastened a pad right to the end of the stick so I could grab it, insert the pad and stick, give it a swift whirl and out. I started making my own bottle brushes since those from the factory had bristles coming out two sides through only eight holes tied by the fine wire. The wire would break sometimes within 15 minutes of use, causing the bristles to fall out. These brushes cost $7 a piece, so I saved the shafts and figured that by drilling eight more holes so that I could have them coming out of four sides instead of two. Then I had Reed get me a new push broom with nylon bristles which I would carefully remove so as not to damage them. By inserting the bristles in these holes in sequence and by shoving an old darning needle up through the center so as to catch the bristles and hold them secure, and the end bristle I secured with a nail. Then I cut a small piece of nylon hose, heated it up and put it over the tip of the shaft so I could throw the bottle on quickly without fear of chipping the top. Boy, that worked slick.

Between all the little things I had improved, the amount that we could put through then of these hard to clean jugs was up to 120 cases per day. I was very encouraged because the bottles could not be cleaned to that extent in the back of some cafe. I raised the price to ten cents per jug. Then our profit margin was $48 per day.

One time when we were down visiting Bob and Bev, Bob said in a casual way, "May's just about taking over down there. Is there anything she can't do?"

"Well, she's doing pretty good. 'Bout the only thing I haven't really let her do is talk to the companies on the phone much." said Reed.

"Why?"

"Well, she's just not got the personality for it. I'm afraid customers will quit us."

"Oh, I dunno about that. I think she'd do alright. She's got a mouth, doesn't she? And ears, doesn't she? So, what's wrong with her?"

"Well, nothing really. I just don't like the idea."

While listening to them, the thought occurred to me, it might be 'cause he just don't want me using the phone, as though I'm going to call someone up and tell everything I know. But why would I do that? No one would believe it anyway.

Then one day a company called up that I had contacted. They ordered 200 five-gallon plastic buckets. Francis took the order.

I asked Francis, "Is the order for Bennett or Roper buckets?" I had both styles, but their lids would not interchange.

Then she called them and asked. The man said, "I have some lids for the Roper, but I need 175 buckets with lids and just 25 without lids.

I asked her again. "Does he want all 200 buckets Roper, or can he use some Bennett's'?"

She said, "Oh hell, call him yourself."

Fine, I did. After that Francis did not seem to mind my contacting the companies on the loads incoming and outgoing.

I called Mountain Beverage to see if we could pick up a load of jugs and the man said, "I have not been paid for the last 104 cases that were picked up."

"Oh, really! Well, I'll check on that and get back with you, Ok?"

"Ok."

I sat the phone down and walked in to see Francis. I asked her, "Hasn't Mountain Beverage been paid on the load we picked up over a month ago?"

"What's it to ya'?" she snarled. "That's none of your business."

"Well, that's fine but they're not going to release another load until they're paid. So, whatever. But Miller ordered a load and we don't have a load for them."

"Just get off my back."

Reed walked in and hearing the commotion asked, "What's the matter?"

"I was just telling Francis we need to pay Hill for their last load so Bill can pick 'em up so we can put them out for Miller."

Francis piped up, "No she's not. She's trying to boss me and tell me how to spend the money."

I looked at her and thought, Good night. Of all the stupid things. Then I said, "Look, if you don't care about what money we have in here or the customer, then that's your problem. But I can't do jugs I don't have."

I went back to the phone and said in a whisper, "Just hang onto the jugs until you're paid. They'll pay ya'. Ok?"

"Ok."

I went to the shop. Reed followed. I turned to him and asked, "Why does she do that? What the heck's the matter with her? She's always mad over something stupid. I can't figure it out for the life of me."

"Well, May, ya' gotta understand. Before you came into the family, she was washing the jugs. It wasn't much but she worked hard. And everywhere she went on a delivery, people would show her love and praise her for her work. Then you come along. Some young whipper snapper that does three times as much and everyone knows you're doing the work. Also, you've been talking on the phone and she's so damn jealous of you she can't see straight."

"Oh, c'mon. How in the world would be anyone jealous of someone with just a lot of Chinese labor? For what little bit of praise I get, you've gotta be kidding."

"No, I'm serious. If you want her to like you, just praise the daylights out of her. She laps it up like a cat laps up cream."

I plopped myself on a jug box and tried analyzing that statement. I could recall for the first three months when I had started washing the jugs before Francis' accident how Reed had told me to shut up and not tell anyone that I was washing them to let Francis get the credit from the customers. It did not seem to amount to the ashes of a rice straw, so I went along with the idea—anything to keep the peace.

CHAPTER EIGHT

I was in the shop one afternoon when all of a sudden, I heard Reed yell from the house, "MAY, GET IN HERE."

I started shaking as I took a deep breath. I walked toward the house. The way he hollered I had no idea what I would be facing. I opened the door. There stood Reed, his pot belly and poor posture with shoulders slumping over, with his bloodshot eyes and deep wrinkle lines in his forehead. His face had a look of agony as he commenced to jump all over me. "Francis told me you were talking to your sister Carol this morning."

"She called and just wanted to know how I was."

"What did you tell her?"

"I just told her I was fine."

"I want to know everything that was said."

"Well, she said she had a new baby girl, that being her fourth child."

"What did you say?"

"I just said I was happy for her."

I looked at Reed and he scared me half to death with his expression.

"You know better than to talk to anyone without my permission." He leaned over me and hollered at the top of his voice. "You're to talk to business customers only and if you don't quit talking to everyone else, I won't even let you do that. DO YOU UNDERSTAND?"

"Yes." I muttered.

"Well, you'd better."

"Can I ask you something? What should I have done? She called me. I didn't call her."

"You should've just hung up. If you'd keep hanging up when she calls, she'd quit calling. Now, wouldn't she?"

I looked over at Francis crocheting on the couch. She looked up with a smirk as though she was delighted in the scene. I said nothing to provoke him further, and after a while he quit hollering and I was excused. Oh, dear me. I was glad to get outside to get my mind off the hell. But I would remember what I was told. Oh yes, I would remember for how could I ever forget even if I wanted to.

I dreaded to even go in the house and I would not even go in to eat until I was about ready to die of starvation, if there were contention going on. I would rather wait until whatever battles there were would die down so I could eat in peace, if possible. I had just come in from the shop again when Reed said, "Get in the truck. We need to go after a new carburetor."

A friend of ours, Bob, told Reed that when we needed parts, we could buy wholesale from Genuine Auto Parts. By telling them that we had an exemption number, we could buy at wholesale prices. Bob then gave us his tax exemption number to use. But Bob said, "Be positively sure that you pay the tax because if you don't, they'll come at me for it."

I thought I understood that pretty plain.

So, when we got there, Reed had picked out the parts that he had gone after and the salesman asked, "Is this taxable?"

Reed said, "It's wholesale and here's the tax exemption number."

Standing there by him, I said, "But we want to pay the tax anyway."

Reed turned to me gritting his teeth, "Shut up."

"But Bob said for us to be sure and pay the tax."

He turned to me again with a horrible look on his face with a little saliva running down the corner of his mouth, bringing his hand around, applying a blow to my head as hard as he could hit. "Get to the car," he commanded.

I stood there for a few seconds then said, "Reed, I'm telling Bob."

He turned to the salesman, who was surprised at all the commotion, and said, "I'll pay the tax this time." It was under $2. Then all the way home, he screamed and hollered at me telling me how I had no right to correct him on anything. It was a horrible thing to ever cross his path.

I remembered the many times I had seen Zella beaten, once or maybe twice a week. Her face would be black and blue and all puffed up with bruises all over her body. I saw no point in having my body put through that type of treatment. Therefore, one could say I was very obedient.

Zella was, by nature, a rather easy person to get along with. She liked to be somewhat quiet and off to herself. I asked Reed in private why Zella always wore the same clothes day and night with scarcely ever a change.

"Well, I'll tell you. But don't tell her I told you. When she was in her teens, her grandfather came up to her room and caught her in the nude without a stitch on. He beat her for it so bad that since that time, she has had a real complex about getting undressed for sleeping, sex or anything."

Francis and Reed would try to impress upon Zella the necessity of bathing and taking her clothes off to go to sleep at night. There was much railing that continued along those lines.

On one occasion when Zella had not bathed for over three months, Francis got awfully mad. Between her and Reed they held her down on the couch. Francis pulled one of Zella's stockings off. There was black muck on her feet and between her toes. Zella liked to wear dresses that almost reached the floor and heavy wool socks. Zella had a leg injury that Francis took care of rather than take her to the doctor. If Zella did not bathe often, this sore on her leg would become infected and full of pus and rotting flesh about three inches in diameter. Much of Zella getting beat seemed to be over this problem. The house seemed a little quieter most of the time after Kathleen's birth because Francis would insist that Reed not holler so as not to wake up the baby.

Autumn was upon us and the children next door were selling pumpkins. I came in from the shop and commenced to get something to eat for myself. About 15 minutes later Francis came in with Reed behind her. Zella was also in the kitchen feeding Kathleen in the high chair.

Francis said while standing next to Zella, "Have you changed that baby?"

"A little while ago."

Francis inserted her finger between Kathleen's diaper and her bottom, "You haven't changed her diaper." As she came around with her hand slapping Zella's face, Francis turned to Reed, "She's trying to feed that baby with her diaper full of shit. No wonder the baby doesn't want to eat."

She then turned to Zella, "You nut. How would you like to sit down to eat in shit up to your waist?"

Reed butted in, "Change that diaper or I'll change it and if I do, I'll mop your face with it."

"Well, hell, Reed. Do you think it was my fault that she just messed?"

Then Francis yelled, "Yes, I think it's your fault because you never check to see if she needs changing or not. Her little bum is so damn raw now just because you don't give a damn."

Reed then grabbed hold of Zella's hair, "You change it right now." He yanked her hair for a little bit and then let it go.

Zella was bawling, the baby was crying and had knocked the food all over the floor.

Francis said, "How come every time I check her diaper, it needs changing. If you were doing your job, you'd have it changed already."

Reed again stated, "If you don't take to changing her more often when I come in and find a messy or pissy diaper, you will get it in your face." He grabbed hold of her hair again and shook it. "Do you understand?"

Zella screamed, "Yes!"

I was sitting there watching everything like a church mouse. I had heard quite enough so I put my dish in the sink and said while leaving the door, "Thanks, Zella. Those potatoes were delicious." Then I went back to the shop

Bill could always pick up and deliver bottles in one fifth the time it would take me to wash them. I asked Reed if it was fair for Francis and Bill to run around visiting relatives, going to dances and shows, while I was just stuck with the work that went on and on.

Reed said, "Don't worry. The Lord sees who does what. Just don't concern yourself with what Francis and Bill are doing. It's what you're doing that you should worry about. God will see that you will have rewards far and beyond what Bill gets if you do your part regardless of whether he does his part or not."

"I understand that, but Bill thinks it's cute just to leave the truck for me to unload all the time. He's such a goof off. When five o'clock comes, he acts like he has a perfect right to quit. He doesn't care if it rains during the night and ruins all the cases or what. But if I talk like a Dutch uncle for half an hour, then sometimes he'll help me. Heck, if this is supposed to be United Order, then shouldn't he do fifty percent?"

"Yeah, but Brigham Young said that a person isn't worth his salt if he couldn't support ten others besides himself."

"Well, doesn't that apply to Billy, too?"

"What do you care what rewards Bill gets?"

"I know but you're talking one hundred years from now. I'm not worried about all this reward business when I get in heaven. The Lord will probably say, 'Here's what I need for you to do,' and I'll have work over there, too. So, heck, I'm just wishing I had some help now."

"Billy does give you some help, so be glad for what little bit he does, that he doesn't just leave it all to you."

"Yeah, but you know what? Just to show you what I mean, when we have to take a load for Adria Maintenance Company and I'm the one to load the truck,

Francis says that I need to take each bottle out of the case and screw a lid on it and put it back upside down. But when Bill is going to load the truck, he just loads the bottles on and puts the lids in a box and tells Francis they can put the lids on up there. And she says nothing. But if I try that, I get the third degree. She tells me that I'm just damn lazy, that I'm not doing what the customer wants. I really don't care one way or the other, just so it's the same. You know what I mean? I wish you'd ask her about it."

There was silence for a while then he said, "Well, the customer likes it that way so it is better if you do it, that's all."

I got a bright idea. The next time I was delivering a load I said to the manager, "Would it be all right if we brought your lids in a box or do you need to have them screwed on each bottle?"

"Oh, a box is just fine."

"Ok, thank you."

Reed heard it so that took care of that.

On our way home I asked if we could stop to get me a candy bar. Reed said, "If you want us to spend a dime on you, then you should see to it that you earn an extra dollar, so that nine other people in the family besides you can have a dime also."

That seemed only right. But even though mine was the only money coming in, they would never say what they spent it on, only that if I wanted something, I had better work harder.

We would save lids. If I sorted through five boxes in an hour and a half, separating the aluminum from the tin, we could sell the aluminum for $4. So, I would do this in my spare hours, rather than waste the time even though it was not much. Also, between the demand of incoming and outgoing loads, I had a huge stack of bottles in back, approximately 2,000 cases that I would work on cleaning up in slack time. Between that and working at Old Mill, or babysitting, I liked to think that I brought in as much income for the family as I could, just as a working man would feel trying to support his family to the best of his ability.

Even so, I hesitated to ask even for a candy bar or anything else. Rubber thongs (sandals) cost $1 back then, but rather than ask for a $1 to buy a pair, I made some out of wood. Ha! I cut the wood in the shape of my foot then drilled holes where my big toes were and on the side of my foot so I could run a rope through them. I put them on and wore them a little while and had a good laugh at myself. After all the work I had done they were too uncomfortable to wear.

Bob and Bev came to visit us one afternoon. We were standing there in the yard and Bob was telling me that he knew the famous artist Robert Wood personally and that he could get me into taking lessons from him if I wanted to. Knowing Reed's attitude, I said to Bob, "Maybe if you could talk to him and see if there's any way of talking him into it."

Bob said, "Ok." So, he approached Reed off by himself. I came up and joined the two of them after a few minutes.

Reed said, "No way! There are too many artists starving to death now. She already has a job. She needs to be here to help the family and keep the business going."

I thought that was an opportunity of a lifetime, but Reed could not have cared less. When I was talking with him in the house later, he started railing at me, "The religion that doesn't require the sacrifice of all things doesn't have the power within it to save. You need to be concerned with what the Lord wants you to do, not what you want to do. There's a billion people out there all sending themselves to hell because they want what they want, and there's no way they'll allow the priesthood to guide them in anything."

"Look, Reed." I thought I would change the subject. "I know we're supposed to sacrifice everything, but is it really that big of a sin to have a vacation once in a while? I mean, what can it hurt?"

"What do you mean a vacation! You get a vacation every time someone dies down south. So, what are you complaining about?"

"Well, let's put it this way. Who would work as long as I do without vacations like, it's been nearly nine years. You'd think I was abnormal or something."

"Well, you're not normal," he laughed. "If you was, you'd be coming after me for more sex instead of wanting to do all this dang work."

I thought when he walked away, What a stupid statement. I've got a family to support and that's far more important. But, boy. What a godsend it would be if I just could have one day by myself just to think.

One afternoon I noticed Billy and Francis talking to a gentleman in the yard. After the man left, Bill came in and said, "That was Francis' brother, Leo. He asked us if you were mentally retarded."

I wondered how the man could say such a thing when he didn't even know me. I had never talked with him, but I had the strong feeling that Francis and Bill would prefer people to look at me as a nut. But I told myself just to forget it. It did not amount to the ashes of a rice straw anyway. I told myself that someday a woman with my integrity and honesty would be in short supply, and I would be appreciated.

CHAPTER NINE

Mom and I were in the kitchen, I had fixed some supper for us and we were eating. I could hear Reed, Bill, and Francis in the front room. Reed was telling Bill that he needed to be more diligent in helping with the business and Francis chipped in, "Well, Bill just figures, why should he? You say May's doing it all anyway. So if he doesn't get any credit, why should he give a damn?"

Then Reed hollered at Francis, "I didn't say May was doing it all. I said she was doing most of it. So just shut up while I'm correcting Billy, will ya'?"

"Yeah, but he's told me many times that he wants to leave and get a house of his own. He doesn't tell you everything that he tells me."

"Well, I can't help it. What he needs to do if he is going to be worth something is either help May to build Reclaim Bottle, or he could even start a business of his own, if he thinks he can make more money."

Francis said, "Well, he feels like it's just a bunch of shit. You've got your wives and he wants to marry more women too. He feels like he's just not getting anywhere."

"Well, hell, that's what I'm telling him." Reed slammed his book down, "If he is ever going to gain influence in the eyes of the priesthood council, he's got to be making good money, so they'll give him recognition if he wants to influence them to give him any more women."

(When men pay more tithing, it is like a boy getting brownie points, it all adds up, enough either money or service's and they stand in line to receive a young wife. It is the young female flesh that is the grease that keep's the wheels of these polygamist groups turning.)

Mom and I were still eating our sandwiches when Bill said, "What I would like to do is start raising cows. I can get calves for about $30 sometimes in the auctions, and I can get a cow for about $150 if I watch the ads and then feed the calves, we have all this pasture."

Reed thought for a while.

Francis said, "Anyway, if he doesn't get something, then he'll leave, and I know it."

"Well, go ahead and get him a cow then, if he is sure he wants all the work of raising calves."

I jumped up and butted into the conversation, "Even calves do good on goats' milk."

134

Francis said, "Yeah, they do."

Reed said, "Well, you're still going to have to help May in the business or we won't have enough money to buy the hay or grain."

I thought, we might have a little meat to eat now and then.

Bill worked long and hard to get old lumber he could get free to build sheds. Then when I got inheritance money from my Mom's old estate that totaled $2500, Francis used it to buy hay for the cow and the goats, also for fencing materials, and posts. Bill fenced the whole pasture which was four acres. I thought it was kind of neat to see Bill care about something. They also got some sheep and some more cute little baby pigs. It was my job to feed these little pigs, at least I took over the job because they were always hungry, and I did not see anyone else feed them. Feeling sorry for them, I saw to it that they got fed.

Anyway, one day I was adjusting the portable picket-like fence that was around the pigs when one little red pig got out. He was only about a foot and a half long, but boy, did he take off. Heck, we paid three dollars for him. I could not just let him go so I took off after him, I was not far behind him on his trail. He ran through the front yard, across the street, through Mr. Pill's fence, and into a huge pasture. I thought, Surely, I can out run this little twerp. Oh, dear me, he just kept going. I was about twenty feet away from catching him. He ran clear to the end of the field then over and through the fence again, and across the street and over towards the canal. He seemed to have got out of my sight, so I carefully looked around and then I spotted him in the canal hugging the embankment. So fine, I got in—shoes, clothes, and all, and went across and got him. Then I got out and commenced walking home.

I noticed a girl from a wealthy family whom I had known when I was young, passing me on the same side of the street. She was dressed very nicely, her hair all pretty and everything. There I was if you can imagine how I looked. I swallowed and breathed deeply as we passed. Oh dear, I would have liked to have been spared that. But as I walked home, it was just a lovely warm summer day. I enjoyed the walk home even if I was holding Mr. Piggy.

I was soon to get a little pet. The sheep that Bill had picked up at an auction was having a baby lamb. "Easy, gal, easy. It's Ok," I whispered. But she was so wild, spooky, or nervous that when the little thing had only its head out, she turned quickly and caught the lamb's ear on a nail sticking out from a board in the hall and ripped it. I let her go into a pen in the back of the goat shed and took her some feed and water. She was so darn rambunctious that she accidentally stepped on the little lamb's front right leg and broke it. Two and a half hours later when I came back to check on them, she had stepped on the back-left leg and broken that one too. That was just enough. I said, "To heck with you. You ain't goin' to have this baby no more." So I took the little thing to the house and commenced putting some splints on its legs and some salve on its ear. I held the little thing in my lap and petted it, "What a sweet face you have with pretty blue eyes just so innocent. Poor little thing." I felt so bad. I made a box of straw for him and fed him goat milk from a pop bottle with a nipple.

The days passed by quickly and he was standing on his legs. I was so happy. But the sore on the lamb's ear had not healed completely and I saw maggots on it. That made me mad. I went and got some tweezers and picked them all off, then I washed his little ear and put a bit of Vaseline on it, just enough to make powdered golden seal, an herb, stick to it. Every day I packed it with more golden seal until it healed up. Then when this darling little lamb was fat, well, and healthy. I staked him on the front lawn every day under the huge shade trees that lined the driveway. "Have a good day," as I gave him a hug. "You darling little thing. I will see you later."

Now we had cows, goats, pigs, chickens, geese, my cat Pester, and Bill even bought a few ducks. What a joy to see a mama duck take her four babies into the pasture, down the hill, through the grass, and into a small pond fed by a flowing well. The sunlight glistened through the trees and sparkled on the water. Those ducks had the time of their lives. While in the rapture of those moments, I could forget much pain.

I had no objections to bottle money supporting Bill's cattle farm, but what would irk the hell out of me, and I felt it just was not right, was that Bill was always running off to auctions, sitting on his butt, or going to his dances, claiming he was going to find another wife, or off to shows just because he had connections with friends who would let him in free. I would think, where is there justice? I would work on my feelings to keep them from cropping up like a weed in the soil. I would keep stomping them down.

Over and over I would try to ignore his sluffing his work, leaving it for me. I had the hardest damn time with myself not to get mad when he would go off to play. He would always have some fun thing going on. If it was not a free show, it was watching TV or going swimming. I just could not see it. Heck, I liked to watch Mission Impossible, and Red Skelton once in a while. That was like two hours a week compared to his playing every day. I liked to hear Red Skelton's jokes so I could repeat them to make Mom and Zella laugh. To this day I like to remember all the good jokes I dare repeat. But seeing Bill quit at five o'clock every night like he was better than I or something, I just could not swallow that. I felt to seek my God all the more, for truly, if there were anyone who might care, I felt it would be the Lord. I did not know of one person on this earth that would give a care. My mother cared, but even she figured that I was just doing my duty. That's fine.

I began to sing in the shop one night with the rain beating against the glass on the shop door:

Put your shoulder to the wheel push along.
Do your duty with a heart full of song.
We all have work, let no one shirk.
Put your shoulder to the wheel.

"The World Has Need of Willing Men," words and music by Will L. Thompson, Hymns, page 206.

I would keep on until I choked up with a lump in my throat as I tried to continue singing.

Come, come ye saints.
No toil nor labor fear.
But with joy wend your way.
Though hard to you this journey may appear,
Great shall be as your day.
'Tis better far for us to strive,
Our useless cares from us to drive.

"Come, Come, Ye Saints," words by William Clayton, music from an old English tune, Hymns, page 13.

As I would look at a stack of about two hundred cases that would take me until two o'clock to clean, I could find peace and comfort in the hymns of the religion. Then the pain was not so great.

I would think about all the fun times I would have in my dreams because in my dreams I would go skiing or sleigh riding up in the snowy little villages, there were only about twelve other skiers. Or all the various times I dreamed that I had gone swimming in beautiful locations and all the different lovely environments I had enjoyed. It would just send my soul thrilling. I dreamed many times that I could fly. I could go anywhere without my feet touching the ground, and my body would move with the command of my mind. I could be standing, then when I wanted to go through the air without walking, I would tilt my feet up in back of me. I would be up about four feet off the ground and just move ahead. When I wanted to turn, I would slightly turn my head in the direction I wanted to go, and I would go in that direction. Boy, what a way to travel. But that was a dream and it seemed like I was always dreaming, as I leaned against the cardboard boxes behind me.

Then the pain of reality would give me a jolt, and I could not help my eyes becoming wet again. I thought, this life will never hold anything for me. I could see before me a scene of myself being a ninety-year-old woman still washing jugs. I told myself, my mission is to prove myself and my worth before God, and that's the only prayer I have. For truly, my mind was so darkened with servitude that I could not even imagine one day, twenty-four hours, where a person in my position could get up and do anything or go anywhere that I wanted to do or go. I could not see how that could ever be.

As I began to slap the side of the box, I had just tipped upside down to knock out the dust. Then as I pulled out the liner and flipped it to its clean side and reinserted it into the box, I again looked at the stack and thought, I'd better hurry if I want to get any rest tonight.

We were into the coldest months of the year. Reed and Francis took me to the University Hospital to see why I had not had a menstrual period for about four months. The doctor discovered that I was hypoglycemic. He said that I had either been working too many hours, had spent too much time in the cold, or had been wearing heavy boots. Any of the three, he said, could have caused my periods to stop. I was doing all three! The shop had no heat in it and the floors were icy. I found a pair of old fishing boots at the dump. They were big enough that I could wear several pairs of socks, although that made them quite heavy. So upon the advice of the doctor, when we were at the dump again, I sorted through the old boots. I found a pair of lady's boots that fit me. There was a little hole in one. So I put four plastic bread bags over the one foot and then put the boots on. I liked that style of boot really well and asked Reed if he could buy me a new pair.

He said with a big grin, "Do you think you're worth a new pair of boots?"

He was joking of course. I started breathing heavy and being very sober about the whole situation.

"Yeah, I'll get you a new pair. You're worth it."

It was just like ripping open an old wound and then throwing sand in it. I said, "Don't be in any great hurry. I can get by with these for some time."

A few weeks later we found a local connection where they bought me a new pair.

My neck hurt so bad for want of a chiropractor adjustment from tilting my head back to look at the inspection light so many thousands of times that I could hardly stand it. I devised a little contraption to hang myself from to try to put my neck in place so they could save the $3 chiropractor fee, but it did not work very well.

Even though my neck was killing me, I started up a batch of jugs. The water was straight from the boiler, approximately two hundred and ten degrees. I had just added the caustic and Reed was putting the jugs in the sink filling them with the water being pumped through a hose from a submersible pump. Suddenly the hose slipped out of Reed's hand and caustic was spraying all over the ceiling, I hollered, "Shut it off." Without thinking, I ran around the vat and ran right through the spraying water as I grabbed the string that controlled the switch "Awghhh," I screamed.

The boiling caustic water had sprayed all down one side of my chest, shoulder, neck, and face. I screamed as I ran towards the house. Running to the kitchen through the front room pushing objects out of my way as I headed for the bathroom, Francis, and Zella, seeing me run past them, followed me.

Francis hollered, "What's the matter?"

"It's caustic water. Wash it off," I screamed. I was shaking as I was trying to turn the water on in the bathtub so that it could come through a hose we had hooked up to the faucet.

"Quick grab the mineral water," Francis said.

I was washing myself off then Francis threw mineral water in my face, then that started my eyes to burn.

"Where's the olive oil?" Then she threw that on me as I was jumping and screaming. Then my vision was blurry. All the time I screamed to the top of my voice.

Reed hollered, "Get some of that milk outside. That's supposed to neutralize caustic."

Someone ran and brought some in and they threw it on me. That felt good. "More," I cried.

They kept throwing milk on me and I began to calm down a little. "Ohhh, wrap some cotton on me and pour some milk on it. Can we do that?"

Francis wrapped gauze around me with large pieces of cotton over my burns and poured milk over the cotton. This would ease the pain but as soon as the cotton started to dry out, it would sting again. I laid on the couch in Zella's bedroom and had someone dump milk over me every little while.

Reed came in and looked at me after I had settled down and said, "I knew something would happen to you for the way you acted at Genuine Parts store. I didn't punish you enough or God wouldn't have took a hand in the matter. Joseph Smith said we learn by the things we suffer. You can't defy me and get away with it."

"Well, goll. That's been weeks ago."

"I don't care. God might not punish you for years. He gives you time to see if you're going to repent."

If he was trying to scare me, it worked for I had no answers. I was suffering with so much pain. I stayed there about ten days with third degree burns and huge water blisters hanging on me about an inch and a half in diameter. It was about two weeks before I went back to work.

Someone had offered to buy the five acres in Murray where we were. Francis and Reed were working with a realtor, Jim Long, to try to find us a new location. It seemed like once or twice a week, they would take me with them to go look over a place to see if it would be suitable for relocating the business. This went on for about six or eight months. We saw a lot of nice places, but they finally located a property in West Jordan with a three-bedroom home, large basement where there could be other bedrooms, and a large building in the back which the former owners had used for light manufacturing. It had several other old buildings that we could utilize for chicken coops and what not. They were able to purchase this property of an acre and a half for $35,000. They were selling the home on Fifth East for $70,000. So they located a 6 and ½ acre farm with a nice home in South Jordan and used the other $35,000 for a down payment. The total price was approximately $65,000 with the balance to be paid approximately at $200 a month.

Bill could have his cows on 6 ½ acres in South Jordan. And of course, I would use the buildings in West Jordan for the continuation of Reclaim Bottle.

Zella had four children by then—Kathleen, David, Charles, and Paul. Bill and Berniece had three children—Guy, Susie, and Mary Ann. Seven adults and seven children totaled 14 members of the family that made the move. The City of West Jordan approved our license for reconditioning jugs in that area because it was similar to what had been done there for years.

CHAPTER TEN

I really liked the new home. It was a 100 percent improvement over what we had. A trumpet vine grew next to the house, crawling along the wall so as to protrude a few branches close by the bathroom window. I could see little hummingbirds come to nurse on the flowers there. We spent a lot of time hauling junk from the premises so we could move the bottle business in. With one of the last loads, I took Pester. We were in the back seat. As I stroked her, I said, "You're going to like this new place. It's much nicer." I hugged her and petted her all the way so she would stay, and she did.

After the move was completed, I could concentrate on working in the business. I spent a lot of time on the phone contacting anyone for whom we could do some type of washing, whether it be bottles, glass, or plastic, 1- gallon or 15-gallons, 5-gallon buckets, head pack or cube'a'tainers, or 7½-gallon acid carboys.

I felt eager to begin each day to learn more and do more and try to expand my capacity, hopefully to bring a higher income into the family so that our lifestyle could be improved. However, I could not seem to locate enough work. Then one day when Bill and I were at an eating house picking up jugs, I noticed about 15 cases of 1-gallon cans, six cans to a case, in their dumpster. I thought for a minute as we were carrying out jugs. When we got loaded there was a little room on the back of the truck. I said, "Hey, let's put these cans on, too."

"What for?" Bill asked.

"Well, I'd like to see if maybe I can sell them to the nurseries. I mean, look, Bill if they have thrown this many away at one time, we have to come here all the time anyway to get their bottles. So depending upon how much we can sell them for, that just might amount to quite a bit. You know what I mean?"

"All right."

So we took them home. The next day I called around to every nursery in the valley. I found some sales for them at 6 cents per can, but they wanted holes punched in them, so I asked Bill if he would keep bringing them in and he said he would.

I rigged up a little jig. I took a flat piece of metal, 1"x1/8" that was approximately 2' long and cut a notch in it, 3/4" wide, 3/4" deep, so as to bend a U shape on the end of this flat bar. I inserted a short bolt that I had sharpened to a point into this notched groove so the bolt would be pinned in the U. Then I took a peg that would normally be used for a hinge on a fence post to swing a gate and I looped the end of the U over it for my hinging action. Then I placed a platform just the right height with a stop on the other side so I could place a can into position very quickly. And work the handle to punch holes in the bottom of the can. By turning the can three times, I would have four holes. As fast as I could grab another can, punch holes and pitch it, I was just counting the money that I was making. I started to laugh then I shouted with glee, "All right!" I looked at the clock and waited for the second hand to get into position, then I worked as fast as I could, doing this while timing myself. In five seconds, I could have one can with four holes punched in it and the other one in place ready to be punched. That was approximately 60 cents per minute. Hey, that's all right! It came to about $15 to $20 an hour for my time and the rest for Bill's time to pick up and deliver. It was better than washing jugs because, we could wash bottles all day to do 120 cases at 40 cents a case gross income, if the jug belonged to the customer. Then if it was our jug, we were selling them for $1 a case, which was much better. But I was determined to capture the market on this little deal too, for whatever we could do without going too far out of our way to pick up the cans.

But even then, with all the money I could make on doing whatever, I looked at my mother. She was still wearing rags all the time and it hurt my feelings. It seemed like no matter what, I could never do good enough. When Mom and I would wash 5-gallon buckets, we could do 200 per day including the lid. I would pay $1 per bucket and sell it for $1.50, clean with the lid. So when we had buckets to do, we would make $100 per day.

I was desperately looking for more work to do and went to a place I had contacted over the phone that had 2,000 buckets he wanted cleaned up. He said they only had a little bit of fruit juice and they would wash out really easy. Seeing as how they were his buckets, I said, "Well, I'll do them for 30 cents each."

"That's way too much," he said. "How about 20 cents?"

I hesitated knowing how badly I needed something too, "Well, let's try a few at 25 cents."

"Ok."

So we took 800 of them. When we got home and unloaded them, they were stuck together so bad I had to put sections of them, about ten, at a time in the vat of hot water to soak them loose. As they came loose, all this rancid peach juice would go into the water. After pulling apart 100, I had to drain the water and start up fresh. But it took so long to pull them apart, that by the time I had washed 100 buckets and lids, that was the most we could do in a day. The worst part was getting them separated.

One night I was using the old water that we had used to wash in that day to pull apart the buckets for tomorrow's running. My clothes were soaked with sweat and the sticky, brandy smelling liquid from the buckets all over the floor and me. Just then a knock came on the shop door. I answered it. It was one of the members of the priesthood council in his suit. I told him Francis and Reed were at the house. He thanked me and left. I stood there a moment looking at the deplorable condition he had just seen me in. I felt somewhat forsaken and ashamed, then I said to myself, Good grief, of all the days to show up. Oh well, it can't be helped right now. So I just finished what I was doing.

After a week and a half when I had them all cleaned, it had rained but now the sun was shining, so I went to Bill and told him they were ready to load for the delivery. He said he did not want to deliver them, he wanted to do something else.

So I went to Reed and said, "Are you and I going to make the delivery?"

"Why? What's wrong with Billy?"

"I don't know. He said he had something else he wanted to do."

Reed jumped up and went into the other room. "Like what? Why can't you make the delivery?"

"Francis and I were going to look at some turkey feeders."

"Well, you make the delivery first and then you can run around on turkey feeders."

Bill sat there for a minute looking disgusted.

"Come on. Get up and make the delivery," Reed demanded as he nudged Billy in the arm.

Francis walked in the room and Billy said, "Well, I guess we can't go."

"Why?"

"Because I've got to deliver those damn buckets up-town first."

"Well, I guess we'd better do it first then," Francis commented.

So Bill went out and backed up the truck. It had mud on the bed from Bill picking up old produce from the stores and taking it out to feed his cows on the farm. He started to load the clean buckets without cleaning off the mud, then he shoved them ahead and a stack fell over. I heard the noise and went out. Here were these beautiful white buckets that were such a pain to clean, and they were all muddy down one side of the stack and on the bottom of the others.

I stood there a minute, sick and forlorn with the fury of disgust running through my veins, I yelled at Billy, "You didn't even clean off the truck. Why the hell didn't you just tell Reed you refuse to do it rather than do this kind of crap? Now, I've got to wash them over, thanks to you. You don't even care. I'd rather make the delivery myself than have you wreck them all just because you don't give a damn."

"Well, why don't you then?"

"Fine, I will."

So I went to the house and told Reed that now I had to wash a lot of them over just because of Billy's dirty, rotten trick. "I'd just rather deliver them myself to see that they get there all right."

Reed said, "Ok."

So I cleaned off the truck. Mom and I loaded them, then when Reed and I got up there, the boss came out, looked over the load, "Well, you done a beautiful job, kid."

"Thank you."

"Would you like to take the rest of them and clean them up?"

"Not really."

"Well, what would you charge me to do the rest of them?"

"One dollar per bucket."

The guy gasped, "A dollar?"

"Yep. That's right."

"Well, I can't afford a dollar."

"Well, that's the cheapest I can do it for, so whatever."

We unloaded and I handed him the bill, got the pay, and left. With a hopeless feeling running through me all the way home, the thought repeating itself, there's got to be a better way. There's just gotta be. God help me, we're goin' to find it.

So, in addition to trying to find new accounts, whenever I could spare the time, I would have a few minutes of fun with the children. Even though I was not allowed to have children, I sure was glad that Zella and Bernice had the children that they did.

I took some old chains that we had around the place, climbed up in a tree, sawed off a few branches, and bolted the chain securely so the children could have a little swing.

At the supper table I was going over David's spelling list while I was eating. Reed came in and hollered, "You're playing with the children again. When you get through eating, I want you in the bedroom."

I took as long to eat as I dared then I would go to the bedroom to comply with Reed's damn demands.

It really confounded me one Sunday afternoon, as I sat with Kathleen in the living room. I was reading a story to her about the life of Wilford Woodruff, how he walked 30 miles through mud and swamp land to preach the gospel. Reed came in, "How much longer you goin' to be?"

I lied to him, "Well, I'm not quite through."

"Well, hurry up." He left.

I went on to read another story about Joseph F. Smith about his mission to Hawaii. He told of a Hawaiian lady that took care of him when he was deathly ill and brought him back to health. Twenty years later he returned to Hawaii. This woman, though very old, came to greet him bringing a cluster of beautiful bananas. She was blind. Joseph hugged and kissed her with such love and appreciation that she had come to meet him.

Kathleen and I loved these stories, but Reed kept awful close track of me so I could not read another one. But I thought, Goll, if that isn't strange. I can't even read these stories of Mormon history to his own daughter.

Then on another occasion, Reed was sitting in the kitchen when Paul, his youngest son, came in and in a fun, loving mood, Paul jumped up on Reed, throwing his arms up to put them around Reed's neck with the biggest smile on Paul's face. Reed grabbed Paul and threw him half way across the room, slamming Paul into the wall. Paul's expression was one of shock as he gasped. He looked at me, puzzled, so I put out my arms and went over and grabbed him. I smiled like "come to me," since he was looking at me not knowing what to think. I said, "Oh Paul, come and give me your lovin'. I just love it and you can just love me all you want to," as I kissed him and held him to me.

Reed said in a heavy voice, "I don't like all that mauling. May likes it. Go to her for your kisses."

I said, "Yeah, I really do."

Paul was sitting down now as I continued to hold him. Reed got off his chair and walked into the bedroom. I rocked Paul in my arms loving every minute of it. Then Paul was fine and went to play. I walked into the bedroom, closed the door, and looked at Reed with daggers, "What the hell is the matter with you that your own son can't come up and give his father a hug?"

"Well, I don't like it."

"I don't care if you like it or not. Just suffer it for his sake."

Reed said, "You love him, if you want to."

"Well, I sure will."

That made me so sick. Paul was the most loving little boy; anyone could enjoy him. Paul and Kathleen were the "lovers" of the family, always hugging each other and kissing each other, although Paul was only four years old.

It seemed like Zella, Mama, Bernice, and I were always trying to do what we could to get along with Francis. Bernice, Zella, and I would pretty much do the cooking. It was like whoever started on it first would do it.

Francis came home around noon from going with Billy on the fruit route to pick up the old vegetables for the cattle. Zella had fixed some lunch for everybody. I was sitting in the kitchen along with a few of the children eating a little bit when Francis walked in. She went to the stove, looked in the pot. Zella had fixed vegetables with stewed tomatoes with a little macaroni in it. It was ok if you put a little margarine or cheese with it.

Francis turned to Zella with the children watching, "What did you fix this garbage for? Do you expect the kids to eat that? They won't."

Some already had. Then Zella being hurt over the statement hollered, "Well, at least it's better than nothing. If you don't like it Francis, you don't have to eat it."

Francis, still hollering, said, "You're always fixing some kind of garbage. Look at all the things you've wasted that's went into that. It's just a bunch of pig slop."

"If you don't like it, then fix something for yourself. See if I care." Zella was crying.

"Don't you holler at me," Francis raised her hand and struck Zella on the side of the head. Then the battle was well on its way. Zella put up her hands to keep Francis from hitting her head.

"Get your arms down."

Of course, Zella kept her arms up.

"You get your arms down or I'm going to get Reed."

Francis walked into the other room. "Zella's got her arms up again."

Reed flew off the bed and grabbing the belt from out of his pants, came in, "You get your arms down," and whacked her across her arms. "Come on. Get them down."

"I will if you'll quit hitting me."

Oh dear, I just wanted to leave the room. I was so damn sick of this scene. When I returned, Zella had so many blows to the face that she looked like a boxer looks after a fighting match, once again.

As the months went by, Francis seemed delighted in making people mad at me, and would continually sow her discord. Because she would accompany Bill on the fruit route every morning, which generally took about four hours, Bill told Reed that he did not know what to do with Francis because she would say all kinds of things about May.

Bill said, "I don't know if they're true or not, but if I tell Francis to shut up that I don't want to hear it, then she gets mad and starts mistreating my wife. But if I don't say anything and just listen, then I find myself believing her and I have to work with May, and this makes it very difficult for me."

Reed said, "Well, tell Francis that if she doesn't stop her damn discord, that you'll leave her home. Then do it a couple of times if you have to. She'll quit."

Then in the house she would say things while talking to Bernice like, "I've seen May take some of our brand-new towels and wipe off her muddy boots." Bernice's job was to do the washing as well as go through the produce. Why Francis would just say such an ignorant thing to try to make Bernice perturbed at me is unknown, but she would.

Strange enough even after I had been there ten years, I was still taking care of Francis every night. Somehow, I was such a "horrible person" but yet I was the only one that she wanted to put her to bed at night and give her a bath. Because she said that anyone else was not careful enough with her sore spots. Although Francis never asked for forgiveness, I would forgive her anyway, and continued to do the best I could for her. But I always knew that if Francis ever really had her way, it would be my throat. One might think that for me to spend all the hours to pamper her every day, that she might say thank you to me once in a while. But no, it was like she thought her face would crack or something.

I had thought about this situation and took my line of reasoning before Reed. "You know what, Reed, even after all these years that I have been here working to support your family, still if anything happened to you, I'd be kicked out without one dime to show for ten years of hard labor. You know how you're always saying you're on borrowed time and you know how Francis is always sowing discord."

Reed said, "Yeah, I know what you mean."

"I just feel like it's hopeless. You can't put appreciation where there isn't any."

Reed went to Francis, "We ought to put something in May's name for all the years that she's been here supporting the family so she'll have something if anything happens to me."

"Well, hell, Billy's worked too. You act like May's been doin' it all and she hasn't."

"Well, if it wasn't for May's labor supporting the family, and Bill's cattle farm, we'd probably have to live off welfare."

They discussed this situation for several days. Then Reed said, "If you don't want to give May anything, then I'll give May my share."

As Francis had put everything between her and Reed, then Francis decided, "Well, fine. I'll give my half to Billy then, and they can work to take care of us."

So the papers were drawn up although the business property of an acre and a half on Redwood Road was half Bill's and half mine. The same as with the 6 and ½ acre farm in South Jordan, with half Bill's and half mine. It was a general understanding that if "cuts ever come to cuts," Bill would take the farm and I would take the business.

I had no idea what would have been fair, but I thought, Let's see now. For ten years' labor and they paid $35,000 for this place, that would be $3,500 per year for my wage. Well, that's OK. That's better than a poke in the eye with cigar butts. I felt somewhat enthused now because I had something concrete to build upon.

There was enough money to make a down payment of $5,000 on a $21,000 home next door. The neighbor had passed away. And we figured that between renting it and what I could make, we could make payments of $186 per month.

It was 1973, and as the months went by, I continued trying to locate work. Craig Thatcher from the Thatcher Chemical Company asked me if I knew where I could get 55-gallon metal drums. I said, "No, but if I hear of any, I'll let you know."

Shortly after that I was calling around to some of the bakeries to try to locate some 55-gallon cardboard barrels for Bill to use on his fruit route. I called a local bakery and they told me they had three metal, open head drums they would sell me for $3.50 each. I asked how often that I could get that many and they said once a week. I talked to Reed and Francis about them. I told them I thought some of the people in the group could use them for wheat storage.

Reed said, "Well, why don't you call them and ask."

So I called around to several of the large families, and several wanted them. Bill picked them up. I cleaned them out by laying the drum on the shop floor and reaching in with a pad and detergent, to remove the lard. I rinsed them with a hose then I would sell them for $6 cleaned.

I called Craig Thatcher to see if he could use open head barrels. They were blue and white and the paint was still pretty good after I finished washing them. I told him they would be $10. He told me he could use all I could get. I thought to myself, All I can get? Oh, boy! That statement got my adrenalin going. I sold all we had and began looking for more.

I called around to some of the dairies and sure enough, we picked up another source for drums. Then we began picking up 15 a week from the dairies. With the bakery barrels, that was approximately 20 drums a week that I had to clean. I had to figure a better way to handle them, so I made a rack out of 2"x4"s and a pipe. An angle iron was bolted to the 2"x4" on the bottom. To look at this rack sideways, it had the shape of a triangle. I could clean the drums out much easier, then I contacted an even larger dairy in Ogden and started buying all their open head barrels—approximately 70 per month.

They said, "If you don't take the closed head barrels, we can't sell you the open head."

"Ok. I'll take them too."

But I had no way of cleaning out the closed-head drum. After I had accumulated 25 or more drums, I told Francis and Reed we would have to buy a submersible pump to wash them. It would cost $60.

I went to work making a rack to go over the bottle vat by using 1-inch pipe. I borrowed a cutter and threader and got the T's and elbows I needed to put it together. A drum weighed approximately 35-45 pounds each. I made a step shelf on each end of the rack to rest the weight on, as I could not just lift a drum.

I took a pipe cap and drilled holes in it for the nozzle to give the water somewhat of a spraying effect. With this screwed onto the pump discharge, I could then flush closed-head drums. After washing the closed-head drums, if they were bare metal on the inside they would rust immediately if they did not get dried out fast enough. So I hooked up a little contraption to the natural gas line and put a pipe on the end with a flame shooting out of it into the drum. But after the oxygen in the drum was burned up, the flame would go out. So I had to develop a better way of drying them.

I found a little 5-gallon barrel in the junk pile out back, flushed it out, then I put it on top of a little natural gas burner. I built a little skirt around the drum so the flame would not blow all over with the one side open so that it would get enough air to continue burning. I then drilled a couple of holes in this little barrel with a circle saw, inserted a vacuum hose on the one side going up to the barrel. Then, the air from the vacuum going into the little drum, which was being heated on this little burner. Then, that would dry a drum over a period of time. But it was not nearly fast enough.

I called up a friend, Joseph Tanner, who had installed the hot water boiler at the old bottle barn years ago. He had been in the plumbing and heating business for years, and we discussed how we might make something more efficient for drying the drums.

I was also thinking about what a man who worked at Van Waters and Rodgers Chemical Company, was telling me about a little machine that would hold two barrels and tilt them from their tops to their bottoms while rolling sideways, with chains in the barrel to scour out rust, as some of them were too rusty to sell even after washing. I took some plans of what I thought a chainer might look like to Bob, who was a welder by trade, to see if he could make me one. I continued to wash mainly open-head and save up the closed-head until we could have a decent dryer and a chainer made.

Without painting the drum, I could do about 20 open head a day from start to finish. I was still working on bottles two to three days a week. When it came time to license, I said to the lady while handing her my money, "What do I do to change the name of my business?"

"Just tell me what you want me to put down here."

"Ok, put 'Reclaim Bottle and Barrel.'"

After approximately a year's time, Bob had what we figured would work for a chainer. A little frame with wheels on each side, and a shaft with wheels in the center, and a motor with a sprocket attached with the chain going to the center shaft to make the center shaft turn. This is what would cause the drums to roll. But the only way we could get the barrels to go on their top was to go on that side of the chainer and push down, and then put blocks under both sides to hold it in that position. Different blocks were used when we wanted to hold it level and the same for the bottom, but this was quite time consuming.

Then the little chainer developed some serious cracks in the frame. I asked Reed, "What are we going to do to fix it?"

He said, "Well, load it on the little pickup truck and we'll take it over to be welded."

So I unhooked the electricity that went to the motor and rigged up a skid braced with the little truck and figured out how to use a "come-along" winch. After working the better part of a day, I had it loaded and ready to go.

Reed drove it over to be welded. After 20 minutes welding we were on our way again. I said to Reed, "We're going to get a welder."

"Why? Nobody knows how to weld."

"That's all right. I'm going to learn."

So we did. I learned to weld in 1975. I started out doing a lot of "turkey pucking" with a little buzz box. My horizons had expanded, and I loved doing it! The work was not a masterpiece, but man, I could make all kinds of little things to assist me in creating more effective equipment.

I had put together another 20-gallon barrel with a flame under it for drying closed-head drums. I welded a few baffles on the inside to restrict the air from just whipping through for a better, hotter drum dryer. I bought a commercial insulation blower and hooked that up for my air supply. That worked fairly decent for drying a closed-head drum. Then I asked Wayne at ChemCentral if he wanted to buy some of my closed-head drums.

He said, "Sure. Send me about 20 of them."

I had washed glass gallon jugs for that company for years. The only thing I had for painting was a paint brush, but Wayne said he wanted them painted. I did not know the difference between latex and oil base paint, so I got some latex paint and tried thinning it down with turpentine. I mixed and mixed, but this was the strangest stuff—it just would not act right. After about half an hour stirring, I thought, What the heck. I took the brush and commenced to paint the drums. Boy it looked really strange. It was not covering or anything. So I painted them again. I used black oil base paint for the sides and this white latex for the tops. Well, needless to say, the tops looked like they needed to be painted again. So I gave them a third coat. I thought, Well, that's about as good as they are going to get, I guess.

We loaded them on the truck and made the delivery. We unloaded them at ChemCentral and Wayne looked at the drums with an observant eye. I said quickly, "Do you have a bung wrench? We can unscrew the plug and you can look inside."

"Oh, if you washed them, I know they're clean." Still looking at the drums, "But boy," he exclaimed, "You're sure one hell of a painter."

Next to me, standing on pallets, were other reconditioned drums. I gulped with envy looking at the product my competition was producing. Boy, they looked almost like new. I thanked him for the order, and we left.

I asked around with some different people on spray painting equipment. The best deal I could find was at Sears. They had an offer of a little compressor, the hoses, canister, and gun for $70. So I told Reed we needed to get that. The little cup would hold one pint of paint and I learned all about the difference of latex and oil base so as not to have that problem again.

Soon after that I got a 30-drum order from Flo Rep to be painted orange for antifreeze. My mother would bring the drums to the doorway for me to wash, then after I had washed them, she would put the drums on a 2-wheel cart and take them to the old chicken coop, which we called our paint shed. It took all day to do 30 drums, so at ten o'clock that night Mother and I were ready to paint.

Orange is a rather transparent color. The painting setup consisted of two turntables made out of 3/4" plywood with some casters which I had bolted on the bottom of the plywood, with a pipe flange bolted in the middle. The pipe from the plywood would drop in a bearing block bolted to a flat steel plate on the floor. I could sit on a little stool I had made out of grocery cart casters bolted to a little piece of plywood and a cushion glued on that. I would kick the tables with my foot to turn them while I painted. I had no exhaust fan at that time and the fumes were heavy.

After I painted the drums, Mom and I looked at them and the original color of the drum was showing through the paint really bad. There was orange paint all over the floor and there I was half stoned from the fumes. I looked at Mom and started to cry. It was an orange nightmare.

Mom said, "Come on, May. Can't we just forget it for the night? We can't kill ourselves just because we have an order. You look tired and I'm tired."

"But we need to deliver them in the morning, so we've just got to do them over."

"OK. Let's hurry then and I'll help you."

So we began to paint them again. Reed came down to the shed. He started railing at Mother, "You're supposed to hurry so that May isn't waiting for you instead of being so damn slow."

"Well, Reed. When you get as old as I am, then we'll see how fast you are."

"Well, I'm sure I'll be faster than you. You're slower than cold tar in January."

I stood up half stoned, "Well, she is helping me, and I appreciate it. Heck, I don't see anyone else around that even gives a damn 'cept Mom. You're too busy watching the boob tube to even care what's goin' on."

"Don't get smart with me. I'm the one who allowed you to go into this barrel business to begin with. And I can just as easily stop it if you don't show me more respect," he yelled as he hit me on the shoulder.

Standing on slick paint with my footing not being too sure, I fell and landed on my bottom. I picked myself up off the floor, my head spinning, "Well, yeah, but it's benefiting all you guys too because of what we're doin'."

"I was benefited just as much and more by the bottle business."

I stood there and a hopeless feeling came over me. I just wished he would leave. I stood there saying nothing. We were looking at each other. I said, "Well, can we please just finish."

"Well, I'll go but you'd better get your head screwed on straight."

He watched us for a while then left. We finished about 2:30 a.m.

CHAPTER ELEVEN

I wanted to drop the bottle business and go strictly into reconditioning drums. I approached Reed with this thought one afternoon. We were in the kitchen sitting around the table, and I said, "Ya' know, I think I can get enough barrel accounts to where we could just flat out drop the bottles and do pretty well."

"You're just barely starting into something. You really don't know hardly anything. You could have OSHA, or West Jordan City, or anything shut you down. You'd better not drop the bottles until you are positively sure of what you're doing."

So I continued on for approximately another eight months doing both bottles and barrels. It was such a disgusting thing to me to continually set up to wash bottles for a day or two and then switch back to my barrel setup. I wanted to locate more accounts so that I could wash their drums. There were a couple of oil companies that I thought were large enough that I could work steady for. One afternoon after washing a batch of bottles, I said to Reed, "I think I've got enough accounts to work for to make a decent income that we don't need the bottle business anymore."

His comment was, "I'd rather you stay with the bottles. I know you want to go to the barrels. I knew you'd come to this someday, but I think it is a job for a man, not a woman. You'll probably spend the rest of your life putting back all the money that you make into building the business and never live long enough to enjoy the fruits of your labors. I think it's way too damn much work."

"Hey, work I already know. But at least it's got a future."

"Well, I'll tell ya' one thing right now. If you feel that you can do well enough on the barrel business to support my family, plus the cattle operation along with the fruit route, and still have time to take care of me, (sexually) then OK. But if any of those things need money, you're not having any to build your barrel business. But after those things are taken care of and if there is anything left over, then you can use it to build your business."

I thought of all the shows I had seen on Mission Impossible. My body tightened like I had gravel in my guts and spit in my eye. "Let's go for it, I said to myself. My time would be extremely well organized to accomplish the most amount possible. I thought to myself, it's a matter of getting the right contacts. If I could get some half decent drums in here and get set up for better production, I'd have something."

But I had to pay more so that my incoming contacts would sell me their drums. When selling I would have to sell for less to have the customers take my barrels, which were not as nice looking as my competitors' drums. I contacted a paint company and arranged to buy a load of about 80 resin drums for $300. They told me the resin would wash right out with hot caustic water. But when I tried running them through, they would not come clean. I had tied up $240 on that load and had no idea of how to clean them. I went to bed that night after trying to wash them and perspired from the pressure, searching with my mind going through space trying to pick up any particles of light on the subject.

Reed was already threatening to make me stop on the drums. If he knew I was at the pit of despair, he might try to stomp out my dream of someday having something worthwhile. Where could I go? Who could I ask for the knowledge that I desperately needed? I shook, tossing and turning, in a cold sweat until morning. I got up and built a rack that would hold five drums. I held the drums on a tilt so the resin would drain towards the big bung hole. I took a cream scoop from the house and bent it so that I could extract most of the resin that had settled there. Then I took the drum and put thinner in it, put the plug back in, let it sit for a day, then put them through the wash. They came out clean enough for me to sell. I painted the load. Thatcher Chem said they would buy them for ten dollars, but after getting the load, they said they were slightly sticky inside and that they had to rinse them with acetone before they could use them. So they only paid me six dollars per barrel. Anyway, I learned that that method of cleaning worked fairly well.

I contacted another paint company for their resin drums for one dollar. One hot summer day while I had drums on the rack, I forgot to screw out the small bung on top before I unscrewed the large bung on the bottom. The pressure from the heat of the day built up inside the drum so that when I unscrewed the bottom bung, it went poof! It blew resin all over my face and eyes. There were some nasty words that crossed my mind. I had to wash myself quickly with paint thinner.

Mother was doing most of the chaining—that is what we called it when we put drums with chains inside on the little machine Bob had made. After I had extracted most the resin, Mom would put thinner into the drum about one gallon and put it on the chainer. Then after they had rolled on that for 15 minutes, the drums were tipped upside down on a rack outside the door to drain into a sludge holding tank underground.

One morning for some unknown reason, the rack was not there outside the door and Mom put a drum over for me to wash that was right side up and had been chained with thinner. I brought it inside without thinking much about it. After I washed the outside then boosted it to the washing rack, the thinner splashed out onto the floor which quickly caught fire from the flame underneath the vat that heated the water. This caused an explosion that blew out the shop windows. Fire was all over the floor. It was a wonder that drum did not blow up and kill me. The hose was in the middle of the fire. Standing there, Reed yelled to me, "Grab the hose!"

"I can't. It's in the fire."

"Grab it anyway."

So I did and commenced to spray water everywhere. I was able to put out the fire from all the things that were burning around me, but I got third degree burns on my arms between my gloves and the short-sleeved sweater. I no sooner had it under control when Reed, with a smoky face, started hollering, as if I needed chastisement, "You're going to kill all of us before you're through." What could I say? So I did not say anything.

Reed got a small burn on the ankle and Berniece had a small burn. I was glad that I had gotten the worst of it if someone had to be burned, because it was my fault. The whole shop was black and smoky inside, but I was thankful to still be alive.

After several months of working to earn all I could, I finally made enough to buy a few improvements. I had installed a small exhaust fan in the paint shed and bought a couple of three-gallon paint pots along with a paint gun. I now had a 10-horse-power compressor.

One day I was in the paint shed switching the material line from one paint pot over to the other for a different color. The bleeder valve that releases the air acted like all the pressure was out, so I commenced to undo the quick coupling. "Oh, hell," I exclaimed. The pot had full pressure. It shot paint all over me from head to toe. I was dripping with blue paint. I stumbled past whatever, to get to the bathroom where I had to use thinner to clean myself up. Reed walked in. I had one eye opened.

He began to laugh. "Ha, ha. That's the best thing I've seen all day. Oh, I shouldn't laugh, but you ought to see yourself. Ha, ha, ha, ha. I hope it makes ya' happy." I was glad I had free thinner which had come in the drums because I sure used a lot of it.

I had figured that I could do possibly 50 drums a day instead of 20 if I had a high-pressure sprayer to wash off the outside of the drum, which would increase the income to $200 per day. I bought a pressure sprayer, but I needed three-phase power. I proceeded to try to get the power company to install three-phase power on the property. Everything was approved, the date was set when they were to come to do this. I called up in the afternoon to find out why they had not shown up. The man in charge said that he had a note on his desk that morning from the City of West Jordan that said there was to be no three-phase installed for Reclaim Bottle and Barrel.

I asked who signed it. He just said, "The City of West Jordan."

Oh dear. I called an attorney and explained that I had put "barrel" on my business license along with the "bottle" and that if they were going to shut me down, why did they not do it then, 'cause now I have spent several thousand dollars on equipment to recondition drums. I told the attorney that for every day my high-pressure sprayer was not in operation, I was losing $200. I have no idea what he did, but the next day the power company was down there putting up the three-phase. With appreciation I thought, Whenever they want drums for something, they'll be happy I'm here, 'cause I will just give them a heck of a deal.

Mom was out chaining drums on a wet, drizzly day. I was washing, trying to get a rush order through. Mother came over to me and said, "May, the chainer's on the blink again."

I came out and looked at it and said, "Oh shit."

The motor mount frame had cracked on the side and the motor had dropped in the mud, ink, and oil below. "Heck" I said, "I just welded that thing half an hour ago." But I never could know where the next breakdown was coming from, because this thing was so coated with crap. I felt like I was under such tension. I looked up in the air as I clenched my fist and gritted my teeth, and just wished that I had a nice little room I could go into that had a foot of insulation all around the walls so I could scream bloody murder to my heart's content, and then come out and go back to work and fix it. But I had no such room.

I looked at it and looked at Mom, rain dripping off the plastic bag she had on her head. The feeling of hopelessness running through me, I slid down against the shop's outside wall. I sat there looking at my problem, then started to bawl. I just kept crying with the rain washing my face, along with my tears, my arms braced on my knees as I sat there in the mud. Then I began to think. That's an explosion proof motor. All I have to do is hoist it back into place and spray the mud off. It'll be fine.

I looked back up at Mom as she said, "Oh, come on, May, what are you going to do about it? Let's hurry."

"Would you please help me up?" I held up my hand for a lift. She helped me up. "OK. We've got to move all these thinner drums so I can weld after we wash off the motor with the high-pressure sprayer."

I got the welder out to secure the motor rack up in place. As I was standing in the muck trying to weld, I kept getting shocked. I felt like everything was after me to blow my mind. I got it repaired and felt much better.

Mom said, "You know, May, we're just like pioneers."

I smiled. Huh, I had never thought of that, but I thought that was cute. Mother was always willing to help me. I would gladly let her rest if I thought she would get to rest, but it seemed like every darn time she was not with me, I would find Reed had her cornered somewhere, either railing on her or slapping her around or some damn thing. It just seemed a lot better for her to help me at whatever pace she wanted to go. I needed her spiritual strength and encouragement. She was the only one that maintained confidence in what I was trying to do. I never heard even one discouraging word from her.

Mother's Day came and that was one thing Reed could not stop! My sisters would come over and bring my mother something. Previous years, Reed had tried to stop the girls from taking Mom to Chuck-a-Rama on Mother's Day. My sister Esther said, "I'll call the cops. I'll just tell them you've got my mother locked up and you won't let us see her."

Reed did not like that idea too well, so fine. Twice a year—Mother's Day and on Mom's birthday—Mom and I went with my sisters to Chuck-a-Rama. Francis was welcome to come with us, so she did. Sarah and Esther, my sisters, had bought Mother a new blanket, three new dresses, and a new sweater.

The next day, Mother was in the kitchen when I walked in. Reed had a hold of Mother's hair and was screaming at the top of his voice, "I don't give a damn who gives you what. Anything that comes in this house comes into the family and Francis will decide where it goes." Then he let go of her hair as he shoved her head back. Mother put her hand up so as to straighten her hair a little bit, "Well, I'd like to keep those things that my girls brought. But if you don't want me to, it's ok. I like Francis."

With all the railing that was always going on, I said to Reed, "You know there's one thing about it that you have to admit. Of all the things that people do to Mama, I've never seen her, not even one time, take revenge or say anything bad about anyone."

"Yeah. Yeah, that is one thing that's good about the old devil," he commented.

I thought about how Reed was always forcing people to do what he wanted. I asked him, "The brethren said that force is of the devil, that God don't force anybody."

"Ha," he said. "When an angel stood before Joseph Smith and said, 'You either do this or I'll run the sword through you,' now tell me that's not force."

"Yeah, but don't you think you'd get more by showing people love?"

"Are you kiddin'? That's a joke! If you let people do what they want, they'd just sit around and do nothin' and I'd have nothin' but lazy bums on my hands. I'll tell you, before I'd have a wife like that, there'd be some serious ass kicking. Zella is lazier than hell, but I see to it that I punish her for it, too."

"Yeah, but have you ever thought of just being sweet and asking nicely?"

"If you're so smart, why don't you try it and see if it will work?"

"Well, it'd be better than all that damn beating. That's not going to make her work harder."

I turned to go about my own business. I had no more to say, and left the house shaking my head. The blanket ended up on Francis' bed, the new sweater on Francis's back, and the same with two of the dresses. Francis gave mother her old clothes since they were the same size. The one dress that Mom got to keep was black with orange flowers and white and purple designs. I think that is why Francis let Mama have it.

Cleaning drums was still a problem. I asked the man at the paint company if there was a way they could drain the resin drums better. Some had as much as a gallon left in them. "Boy, May, if I could, I would. That stuff's valuable."

"Well, it don't have no value to me."

"The only thing you need is the paste, which is for color, along with lead, cobalt, and ASA then you could use it to make paint."

"Oh, yeah? Well, why don't you write down the recipe for me. Do you have all the ingredients there I could buy?"

"I sure do, and I'll make you a heck of a deal, too."

"All right. Let's go for it."

So I saved the resin and got to making my own paint. The ingredients cost approximately two dollars a gallon, so I really appreciated the savings over our having to buy paint already made.

Reed came out while I was making some blue paint for Amoco Oil drums and asked, "Are you going to come in the house and take care of me?"

"Well, I need to make some Phillips gray, too."

"You're always doing something, and I'm getting neglected. I told you when you first started the barrels that you had to take care of me. I'm not going to suffer over your damn business. Now come on. Get up to the house."

"Well, let me finish with this first."

"How much longer will it take?"

"About 45 minutes."

"Well, hurry up."

He was gone for about an hour and then came back. "You ready to come up to the house?"

"Well, not quite."

"You said 45 minutes and it's been an hour. Now come on. Get up there. I mean it, now quit," as he took the stick out of my hand and put it on a barrel, giving me a nudge in the shoulder. "Come on."

"Now, just a minute. I've got to put a lid on this thing, so it won't dry out."

He stood there while I fetched a lid, secured it tight, then I went to the house with him following behind me

Reed had his ideas of exactly how he wanted to be, as he called, "taken care of." He had this hang up about exactly how I should undress, that being when I walked into the room, I was to go over, fetch a pair of see through pants from under the mattress, slip off my stockings and boots with my skirt and blouse still on, then slip the pants on underneath my skirt and turn towards him showing him my behind while dropping my skirt, then removing my blouse, stand up on the bed while he was fondling his privates while watching me, and I would turn around for him to see my body, then he would say, "Ok. That's enough. Lay down now."

While having intercourse he would pull out just before he ejaculated, lay there and rest for a few minutes, long enough for him to relax, then he would say, "Ok, get up and show yourself again."

This would continue for about an hour and a half, then I could go to sleep.

He would wake me up at two o'clock in the morning by shaking me and kicking me, "Come on. Get up and take care of me again."

After this went on for approximately one hour, then if I slept until five, he would wake up again and I would have to proceed for another hour before I could go to work. But if I did this, he would pretty much leave me alone all day long while he slept and watched television, coming down to the shop occasionally to check on me. He would never allow himself to have a natural climax until three days before my period. Then after he had had a climax, three hours later he would want me to work him up again. He would allow himself to climax once a day. Then during my period, I would not have to have intercourse, but rather I would have to work him off by hand while being in a position so that he could look at my body.

As we lay there, I asked Reed, "Why do I have to be the one to take care of you sexually?"

He turned and looked at me, "'cause you're the one that God has blessed with a beautiful body and you don't get pregnant."

"Well, why can't you sleep with Zella? She wants ya' to sleep with her."

"Ah, hell. She's too damn filthy. She stinks so bad I can't even stand to go in the room let alone lay down beside her. I don't mind having it with Zella if you want to pose (for him to watch me in the nude while he is having intercourse with Zella). If you want me to have it with Zella, that's fine, if you're ready to have three times as much when I get through."

No way I could not figure that out.

Zella came to me in the bathroom on one occasion and said, "May, will you show yourself so I can have intercourse with Reed?"

I replied, "Look, Zella. I have no problem with showing myself so you can have it, but the hell of it is, Reed's told me that I have to have three times as much when I get through and I know that this is the way it has been in the past. What is hard for me to explain is I don't want to have intercourse with him for one damn minute, let alone for hours. I'm sorry, Zella, but I can hardly stand him."

"Oh, May. I'm sorry. I didn't know."

"Please don't tell Reed, 'cause I have to do what he wants, or he'll fight me on every turn I make with the business."

I left the bathroom and walked outside in the fresh air trying to sort out my mind. I was in love with accomplishing something that gave me dignity and self-respect. Over the years of building equipment and coming up with better, faster, more economical way of doing work, I was building my self-confidence. That would become a force to be reckoned with.

I would try to do just enough for Reed to keep him happy. So I was then free to run the business as I saw fit, pretty much. Being determined to rise above the poverty level, I dedicated my body, mind, and soul to build Reclaim into something.

The little chainer that Bob had made for us was altogether too light. Having to repair it anywhere from three times a week to four times a day, I gained quite an education on mechanical engineering, also metal stress and strain, by oversizing to adjust for the continual shaking and hammering on the carriage. By the time I had repaired the little chainer as many times as I had, I thought to myself, I could have built a whole new machine three different times.

As the months went by, I could afford bigger air compressors and I came up with a design for making my own paint pots of an approximate 20-gallon capacity. I ordered 10 pieces, 3-feet-long, 12 inches in diameter of 1/8 inch pipe. Also 20 convex end caps that would fit snugly inside the pipe. I then welded the bottom cap inward and the top cap round on top and made 10 tanks. I welded a pipe going down from the top just up two inches from the bottom for a material line and an air supply coming in from the top and a bleeder valve to the side on top, and I rigged up the plumbing so that by merely turning a few valves, I could stir the paint with air. Shut off some valves, turn on others, and I was ready to paint. This allowed me to have many customers' colors on tap to expand our abilities.

I felt that I had enough air pressure from the compressors that we could de-dent drums if we had a de-denter, that is a cage that secures a drum so that air pressure can go in the drum to pop out the dents. I knew where I could locate approximately 100 drums a week. I could get them just for hauling because they were so dented. They were an 18-gauge bare metal drum that I figured I could sell for $10.50 after de-denting and washing them. That was approximately $1000 extra per week, gross, if I just had a de-denter.

I asked Reed about making a de-denter. "Save up your money until you have $12,000 then buy one."

I was not contented with that thought. It will take me forever to save up twelve grand."

"If you start messing around with air, you don't know what you're doing. You could kill yourself."

That ended the conversation, but it did not stop my mind from wishing. When I was off by myself, I drew little sketches of what this thing might possibly look like in order to do the job. I thought of the size and height, and just how possibly, it could be put together, so that it would actually work. I considered all the materials I had on the yard that Billy had accumulated from who knows where. Then I waited until Francis and Reed went somewhere for about three hours.

I dragged the materials in and began measuring and cutting as fast as I could. Reed came home, walked into the shop, and asked, "What are you doing?"

"Well, I'm trying to make a de-denter."

"I told you to forget that crazy idea. Now get that crap out of here and get back to doing something you know how to do."

So I dragged the materials out, pretending that I had repented and listened very earnestly to every word that he said, until I overheard another conversation of when they were going to be gone for five hours. Oh my, I had that day pegged. I made sure that at the moment they left I ran as fast as I could, dragged all that material in, and began welding it together.

With the worry of Reed catching me, I hurried so fast that I had not done as good a welding job in one corner as I should have. I was ready to test a drum when Reed returned. I saw him coming. I had a drum in this cage with air inserted through a fitting I had welded into a bung, but this cage had no shield around it. I hollered to him, "Stand back. I'm trying this thing out." As I inserted the air pressure, I was 30 feet away watching this set up through a plastic window in the paint shed. Just guessing, I thought it had enough air, so I uncoupled the connection, waited for it to release, then went to check it out.

"All right," I hollered. "Look at that. Look at that! Hey, I can sell that drum now. Just a minute." I grabbed at another dented drum, rolling it towards this cage. "Here. I'll show you."

I took the one drum out of the contraption as quickly as I could, put the other one into position. "OK. See that how bad that is? Now just watch. Stand back." I went over to add pressure again. Then I came back after the air had exhausted, "See that? Whoopee!" I hollered.

Thrills of joy were running through every part of me. "Isn't that neat," I laughed. "That really works."

Reed stood there with a bored looked on his face, "Well, it is a little bit better."

"Little bit better? Heck, now it's good enough I can sell it. Before it was a piece of junk. You're looking at $2.50 straight profit right there every time I do that."

As I removed the drum to insert another one into position. After doing the third drum, we noticed the frame that I had made out of 4-inch I-beam, the top part being a 2 ½ foot span had a 3-inch rise in it. I talked Reed into taking me to get a 5"x1" steel plate that I welded on both sides of the I-beam, top and bottom. Also some other necessary improvements, like a metal cage with a door to secure a drum from killing someone if it should blow apart. And I rigged up a motor and gear box bolted to a plate that was welded to a couple pieces of pipe with bearings inserted in the pipe that would run up and down vertically on a polished, case-hardened shaft. I had fastened the motor shaft to a three-inch threaded shaft that I had made specially by a machine shop along with a nut which was welded underneath the top part of the frame. The threaded shaft went through the nut with a bearing secured on the bottom of the shaft, fastened to a one-inch solid plate the size of the top of the drum. By working the controls, the motor would take the plate up and down so as to allow us to insert and remove the drums very quickly.

We had a 1-inch thick metal round like a pipe 2 ½ feet in diameter, 3-feet tall. I cut it down in two places and put heavy hinges on one side and a lock on the other side. Then I torched two-inch holes at random in the round so as to allow 10 cubic feet of air under 100 pounds pressure to exhaust in a split second. By using the machine to generate a higher income level, I would make improvements on this piece of equipment as time and finances would allow.

One summer day Wayne Hunter, Jr. was operating the de-denter when a heavy drum blew. There was a flaw built in at the time I originally threw the frame together that I had not detected. The pressure was so great that it pulled a piece of metal apart 1"x1/4". In a split second, the bottom part of the de-denter blew open sending the machine like a rocket up to the ceiling, cracking a floor joist, then down again breaking a huge hole in the cement floor. If Wayne had been on the other side, he would have been killed instantly. I was sick at heart at the thought that my invention almost killed a young man. At the same time I was so thankful to God that he was all right. My mind tracked through time as I remembered how fast I threw that frame together.

As I stood there looking at the mess, Reed walked in the door and began to holler at me, "See what I told ya! You don't know what the hell you're dealing with when ya start dealing with air."

He did not need to say that. I already felt like two cents worth of dog meat.

I looked through the scrap pile and found several lengths of 1" pipe, approximately four feet long. I dragged them in. By using a wrecking bar to tilt the de-denter so I could put the pipe under it, I could roll the de-denter on the pipe and rotate the pipe. With the help of Reed's boy, David, who was about 10 years old, I managed to get the machine to the other side of the shop. Then I drilled a hole in my office floor directly above so I could lay a steel bar across the floor and bring the hook up from a come along and hook it on the bar so I could jack up the de-denter.

I did not know how I was going to fix it, but the next morning I was up at four o'clock because I knew my clean stack of drums was limited and companies were depending on us. I knelt down and asked the Lord to please inspire me to know how to fix it right so that I would never have to worry about it again and to give me the strength to do it.

I walked out, sat down on an old cinder block in the shop and stared at the mess, still not knowing what to do. Then I decided to cut off all the twisted metal junk and hope for some ideas. Sure enough, I did figure out as I went along, how to repair it and then to reinforce any possible weak spots, then to reinforce as a third precaution. I went entirely through the machine and reinforced as a fourth precaution, anything that could possibly have a chance to give way. By the time I was nearly done, I really felt good that this was five times the machine that it was before. No matter how many drums blew apart, I would know that everything was fine.

Joseph Tanner was out of town and Reed would not help me. After two weeks working from 4:00 a.m. to 10:00 p.m., the de-denter was almost finished. I had built an all new undercarriage for it and the locks worked like a charm. The top part where the bearings were mounted so the motor could go up and down was lined up perfectly. I had tried to finish it totally that night, but my strength would not allow me to.

I came in the house. The scene that hit me as I entered was filthy walls. The kitchen floor had not been cleaned for at least a month. The sink and sideboards were filled with dirty dishes and the table was a filthy mess with baked on crap like it had not been cleaned for days. No supper was prepared. I was very hungry since it was 10:00 p.m. and I had not eaten since 1:00 pm, doing cutting, grinding, and welding all day. I went over and got a bowl to put Keebler graham crackers and goat milk in. I moved enough on the table where I could put my bowl then sat down. As I sat there, I had hardly enough strength to feed myself.

When I was finished, I crawled along holding onto the walls to make it to the bedroom. I opened the door and Reed lay there with watermelon juice on his underwear and the sheets, the plate still on the bed with the rind on it. Candy wrappers and peanut shells covered the floor, and some were on the bed. Reed sat there with buffing dust on his face which he had gotten from going down into the paint room while my help was buffing drums earlier in the day. I looked at the watermelon juice on his chin as I entered and took the plate off the bed and set it on the dresser next to a six pack of pop. I pulled the blanket over the watermelon juice and fell on the bed.

Reed said, "Well, come on. Get up and take care of me."

I lay there in silence. He raised his tone of voice. "Come on. Get up. It's your own damn fault you work as hard as you do. I've been waiting for you all day and

I'm not goin' to suffer just 'cause you want to work like a fool. Now, get up!" He shouted, "Come on, get up!"

I lay there while he was kicking my leg with his foot. He had hold of my arm and was shaking me, then he grabbed my nose and shook my head back and forth.

"I'm not going to let you sleep until you've taken care of me."

I laid there as long as I could and then said, "Reed, I should think you would appreciate having a wife that would work as hard for your family as I do."

"Well, I do appreciate it. But I'd appreciate it a whole lot more if I had a wife instead of an old work horse."

"But if I don't get the de-denter finished, pretty soon we will be losing orders 'cause our stockpile is all gone."

"Well, I can't help it. I'd rather you lose orders than neglect me." What could I say? I remained silent and lifeless.

"You're not going to sleep," he hollered as he continued to shake me. Then he commanded, "Get up and do something for me or I won't allow you to work at all tomorrow if you don't take care of me tonight. Now, come on, get up! You could've come in sooner, but you didn't. So it's your own damn fault."

"I'm so tired I feel like I could die. I just can't."

"Oh, yes, you can," gritting his teeth, "and you will. You're not going to make me suffer anymore."

He put his foot on my hip and kept shoving until I fell from the bed. I put my arms and legs out to break my fall, then I lay there on the floor.

"Come on. Get up," as he grabbed my hair.

Accelerating my disgust for what seemed to be a nightmare rather than reality, it took all the constitution I had to hold myself like a lump of coal without flying apart. I stood up, looked at him, crying inside, and dropped my clothes. My mouth was closed tight.

"Come on. Put some life into it. Don't act like you're dead."

Just as he said "dead," I fell back on the bed. I could hardly hold myself up anyway and I was not about to entertain him if I did not have to. He grabbed my nose again and shook my head back and forth. I raised my hand and hit his arm and said, "Do you think all this is going to help you Reed? Whatever love I ever had for you in all the world, you're killing it. And once it's gone, I don't think I'll ever be able to bring it back." It was not LOVE that I felt for him, but pity. And I tried to show him respect as the head of the home, While I lay there enduring his loud voice, in my heart I made a covenant with myself to never do anything for him that I did not absolutely have to do.

He kept kicking my leg while pushing me out of bed again, as though I meant no more to him than a warm piece of meat. Where are the answers? What is it? I can't even think. There is an intelligent solution to every question.

I was confounded to see such inconsideration. Somehow, I had supposed that he appreciated what I was doing. "I need to pee."

"Well hurry up."

I locked the bathroom door and kneeled down pouring my heart out to God. God save me from this hell. Please Heavenly Father I beg You save me. I try to serve You, but I can't take this humiliation any longer.

"BANG, BANG, BANG! Was the loud knock on the door. "What's taking you so long dammit come out of there."

In the shadows of the darkness, the thought kept repeating itself in my weary mind, He wouldn't care if it killed you.

"Come on. I'm not going to wait all night."

With agony of body and spirit, I lifted and moved my body, though I felt no more stamina than a soggy piece of macaroni.

"Can I lay down yet?"

"No. Not yet. Keep going."

As I turned, my body was shaking while my stomach was threatening to relieve itself of graham crackers. "I can't," I exclaimed as I fell onto the bed.

"Damn it! You're going to pay for this."

The next thing I knew, the clock said 5:30 a.m. Reed was asleep. I quickly got dressed and left to start a new day.

CHAPTER TWELVE

I was beside myself over the memory of Reed's inconsideration that was more horrible than anything I had ever known up to that point. I sat in the kitchen while having some breakfast and Francis began to rail at me, "I know you can't keep that business going much longer. It's going to crash. If Bill doesn't get more than $5 an hour, he'll just quit bringing in the drums for you."

She had been telling me two days beforehand that the reason Bill had been charging diesel fuel on my account and having the attendant give him cash with it, appearing on the receipt as fuel, was because I did not pay Bill enough. But I paid him $5 per hour even for the time he was on the fruit route to pick up cattle feed, as well as, barrel pickups. The good produce that Zella and Berniece would take out from the barrels that contained cattle feed, and set aside for the women in the polygamist group to pick up and utilize, I felt was a very worthwhile project. I seemed so vulnerable to Francis' and Bill's tactics of stealing money from me. They would always come up with different ways that I would not suspect.

I sat there while she continued, "He's going to quit and get another job. Douglas Excavating would hire him tomorrow at $7 an hour if he wanted to work for them."

Her words were like drums pounding in my ears. I walked outside and Reed hollered out the window, "You'd better quit early tonight, if you know what's good for you."

I just walked to the shop with a blank stare on my face. It seemed as though I was trying to forget so much that I was beginning to feel like even the space around me seemed to be coming closer at times so as to squash me. My spirit was slowly dying, as I was slowly but surely becoming somewhat demented. I had little faith in myself, and as I worked and things were accomplished, I would stand back, look at the project, and exclaim, "I did that? But how did I do that?" I would look with amazement at my own accomplishments and say, "Could I do it again? I don't know. It looks kinda' complicated. I can't even remember how I did it." I seemed to get more stupid every day.

I went upstairs to the office and sat down to dial Dunn Oil to see if they had a load of drums we could pick up. I was half way through dialing when it occurred to me that I was dialing their address. "Scrud!" I exclaimed. "How stupid." My head dropped into my hands while I listened to the ticking of the clock keeping time with my fast pulse. My mind was racing a mile a minute. Reed's damn demands, Fran's demands, Bill's demands. Somehow, I must please them all.

Brrring. "Reclaim Barrel."

"This is Union Pacific Railroad. We need 50 open head drums delivered to Store 240 in Salt Lake City. Use the same order number as last time, as soon as you can."

"Ok."

"Thank you."

As I hung up, I exclaimed, "Oh, for good. Man, that's neat. I've got 65 out there already to go." Just two days before, I had had it out with Mr. Miller at Miller Honey Company on a load I had sent to him two weeks ago.

Berniece was doing the washing for 14 people and the old time Maytag had broken down leaving her to wring all the clothes out by hand. I looked at that and said to myself, This is a bunch of bull. There's no dang sense in it. You need an automatic washer and dryer and by crackie, you're going to get one. So I called up and asked to talk to Mr. Miller to see if they could pay us the money they owed.

"Hello. This is May at Reclaim. Uh, do you think it's possible we could be paid on the load we delivered two weeks ago? I'd sure appreciate it."

"I don't think we can pay you until after 30 days at the soonest. That's the best I can do."

Bang went the receiver. I sat there looking stupid holding an empty phone. I quickly dialed him again.

"Could I talk to Mr. Miller again?"

"He's on another line right now. Would you like to hold?"

"Yeah, hello. I'm sorry to bother you again. If I didn't need the money just really bad, I wouldn't ask right now."

"You mean you called me back again just to tell me that? I was on a long-distance call," he retorted in a loud voice. "I've got more to think about than you and your damn barrel business." Bang!

I sat there for a while thinking. After about ten minutes, I decided. It ain't right. I don't think he'd give a hairy rat if I was cold, hungry and in the dark. He wouldn't want to pay me one day sooner. So, what am I going to do about it?

I called again and left a message. "Could you please tell Mr. Miller that the driver from Reclaim will be in there tomorrow to either pick up a check or pick up the drums. I'm sorry but this is just really important that I get the money. And if we pick up the drums, then he can find someone else to do your reconditioning."

"Ok. I'll give him the message."

"Thank you."

So the next day Bill ended up bringing back the drums. We unloaded them in the paint shed, as I thought, A lot of good that done. Now, I won't even get paid in two weeks. Who knows when I'll sell them. "Thank the Lord!" I said out loud, as I quickly raced through the invoices to find the blanket order number for Union Pacific with gratitude running through me. Here it is. I began to copy the heading: Union Pacific RR. P.O. Delivered to Store, Salt Lake City. For reshipment. Shit. To Pocatello, Idaho. What? "Oh, no! Mercy sakes a living. I don't believe I did that. That invoice has already been sent off for payment. Heck. I hope they pay it." Oh, May. Wake up! I said to myself. Gheez I ran downstairs to the house.

"Bill, do you want to back up the truck and load 50 of the open head in the shed to go to Union Pacific? Here's the invoice."

I went to find Berniece. "Ya know what? We just sold those drums. I'm going to use the money from them for a washer and dryer. We could start looking around to find a deal."

"I'll be so glad to see that."

I was looking at her smiling face. "Yeah, that will sure be nice."

Within a couple of weeks, the new set was installed and working. We were all happy.

The water line coming to the shop was also hooked up with the house. I had started up a batch of drums. While trying to rinse one, all of a sudden, my pressure was cut down to a tiny stream of one foot high, making it impossible to continue. That along with all my other agony, I stood there and bawled. I just wanted to cry and kept crying. Somehow it made me feel better just to be a boob.

Day after day after day, every time anyone would use water at the house for anything, it would shut me down. Deeply frustrated, I felt like screaming, pulling my hair out or bawling, all of which did not help. "I either have to get some decent water flow or go nuts," I cried. "I've got to get this problem fixed."

This was happening way too often. So I called up some friends in construction and asked them what the price would be for them to run a 1" line back to the shop. The price was high but I would just have to do it. I had them start installation immediately.

Several months later with that improvement of having plenty of water pressure, I decided to hire a little more help. I already had two guys working part time helping buff and paint.

If I could find small jobs that Reed could do to help me make better equipment, I asked him if he would come down and help.

He answered, "I'm not goin' to help ya'. You're the one that wanted all that damn work. I don't. Why don't you go get Joseph Tanner to help ya'?" When Reed was in a good mood, he would help for maybe an hour until something good came on the television.

Even though Joseph Tanner was an expert in his field, his wage being from $50 to $200 per hour, depending upon the type of work, Reed felt that Joseph would help me without charging me anything. I did not like to impose upon Joseph but he had such a sweet, willing attitude that I called and asked if he would come help me.

Joseph was 62 years old. Reed was only 48. When Joseph came, he would grind off slag from the pieces of steel that I cut and he would help me measure things and line things up for whatever piece of equipment I was working on.

We were working on the development of an even more efficient drum dryer. After he had helped me all day, we sat up in the office kitchen.

"How much do I owe you?" I asked.

"Don't worry. I'll send you a bill."

"But you've been saying that for over the last two years now."

He wore a big smile as he gave way to a jovial little laugh.

I said, "How would you like some fried chicken? Zella's cooking some."

"That sounds delicious."

"Fine."

I ran to the house, made a quick salad, and grabbed three plates with salad and chicken. I took one into Reed and went to the shop with the other two plates.

As we sat down, Joseph asked the blessing. While we were eating, I said, "You know, Joseph. Seriously, I realize you charge $50 per hour when you work on other jobs and I don't have any idea how many hours you have worked here. You know, I have to be able to pay this bill and I expect it's pretty high already."

There was silence for a while. We looked at each other and he began to answer in a very tender voice, "I have never in all my life seen anyone work so hard to support so many with so few rewards for herself as you have. I decided years ago that if there was anything, I could do to help you, I was going to do it."

I sat there thinking of what he had said with tears in my eyes then said, "Thank you."

He continued, "You've really got a head on your little shoulders."

I had always looked at Joseph as a highly intelligent man. What a statement coming from him. He was such an expert in his field. These sweet words lay so gently on my soul. I smiled and said, "Would you like to see a drawing I done of the air dryer we're making so the man from the gas company can see how it works?"

He smiled, "Sure."

I quickly got it and brought it to him

"Uh huh. That's pretty good. And that's a very efficient design we've come up with, too. They ought to like that."

"I couldn't have done it without your help," I said.

"That's ok. Anytime you need any suggestions, just call me."

We were walking down the stairs from the office now. I walked down to his truck as he was about to leave. There was a longing in my spirit that was saying, Oh please don't go. So I talked about everything under the sun that I could think of so he would not go. But after about two hours, the sun was about to go down and I said, "Well, thanks again."

His hand was on the door and I put my hand down on top of his as I applied a little pressure while looking into his eyes, what a humble expression his face contained. "Thanks," I said, again coming from the bottom of my heart.

"You're welcome."

I removed my hand and backed up to allow him to leave. As I worked in the shop, I was thinking of the lovely words of encouragement he had given me. Something inside would say, Joseph thinks I'm smart. I would smile as gladness filled my soul.

I would call Joseph and discuss new ideas and all kinds of things. Just talking to him was such a spiritual strength. I soaked up his encouragement like a sponge.

When I went to make an improvement, Reed would say, "That's not the way you're going to do it."

I would go in, get Joseph on the phone, and explain my plan to him and he would say, "That's really a good idea."

"Could you please talk to Reed. He doesn't want me to do it."

So Joseph would talk to Reed and he would tell Reed (I would know because I was on the other phone listening), "The girl has a good idea. Let her do it."

I noticed Reed would never argue with Joseph because he knew that Joseph was such a well-educated man on many things.

Whenever Joseph came, I could not help but notice his clean, neat work clothes of navy blue and a smell of Old Spice pleasantly arraying around him. Even though he was helping me with dirty jobs, somehow, he would manage to keep his glasses clean. I also noticed every time that Joseph came on the yard, Kathleen, and David, and the two youngest children, would come and hug him. Seeing this, I tried to control my feelings but was wishing inside that I was getting a hug, then I looked away.

As the days went by, I felt a force coming over me more and more. I could not seem to control my innermost feelings. Could I be falling in love? For the first time in my life, I wondered. I had never felt this strongly about anyone before. As I fought with my feelings, I said to myself, Golly, May. He's in his 60's and he's got a big nose. No sooner had I thought that than the other part of me said, I love his big nose And I think he's darling.

The only time I was happy was when I was talking to or was around him. Then when he was gone, I would contemplate his return. I thought to myself, That's what's the matter, by George, It's true. You're falling in love, Mazie."

I told Reed one afternoon while we were in the buffing shed, my two part-time employees were listening. "Do you know what, Reed? I love Joseph."

"Oh, you don't love him. You just appreciate him."

"Oh no. I love him."

"Well, I don't care if you do, just so you love me more."

Every day my mind and my heart were upon Joseph, remembering the good times we had enjoyed working together and the great expectation of when he would come again. The thought crossed my mind over and over, How would it be if Joseph died and I never did tell him what I think or feel? Oh, that would be so horrible.

One morning when Joseph came to help me, the sun had just peeked up over the mountains at the start of another beautiful day. I quickly walked to the shop. I threw open the door. Joseph was standing by the chime straightener. Oh, my soul felt as though I could melt. He looked better than a million dollars to me. As I proudly walked up to him, opened my arms and he opened his, we hugged as I gave him a great, big kiss. Wow! What a kiss! The thrill from that went through every part of my body. I felt like hot wax that was about to puddle on the floor. I was starved for affection I had never known. As we kept kissing, I experienced something like I had never even had the wildest dream possible. The feelings that I had tried to keep confined now were exploding with joy.

"I love you, Joseph. Do you know that?"

"Yes. I can tell. I love you, too, little darlin'."

To try to keep my head straight and think about accomplishing work that day was next to impossible. My mind was on him. And the thrill of his kiss. That is all there was to it. How in the world would I ever be able to stop? Now, that I had a taste of what love is. And how could I keep a secret, My heart wanted me to just run away with Joseph.

Reed had a cold. Ka, ka, ka. Splat as phlegm hit the wall.

"Oh, hell. Can't you spit in the garbage can?"

"It's on your side of the bed and I'm not going to hold it in my mouth and take a chance of swallowing it again. Just get busy and clean it up."

Oh, yuck. It was enough to make me sick to look at all this crap running down the walls. He had spit there for days. I had put newspaper on the floor but not on the wall. With Reed's body odor lingering in the room, I closed my eyes to think of Joseph's sweet kiss and perfume. Just as I was falling asleep, Reed demanded, "Get up and fix me some spuds."

"Right now?".

"Yeah, right now. Come on." His foot pushed against my hip and I got up.

I said to myself, Reed might have my body and all my earnings and the labor that I can accomplish, but Joseph has my heart and I can't help that.

With Joseph's help, my interest in improving the equipment in Reclaim Barrel was accelerated. Joseph came to help me again one morning about 6:00. I had been working since 4:30 a.m. on a jig to make the washing nozzles over the vat to rotate so that it would clean the drums better. I nearly had it finished by the time Joseph arrived. Being in the shop alone, he walked in, came up to me and grabbed me. Then he gave me one powerful, loving kiss. Oh. I thought that was the end of my knees. Wow. The thrill went through me like a streak of electricity. I went for another then another one.

"Oh, I love you," he murmured low. "You're so sweet." He glanced over at my little project and smiled, "And versatile, too. You're everything a good man would want in a woman."

Joseph truly had all the right words to say. As I stayed there in his embrace, I looked up at his pale blue eyes. They held an expression of innocence and gentleness. His sweet smile had caused deep lines in his cheeks. His cute nose, it looked just like Jimmy Durante's. I laid a big kiss on the end of it as I gave him another squeeze. I stood there just holding him for a moment while my soul seemed to receive a rejuvenation, as a light bulb would if the cord were plugged into an electric socket.

After we had worked that day, the drum dryer was perfected. I had located a blower that would force seven pounds pressure through a 1" line. That air was forced through this heating chamber. After two minutes the drum would be so hot it could not be touched with bare hands and perfectly dry inside.

That night after Joseph had gone home, I thought how Mama loved Daddy and his name was Joseph also. Here was I, madly in love with a Joseph. The magnetism that brought us together was extremely powerful. Like a gnat being burned up on an open flame, I could not resist the fire. Every day I was so full of desire to see him again.

I remembered my statement as a child telling Uncle Walt, "I'd never marry an old man." Ha! Now the laugh was on me for I truly felt a fulfillment of a longing when he arrived.

I had a dream that night that Joseph came to the house and I told him that I would get him something to eat. When I went in the kitchen and returned with a meal for him, he had gone. I looked at the family and asked, "Where's Joseph?"

"He left. He said he had to go on a mission."

"Well, when will he be back?"

"He didn't say. He said that he might not come back."

I flew out into the night and ran down the street. I came to a cross in the road. Not knowing which way he went, I ran down one part of the cross as fast as I could. Then I ran back up and down another part of the cross. I was asking people, "Have you seen an elderly gentleman go past here?"

A man answered, "Yes. I seen an old man go into that white house over there."

I ran to the house, opened the door without knocking, and there was a man lying on the couch with his back towards me. I quickly turned him over. It was someone else.

"Oh, excuse me," I gasped, and backed out. I was heartsick, forsaken, and forlorn. I gave up as he would likely be far away by now as I slowly walked back to the house. I opened the door and the family asked, "Did you find him?"

"No, but if I ever, ever see him, I'll never let him out of my sight again." I sat and wept.

When I woke up to find it was only a dream, I went straight to the shop and called him at 4:30 a.m. I told him the dream, "Oh darling," I cried. "I hope to God you never leave me."

Joseph came as soon as he could to soothe my hurt feelings from that nightmare. When I was in his arms, I said, "Honey, there is something I need to tell you."

"What's that?"

"Well, I'm not Reed's daughter. I'm his wife." I did not choose to marry him. He was never my choice. It was the Brethren that said I had to marry him as his third wife.

"What now?"

"I don't know. But I love you with all my soul." I wanted just to stay in the security and joy of his loving arms around me. It dawned on me that after Joseph came into my life, I no longer had the dreams of heavenly places nearly as often and that was all right. For now, I was living in reality like as if it was a dream and loving every single day.

"Joseph," I said while looking in his eyes, "What if something happened and I could marry you? What do you think about having children?"

"Humm," as he gave me a squeeze. "I can't think of anything sweeter than having children with you. I would probably spoil the little things rotten or just love them to pieces."

What a gorgeous answer. I imagined what our children would look like—little cottontops with pretty blue eyes. I said, "They'd sure be cute with big noses on every one of them."

"Now, if they took after their mother," Joseph said, "they'd be saints. But if they took after their father, they would be holy terrors'."

"Oh, come on," I laughed. "You're as sweet as they come."

"Hmmm. But not as sweet as you, my little darlin'."

We decided to get to work.

He helped me for about three and a half hours then he had to tend to other business. My mind was a furious confusion over the whole issue.

What kind of situation was I in and why? I did not know. Reed refused to give me children and I am married to him under the covenant. When can I have my children as I am getting up in age now? I asked myself. I am 34 and my patriarchal blessing says I would be a mother in Israel. All this turmoil and arguments I had heard for years about Mom shacking up (as Reed called it) with my father on the prairie. The shame of my illegitimate birth that I had lived with.

I went to the shop storage room and put this question before the Lord. As I pleaded before Him, "Why am I going through this? I don't understand. Father, if there is a way that I can marry Joseph, please bring it about. I'm so happy he has come into my life. Please don't ask me to give him up. I'll do anything, anything you want me to. But please don't ask that of me." I whimpered while trying to speak. "I don't want to have a baby out of marriage but I do so want to have Joseph's babies."

As I knelt there, I had ceased praying for a moment while my mind was thinking, What a hypocrite I am, here I am telling God I want His will, while all the while I'm begging for mine. I felt my prayer was likely in vain but the disgust in my feelings declared, If I never have to have intercourse with Reed again, it will be too soon.

Then I raised up from my knees and sat on the floor crying. I thought, I wish to God I had to go to Joseph's bedroom every night then it would be heaven instead of such a hell.

I began to daydream thinking how it would be to have a few privileges like going to the canyon on a picnic with Joseph where there is beauty everywhere you looked. Or to be by the side of someone I loved and who was so sweet to me, and then to have some nice goodies in a basket. Ummm. I was just seeing it all in my mind. Oh yes. I have Joseph's head on my lap so I can gracefully kiss him while he is resting. I loved this thought. Dreamer, I said to myself. You'd dream your whole life away if you didn't have so much work to do. Oh dear, I got up. Heaven help us, as I kicked an empty box out of my path.

CHAPTER THIRTEEN

Joseph began to study plural marriage diligently. He had a wife but did not want to lose me. It was late afternoon when Joseph arrived. I ran to the shop. We went where no one could see us if they walked in.

"How's my darling?" Joseph whispered.

"I've been missing you. I'm so happy you got here ok." He held me while I melted into his arms. "I have been waiting for this privilege ever since you left, just living and counting the seconds until you are here holding me again. Oh Joseph, it takes every ounce of strength in me not to upchuck and to say, 'to hell with it all' and leave."

"What about the business though?"

"Even if I did lose it, you're far more important. We could make it doing something. Heck, even if I was a scrub woman, I'd be happy. Besides, between my guts and your brains, you know I'm sure we'd do ok."

Then Joseph said, "But you've sure worked hard for all this, little sweetheart."

"Yeah, but you just don't know what I have to live with to keep it. Reed come up to me this morning and said, 'May, I saved your life today.' And I said, 'Oh, yeah? How?' And he said, 'There was a shit eating dog headed this direction and I killed it.'"

Joseph reacted, "Oh hell, what a dirty, rotten statement. You know, honey, I just can't figure out for the life of me how in the world a man like him ever got you for his wife. I just can't comprehend it, you know?"

"Yeah, I know what you mean. What I can't figure is how he has the audacity to tell people that he loves me when he's all the time slandering me in front of other people for some kind of kick he gets. For whatever reason, I don't even know." I continued, "Oh, you know what, honey? I made the neatest salad. I think you'll like it. Do you want to wait here for just a minute and I'll run and get you some, ok?"

"Hurry up," as he gave me a little slap on my behind.

I brought back a salad that had pig weeds, watercress, mustard green, boiled egg, and little pieces of cheese topped with thousand island dressing. We had the blessing and Joseph began to eat.

"Ummm. Now that's what I call a salad. I really like this."

"I got almost everything from the field right next to us."

"Man, this is delicious."

"Well, I'm glad you like it. Whether anybody else does or not. Should I tell you what Reed said just now when I gave him a bowl?"

"What?"

"He said, 'What the hell you got in this? Some damned old weeds again? You're always trying to feed me weeds and I hate it.' So I said, 'OK. What would you like?' He said, 'I want grilled cheese sandwiches.' So I made him some, but I'm sure glad you, sweetheart, like it."

Joseph finished eating and I went over and sat on his lap and looked into his sweet face and said, "If I had to give you up knowing now what joy is, it would be like turning from the light back into the darkness. Years ago when I would see someone run to hug someone and they would seem so happy, I was so confounded. I never could figure it out. Oh, but now I know. I look at the world through different eyes than I used to. The sky is bluer, the grass is greener, the sun is warmer. You're like a reward for years of hard labor."

Joseph's eyes were wet. With the sweetest smile and a heavenly look of innocence in his eyes, he said, "Oh May, I would give anything to have you. Like Jacob worked 14 years for Rachel? I would work 14 years for you."

I put my head on his chest and wept as I whispered, "I love you so."

We worked on repairs for approximately two hours then Joseph had to go.

Every other Sunday I took Reed's and Bill's children into the office and taught them Sunday School. As I was teaching the children, I thought, Here I'm discussing religion to help these children become better, and yet, I wonder if my life has a stain because of my love for Joseph. What in the world are we going through all this for? Perhaps it was to prove to me that I was not perfect. Not that I thought I was ready necessarily for the celestial glory, but I would pride myself in the control of my mind, my thoughts, my appetites that I might do God's will over my own. But this was different. How could I fight something that I wanted so badly?

I dismissed Sunday School with the children. As they all ran downstairs to play, I sat there for a moment contemplating on what Joseph had said the day before. He told me that he was impotent and did not know if he could give me children or not. I thought, If God wants us to have children, we'll be able to have 'em. Besides, I said to myself, I'd rather go through eternity just holding Joseph's hand than anything Reed had to offer with his big prick.

Building the business was a perfect way to have Joseph coming over so often. It gave justification. Hopefully, so no one would suspect what was really going on.

I had enough money saved up ahead that I could buy a diesel tractor if I got a really good deal. So I bought an old clunker that was barely hanging together, along with a trailer that would haul 144 drums. I had a larger vat built and with Joseph's help we insulated it to keep the water hot. This new vat was long enough that we had two nozzles washing instead of one and a large gravity flow pump, so that I could have two people washing drums. Wayne Hunter, a good friend of mine, had a son, Dale, who was just out of school and looking for work—a very fine young man. I saw an excellent opportunity to hire a very trustworthy, and a hard-working kid, who later became my manager.

It expanded our procedure from the 30 to 50 drums per day that I was able to do by myself to 140 per day with two men washing the barrels. My being able to answer the phone so that they could continue to wash was far more profitable.

Joseph and I built new paint tables. They were square racks made of angle iron. We bolted four pillow bearing blocks that had two shafts running through the block bearings with cone shaped metal pieces welded on the ends so that the drum could roll and the top and bottom chime would be the only thing that was touching. Then we hooked up an air ram that expands and contracts that would tilt the one end down, so we could take the drums off when they were painted. The rolling was done with an air motor. We made two tables but the first motors we put on were way too small. They were supposed to be 1 horse but they acted more like a 1 mouse. So I got some larger motors installed. We felt that we had the set up pretty much perfected. We were ready to time ourselves.

I postponed doing the painting until Joseph arrived because he wanted to see how fast we could do this. I had some good guys help me take one barrel off one table and put another barrel on while I was painting the drum on the other table. Then I would swing around on my pivoting chair and paint the one they had just put on. I had one paint gun in one hand for black paint and the other paint gun in the other hand for white paint. With the paint pots I had built, I could put 100 pounds pressure instead of 60 recommended pressure on a factory pot. Also, with making my own paint, I was able to add more color for coverage so it could be just a tad bit thinner to come out quite fast.

Joseph was standing by the door with his stop watch out of his pocket. We were all in position. Just raring to go, I said, "Tell me when."

"OK," Joseph said, while flipping the paint fan on, "Go!"

Boy, I concentrated on every second to make the most of this deal. The guys would grab hold of the painted drum with a set of vice grips, flip the handle, and the table would tilt down to drag the drum off. They would put on another drum, flip it up, while the other kid would drag the drum across the room. It took three guys to keep the two tables supplied and me going lickety split.

When we got through with the 144 drums, "Stop!"

"All right. What did we do?"

"Nineteen and a half minutes."

"Let's see. What does that figure?" I asked.

"Well," Joseph scratched his head, "I think that's around 7 drums per minute, isn't it?"

"Boy, are you sure?"

"Yeah, that's about right."

"Wow, are we good or what!" We all stood around laughing.

"Wahoo! Can you believe it! That's so neat I can hardly stand it. Do you know what that means? Course, we was just showing off, but heck, realistically, think how fast we could do 300 drums if we needed to. Man, that's so neat."

As the days went by, I tried to locate more business, but it seemed like all the accounts that I ran into had quite a bit of chaining to be done. Our poor, little two-barrel chainer could not keep up with the demand. Mama was working nearly day and night chaining drums. It seemed like there was only one answer. I checked into the cost of a 6-barrel chainer. The man quoted me $45,000 with half in advance, the other due when the chainer was finished, and they could not promise a completion date. Forget that, I said to myself.

I went to Reed and said, "I'm going to have to build a 6-barrel chainer."

"Are you sure?"

"Yes, I'm positive. There's no way that I can get enough business in here without one. Just like ChemCentral's account, we could do all theirs but they've got over 75 percent chainer. I mean, we're talking 300 drums a week to be chained and there's just no way in all the world that I can ever pay $45,000, half in advance, and they don't promise a completion date either. So I know what I've got to do."

"Do you think you're smart enough?"

"Well, there's only one way to know and that's to try, and if I screw up, I try again. But I've got to figure this thing out before I make a move to know just exactly what the heck I'm doing."

"Well, ok. It's fine with me if you think you can."

I was getting approximately 150 drums per week that had large dents so I got them for nothing. With the de-denter perfected and the washing system adequate, I could sell them for $10 to $11 a drum. This was producing enough income with what accounts I already had to where I felt I could afford the chainer parts.

I had never had any experience in mechanical engineering except for all the work I had done in repairing the little 2-barrel chainer along with fabricating several pieces of equipment for Reclaim. But this was a monster of a job as far as I could see. That's all right, I thought. Joseph had such confidence in me, I had to give it all I could, no matter how difficult it was. I could not disappoint him.

So I measured, calculated, drafted, and drew plan after plan with different ideas, taking the best from each idea and applying it to another one until I figured that what I had drawn would actually do the job. Then I showed the drafting papers to Joseph. He approved. I continually went over my drawings, pinpointing each intricate part then drawing a line out to a large circle then drawing that part out to scale so that I would know exactly what it needed and how to put it together with what needed to be done first and so on.

I spent hours on these plans. Reed came upstairs where I was drawing, looked at me, and said, "You're just wasting your time." He pushed my drafting papers away from me. "If you'd just get down there with a torch, I'll show you how to build it."

I was offended by his ignorance and while pulling my papers back to me, I said, "I can't just do that. I have to know exactly where every single part goes and what size it is. It's a whole lot easier to erase a mistake on paper than to have to weld metal back together because it was cut in the wrong place."

"Well, I don't think all this is necessary. I think you're just wasting your time."

"Look, man, I'm the one that's got to work to earn the money for the parts. Right? And if my plan is wrong, then I'm the one that's got to correct it. Right? So, I would at least like the privilege that seein' as how it might be a screw up, at least it'll be my screw up. Ok?"

"Well, all right." He left me to myself.

When I felt confident that I knew exactly what I needed, I ordered the parts. Some things needed special machining so it took nearly a year for all the parts to arrive. During that time I also fabricated a water vat for testing the drums for leaks. A pneumatic ram was fastened above the vat with a bracket that pushed the drums under water with the air pressure. Also, I located a machine that would straighten and reseal the top and bottom chimes of the drums, thus improving their appearance considerably. Our reconditioning methods were approved by the Department of Transportation and a DOT number was issued to Reclaim Barrel. We were then able to have DOT certify our drums, and therefore picked up more accounts.

When all the parts arrived for the chainer, I was anxious to begin construction. But between managing three employees, organizing the loads coming in and going out, secretarial work, cooking for the children, taking care of Francis, and meeting Reed's sex demands, I could only spend one to three hours a day on the construction. So, to allow more time towards this project, I designated all of Saturday and Wednesday of every week toward working on the new machine.

All during the project, Joseph would give me whatever time he could spare. After seven months I looked at the monster machine and thought, will I ever get this monster built? But every hole that was drilled, every weld, every bolt that was sunk, put us that much closer to the completion date.

After a full year of untold hours and $20,000 spent for the many parts, the project was finally done. Joseph was so proud of me that he just beamed, "Boy, I know of a lot of men who would not believe me if I told them a 108 pound young lady constructed that machine!"

We had professional movers remove the machine from the shop, take it outside, and put it in place. Joseph and I hooked up all the lines from a hydraulic motor to the tank. We had a man come to wire the electricity, but even after it was running, I still had a few problems that I had to fix.

It ran about a month when the main shaft broke in half. It was 1 and 1/2" thick and there was just too much work load on it. Oh, hell, I thought, we have all these companies waiting for us to recondition their drums, and this will take some time to repair.

I had my help remove all the flammable drums from the area then we sprayed down everything with water so I would not catch the place on fire. I got the torch out there and cut away all the old shaft and removed the bearings. I went to town and picked up the bearing blocks and shaft with three new chain sprockets for drive. Everything was being switched to 3".

Several months passed and the business did fairly well. In addition to paying the bills, so Francis would not need to worry about them, I also gave her $120 per week to do whatever she wanted to with it. At that time I was buying the groceries, hay for the cattle farm, paying for the diesel to go after barrels for the barrel business, as well as barrels of produce for Bill's farm, and I was also paying $186 a month on the white house next door and all of Reclaim Barrel's debts. We had never been better off financially.

One day I walked into the house and went over towards the sink, thinking that I would make some soup for lunch. I took some vegetables and washed them, cut off the bad spots, and was dicing carrots to put in a kettle. The children were running up and down the stairs as usual when Guy, Bill's boy, ran up from the basement into the front room. I moved the kettle of vegetables over to the table so I could sit down while I was preparing them. I saw Guy whisper something to Susie, his sister, then they ran downstairs together. A moment later, Susie ran back upstairs and into the front room, then into the bedroom, to find Mary Ann, her sister. They were very happy over something. Then Susie whispered to Mary Ann and they went running by me to go downstairs.

I stopped Susie and being anxious to know what they were so tickled over, I bent over and whispered to Susie, "What's the secret?"

She looked at me and smiled. "Well, I'm not supposed to tell you."

"I won't tell anybody. I promise." I tickled her under the chin. "I tell you my secrets."

Then she said, "Well, Francis found some candy in one of the barrels and she said not to tell you or you might want some."

The smile dropped from my face and the kids rushed down the stairs. I sat there in shock. Sick to my stomach, I was totally confounded. There was not a thing that I had that I would not share with the children. But this was Francis. I wanted just to forget what I had heard and pretend I did not know about it, but I could not. It offended me to such an extent that I was weak and felt a little faint. I sat, resting my head in my arms on the table, whimpering like a baby. Even all that I gave and did for Francis, I had done it willingly because I did have some love for her even though I never could comprehend or understand her actions. I did not know what to do. I just sobbed. Reed came in and went to his bedroom. I thought to myself, I don't know if I should say anything or not.

I went in and sat down and said, "Can I tell you something?" Then I told him.

Reed jumped up. "I'm not going to let her get by with that. She's so damn selfish, she stinks." He went downstairs and sent for all the children. I was standing there listening. He said to them, "I want to tell you something. For as hard as May works, she is the one that has earned the money to buy fuel for Francis to even go to get the candy. Francis is just so damn selfish because she is jealous of May. That's the only reason she doesn't want May to have anything. Do you understand?"

I looked at the children and said in a soft voice, "I want you to have the candy because I love you, not because I didn't know about it. Ok?"

I was thankful for Reed's sticking up for me, but it took a long time to get over the hurt. It seemed so unreal.

One day, it was a cold, and drizzly wet. I was in the paint shed with three of my employees. They were standing around waiting for me to replace the worn pulley belt on one of the paint tables. Because the employees were all waiting for me, I was hurrying as fast as I could to undo the bolts, replace the belt, line up the wheels, and tighten the bolts up again.

Reed walked in. He started hollering at me with these employees listening. "Why don't you ever look over the equipment to see how it's doing to avoid some of these damn breakdowns around here? If you were doing your job the way you ought to be, you'd have seen that hose wearing where it was rubbing against the steel long before it wasted all the hydraulic oil. If you'd put a bend in the middle of that metal line so that the hose would have been far enough from the side of the chainer, it wouldn't have worn a hole in it."

I looked at the guys. They seemed somewhat uncomfortable at what Reed was saying, but he did not care. He just kept on hollering. Then one of the guys who was timid by nature spoke up and said, "I don't see where it was May's fault. Actually, I don't see where it's anybody's fault."

I appreciated his words but Reed continued to rail on anyway. Then Reed left because we were ready to paint. When the drums were painted, one of the guys, while walking out of the paint shed, slapped the "No Smoking" sign on his way out and said, "May, how the hell do you ever stand that man? You must have nerves of steel. I couldn't put up with that for five minutes. Boy, I'm afraid I'd kill the sucker."

Just two months before that time, I had an employee doing the chaining who was continually perturbed at Reed. He threatened to kill Reed flat out to his face. With the fury of that fight, I hated to dismiss such a good worker, but boy, I did not know if he was serious or not. So this more recent statement came as no surprise. On another occasion I was in the office and I had just gotten off the phone. Dale stood waiting to talk to me when Joseph poked his little nose in the door. My spirits picked up. "Hi," I smiled.

His deep voice came across the room, "How ya' doing?"

"Just absolutely fine." I rose from my chair and turned to Dale. "Can I help you with something?"

"Did you want to paint that load for Rinehart's Oil, or do you want me to?"

"Would you? I'd sure appreciate it."

"Ok. What colors are they?"

"Let's see. There's 40 hex bung and the plugs, black, white, and 60 round bung Amoco blue and white. Ok?"

"All right."

"Thank you," I said and Dale left.

Joseph pushed me against the door giving me a greeting kiss.

Knock. Knock. I opened the door. There stood a delivery man.

"My, what good things you bring me today?" I asked.

"It looks like 200 rings from Titan Drum Ring Company."

"Oh, ok. Yeah, let's just unload them right there."

I pointed to the cement platform at the bottom of the stairs. Reed was coming up the stairs with one of the employees behind him.

The employee said with a worried look on his face, "Uh, I was de-denting and I accidentally had the control switch in the "up" position when I pushed the power button and the top plate it wedged against the frame and I can't get it to release."

"Ok. What we'll have to do is get the 36" pipe wrench and that 6-foot pipe for leverage there in the corner of the tool room by the door. If you can get a good hold on the threaded shaft, you might need to have someone help you to break it loose. But be sure you're turning it the right way to unscrew it, ok?"

"Ok." The young man left.

I hurried to my desk to make out a check to pay for the delivery of rings when Joseph said to Reed, "May is handling the business pretty good it looks like. She knows how to keep things running." There was a slight laugh in Joseph's voice.

Reed responded rather loudly, "Yeah, it's May's job to run the business and my job to run May." Then he cracked up laughing.

I hurried out the door to give the check to the driver. Upon my return Reed was saying as he looked at me, "She could never run this place without me. Someone has to keep her in line."

I turned to Joseph, "I need to inspect just a few more drums outside so they can bring them up to run. But weren't we going to plumb in a bypass with a ball check valve in the hydraulic line?"

"Did you get the ball check valve?"

"Yeah."

"Ok. I'll start working on that right now."

"I'll be there to help you with it in just a couple of minutes." I picked up my overcoat uniform and gloves to protect my clothes from the greasy oil barrels. We walked down the stairs.

Reed said, "Well, I'll leave you two. It sounds like you've got your work cut out for you."

The three of us went in different directions with Reed returning to the house.

As the weeks went by, it seemed that we were doing rather well in many ways, but I would keep looking at Mom in her rags the damned old stuff that Francis would give her, and it really bothered me. I thought to myself, How in the world can we get some decent dresses at Deseret Industries to make Mom look and feel better? A faded memory came to my mind. Mama would love wearing white nurse's uniforms like she used to wear many years ago.

I went to Francis to hand her $120 and I mentioned, "I wonder how much extra you would need to get Mom some decent dresses from Deseret Industries."

"She doesn't really need anything nice to work in with those old greasy barrels. She's got a best dress."

"Well, heck, it shouldn't really cost that much. Can you at least see if you can find her something and then tell me how much it costs?"

"Yeah, I'll see what I can find when I'm over there."

So as the weeks and months went by, I would ask her, "Have you been able to get Mom something yet?"

She would reply, "No, not yet."

I knew if Reed got involved that would be "all she wrote." I could only wait upon Francis' mercy, which never did prove fruitful. I was sure that Daddy would roll over in his grave if he knew how Francis and Reed were treating mother. Mama would sometimes come into the house with grease on her clothes from working in the barrels. She wore an apron but her clothes still got dirty.

One-night Francis came at her and said, "Don't you come up here, you filthy old woman. You get downstairs." Francis struck Mother with the side of the knife she had in her hand. Mom was going downstairs as fast as she could. "May can bring your food down to you. You're not coming up here to touch anything."

Then when I commenced to fix a plate of food for Mom, Reed shouted, "Don't you give her anything but leftovers."

"Why?"

"Because I don't want her having any of this good food while the stuff in the fridge is going to waste."

"Well, the things we're having today will be leftovers tomorrow, so why can't she have it today while it's fresh? It isn't her fault that Zella cooked too much of this stuff yesterday. Why should she be punished for it?"

"You quit trying to give your mother the good food and never mind."

Mom was standing on the stair landing waiting for me to hand her a plate. Reed walked over and said to Mom with a sick grin on his face, "Oh, Edith. I'm sorry. I forgot you needed to eat. I flushed the toilet already."

I heard Mom reply, "Reed. Can't you get your mind out of the toilet?"

Then as we sat down to ask the blessing, he said to Mother, "You get downstairs. I don't want the devil present while we ask the blessing."

I took Mom's plate downstairs to her room. My eyes went over every nook and cranny as I glanced around her little room. Approximately six feet wide by eleven feet long, it had been painted with silver gray paint. There were fruit shelves around the sides with old bottles of fruit that had been there for years. The window on the north side was about 18"x30" with a dirty, old piece of material hung up by two nails. The pattern was gray with large pink roses on it. There were little cracks in the walls and larger cracks in the floor growing a black moldy fungus where water would trickle in.

Reed and Francis had taken all of Mom's chests of drawers when she came to live with us. She was left with cardboard boxes in which she kept her old ragged clothes. Her little cot was pushed against the wall on the south side of the room under the shelves of fruit with about 2-feet of clearance between her bed and the shelves. If she got up quickly, she would hit her head. When Mom stepped out of bed, she would either have to step into her boots or step into the water. I had brought in a board about 2'x3' so that she could step on it when getting up.

I saw this deplorable condition every day. A desolate feeling came over me that night as the stench of mildew added to my disgust. I stood there organizing thoughts as I looked over this mess by the light of a 40-watt bulb I thought what would it take to change this condition without a lot of money? I figured I could take all the fruit bottles and stack them in boxes in the furnace room. Then I could pull out Mom's cot, rip out all the shelves with a wrecking bar, and sweep the dirt and cobwebs down off the walls and ceiling. Then if I had some of the stuff, I had heard about that you can shove in cement cracks that is supposed to swell and seal to keep the water from coming in, that would take care of the walls. I could get a paint roller and some of the barrel paint and just paint the whole thing white. Now let's see. If I could get eight redwood 2x4s, 12-feet long, and three pieces of 3/4" plywood, I could put paint resin, like varnish, that I got out of the drums on the plywood to waterproof both sides. I would use this to make a false floor. I figured that this would take me a day if I really hurried. But how could I do it without Reed's sanction?

I went to him, "Reed, I have an idea that won't take much time or money. What I'd like to do is go to JB's Home Center and get some redwood 2x4s and some 3/4" plywood to make a false floor in Mom's room so she doesn't have that damn water all over ruining stuff. And I figured I could take out all those fruit shelves and if I hurried, I think I could clean it up down there and paint everything white and it wouldn't take me very long."

He sprang up quickly, "If you've got so much time, why don't you take care of me? I need a hell of a lot more of you than I'm getting. You only give me two hours a night when I need five. I go around being neglected so you can get work done, but to hell if I'm going to suffer if you're wanting to spend time with that. You get in here and take care of me first like you're supposed to."

"Well, maybe I'd better forget it. I really need to fix the motor mounts on one paint table before I get another order."

"I want to see you in here early today."

No comment. I went down to the shop then drilled new holes in a new motor mount. It looked good so I put it in place. It worked slick. I washed 100 lids and rings for open head drums, swept the shop, made 50 gallons of green paint for V.W.R.

Reed came down about four o'clock. "Are you going to quit 'n come up 'n take care of me?"

"I need to take out the plugs and inspect this load of drums that just came in before it gets dark so we can bring them up and everything will be ready to run first thing in the morning."

"Yeah, hell," he grabbed hold of my arm and shook me.

"You wanna take time for your damned old mother but when it comes to taking care of me, you can't spare the time. I've been waiting for you now to come up and take care of me first, then if you want to come back down and work on this, ok. Or you can leave it until tomorrow."

"If I don't get these inspected tonight and get them turned upside down by the door, it might rain. That would just make a lot of unnecessary drums to be chained."

"Well, hurry then."

When I came in the house at approximately 10 p.m., I was having some milk and crackers when Reed came into the kitchen in his dirty long John underwear with three center buttons missing and his hairy belly sticking out. What a hopeless, dreary outlook I could see for the rest of the night.

"It's about time you came in. Saved me from goin' after ya'. Ya'd better get Francis put to bed."

"Is she ready to go to bed?"

"I don't know. I'll find out. She says she's not quite ready, so you come lay down until she is."

I did the least I could get by with and yet not provoke his anger more than I already had. Then I went in to take care of Francis. As I sat there massaging lotion on her feet, my mind went downstairs where Mother was. I was sure her feet needed massaging but I dared not think about it. Such thoughts were like pouring salt on old, festering wounds that could not heal.

Several months later as I was coming up from the shop, while opening the door to the house, I heard a horrible, blood curdling sound come from the front room. I ran into the room just in time to see Reed kick Mother in the leg then swing his arm down to give her a hard blow to the side of the head. As Mother let out another scream, Mother's face showed evidence that this had been going on for some time. Her jolly, plump face had black and blue marks all over it. Her hair was in a snarly mess with blood trickling down from the top of her head from his having slammed something heavy down on her head.

Oh shit, I thought. Then I hollered, "What the hell is goin' on?"

Francis blurted out, "Reed wants her to sign over power of attorney and she thinks we are supposed to put up with her around here for nothing."

"What does she have that you haven't already gotten?"

Francis answered, "If I've got to be the one handling her damnable papers and all this legal crap of hers, I'm not going to have her tagging along with me telling me what to do everywhere I go."

Mother's broken words came across, "I don't know why you need power of attorney. I sign everything you want me to."

Reed stomped his foot, "We're not taking you in there to tell everything about my family."

"I don't talk about your family to them." She was referring to the Social Security Administration.

"You damn right you're not. You're not even goin' there."

"Well you guys act just like Francis owns me, but she doesn't," Mother looked up at Reed with her eyes somewhat fluttering as though she feared she might be hit again.

Francis interrupted, "I have to handle your damn mess. You'd just love to work the shit out of me, dragging you around wherever I need to go."

Mother looked as though she were contemplating. The room was silent for just a moment although the tension was so thick, one could cut it with a knife. I knew they would win—they would always win over all of us—they had all the chips in their corner. I was physically sick over the oppressive, domineering methods they constantly used over Mother who was now in her 70's. She did not have a prayer to stand up against them. They would beat her senseless if they had to just to get their way.

I turned to Mother, "Why don't you just sign it? They have all of yours and my money anyway?"

"I know, May, but then they can do just anything they want."

"Don't they do anything they want now? What can it hurt?"

She sat there scratching her head with her eyes upon the floor. Reed and Francis remained quiet thinking Mom would do it. Mom looked up at Francis, "Well, I'd like to see the things you sign of mine before you sign them."

"Well, if you have to see every cockeyed little thing" Francis snarled.

Mother said, "Well, ok. I'll sign it then." So she signed the paper.

I have no idea where Francis got it notarized but she did.

I helped Mom to the bathroom where I washed her face and combed her hair very carefully. There was a little lump on her head with a small cut. I fixed some lunch for us, and after eating I went outside.

A dreary, hopeless feeling weighed heavy upon me. I sat down on the cement edge which circled the driveway in the back yard. A thought scrambled across my mind: What am I? Who am I? I was sick with myself as I said a silent prayer. "Dear God, help us, Mom and I, to let us know what you want us to do. Give us knowledge and strength." I felt so weak and sick that I could have collapsed.

The thought occurred to me that anyone else would come up with a way to stop somebody like Reed from beating up their mother. Not me, I was a damn coward, I just felt like a wimp. I was totally at a loss as to how to combat him and keep him from abusing everyone.

I sat, staring at the rocks while the sun beat down upon my already hot body, as I wondered why they wanted power of attorney when Mom already signed over her checks and gave them to Francis. It did not make sense.

I found out months later that Reed and Francis had taken the deeds to a 180-acre mining claim in Arizona my father had left to Mother. Also, she never again saw her Social Security checks after that time.

Whenever I said anything about the way Reed, Francis, or Bill treated Mother, they would say, "It's just May sticking up for her damned old mother again." I heard that so many times but now it is like music to my ears to think that I did stick up for her sometimes. But I feel like it was not nearly enough. This was all during the time when it was all over the news how Ervil Lebaron, another polygamist leader, of the Lebaron group, also preached BLOOD ATTONEMENT, and (like Reed, who seen himself as a god that made him a self-appointed judge, jury, and executioner) he had one of his wives go murder Rulan Allred, a man from the Allred polygamist group. So to challenge any of these demented bastards who thought they were gods was, an act that was taking your life in your own hands. They were, at that time, justifying murder under the heading of religion. The Lafferty brothers was another example of another murder committed.

Reed also had a hang up about Mom talking to anyone that came on the yard. He would say to her, "When anyone comes on this yard, I've told you to hide 100 times and there you are out there talking to them." He would slap her and pull her hair over and over again while he said, "I'll teach you to hide." Then he would get on the rampage. One could hear it on the other side of the house—Mother screaming while he kept hitting her.

On one occasion some people brought some barrels on the yard. After they left, Reed sent word by way of Charlie to tell Edith to get up to the house. When she got there, I was in the kitchen.

Reed yelled, "I've told you to hide when anyone comes on the yard and there you are out there talking to 'em."

As he grabbed hold of her braids, he had a pair of scissors in his hand, obviously contemplating what he had in mind, as he quickly cut off her braids. Mother's long hair meant a lot to her as mine did to me.

"What are you doing?" Mother cried. "Oh, you stupid old thing! What did you do that for?"

"I've told you to hide. You'll learn. You just insist on letting everybody see you that comes on the yard."

"I wasn't even in the yard," Mom whimpered and began to cry.

"I seen you out there," Reed hollered at the top of his voice. "Out there with that man unloading those barrels."

"Oh, you stupid ass. That was his wife. That wasn't even me at all. Now look what you've done." Mom sat down, picked up the braids that were thrown on the table and wept.

CHAPTER FOURTEEN

Mother mentioned having pain in her privates and as the weeks went by, she talked more about it. One day while she was sitting on the couch, she asked if I wanted to look between her legs, so I did. There was a big "ball" about 3" across coming out of her uterus. It had come out approximately one inch.

"Oh hell." I went and got Francis.

She looked at it and said, "We'd better take her to the hospital."

So they did.

Many times I had seen Reed and Bill kick Mother and I could not help but wonder if that was the cause. Along with the kicking, the heavy lifting they wanted her to do probably contributed to her problems. They soon fixed her up at the hospital by reattaching the uterus and she came home.

After Mom's operation, I thought, Maybe I oughta' have a doctor look at my hernia. I talked to Reed about it and he said, "Well, we can go ask and see how much it would cost."

When the doctor saw me, he said, "Young lady, if you can't afford to pay me, I'll just do it for you anyway."

I thought that was so sweet. I asked, "Well, how much would you normally charge?"

He said, "Well, if we did it in a clinic, it would be $500 for the clinic and $500 for me. But if you need to go to a hospital so that they can give you something strong to kill pain, then that would be another $1,000."

I said, "I can suffer a lot of pain to save $1,000."

He said, "If you do decide you need to go there, we can send you from the clinic to the hospital."

I said, "I wonder if we should try to afford it or just keeping going with it the way it was since I have lived with it so many years."

The doctor said, "No, you ought to get it fixed immediately."

So I said, "I would like to pay you. Is $100 a month ok?"

He said, "Sure."

So we arranged to have it taken care of. When I went to have my operation, it was really sweet because Joseph went to the clinic with me. Reed said it was ok. When I came out from being operated on, although I had a lot of pain, Joseph was there holding my hand.

"How's my little sweetheart?" he asked.

"Kinda' weak. I'm so glad you're here."

"You're sure going to have to take it easy now for a while. You can't just run down there and give them guys heck for a while."

He was referring to my employees. I started to laugh, but quickly stopped as I noticed more fully the pain the doctor had told me to expect.

"I wonder if Reed would let me take you home to my house so I can see to it that you are taken care of."

Oh man. Just hearing that, my heart just thought that was the neatest idea in the whole world.

"I'm going to ask him," he said. So he got Reed on the phone.

Reed said, "She can rest in my bedroom."

I told Joseph, "He lies. He won't let me rest."

I was praying and hoping that Reed would have at least one ounce of compassion.

Joseph hung up and called his wife and asked her if it was ok to bring me over there. She said, "Yes." So Joseph called Reed again and talked him into the idea.

"Oh! Thank the Lord. What a blessing!" I said.

Joseph helped me into the car so carefully as the snow was gently falling down upon us. When he got me home, he made the couch into a bed. Although his home was simple, it was clean and peaceful. He waited on me hand and foot. After a good night's rest, I woke up slow and took a look around me. There were Joseph and Verda, his wife, being so quiet in everything they were doing so as not to disturb my rest. For me to see such consideration filled my soul with appreciation.

Joseph noticed I was awake. He smiled and said, "I thought you'd be coming around pretty soon. I have some nice breakfast for you," as he set down a bowl of hot oatmeal mush, milk and honey with margarine in it for me. I wanted for nothing for three days, even an occasional hug and some tender kisses. Everything he would do said "I love you" without words.

The thought of returning home was distasteful but the business needed me and, in a few days, although I had to walk slowly, I went right back to managing everything.

Several days later the kid that lived across the way came over with an old bike he wanted to sell for $5. I bought it and when I got to feeling better, I straightened the sprocket a little and put a thicker washer on one side so the chain would not keep coming off. The children were so excited. We went to the back of the property.

There was a dirt road where they could ride. Charlie, smiling from ear to ear, declared, "I'm first."

"Ok. You can go three times up and back." He did.

"Now it's David's turn." Then when he returned, I said, "Kathleen, would you like a turn?"

Watching she replied, "Well, I don't know if I can."

"I'll help you. We'll go slow."

Charlie said, "Heck, that's no fair. Kathleen's taking forever."

"That's all right. You had to learn one time too. Ok. Now it's Guy's and Susie's turn." I picked up Guy and put him on the seat in front of me to give him a ride.

Reed was wondering where I was. He came out, "You're out here playing with the kids again. Every time I turn my back, you're playing. If you don't have any work to do, you'd better get up to the house and get some rest."

A sick streak ran through me as he continued.

"They can have fun without you."

"Susie needs a turn."

"Well, let Charlie give her one."

"I don't think he can. Let me give her a turn then I'll be right up."

"Well, all right."

When Susie had her turn, Guy cried, "Don't we get any more turns?"

"Well, I have to go right now but I'll give you some the first chance I get." He was sobbing.

That evening I heard the kids and everybody talking about how "The Sound of Music" was going to be on television at seven o'clock. All right, I thought. The family had a large color television in the front room that they watched it on. I had never seen it because, of course, if I had had time to watch TV, Reed would want me in his bedroom. But he did not like the show so I would never get to watch it. So I kind of figured that I would be doing some fixing of supper and take my sweet time whenever Reed was not on my case. While standing in the kitchen and with the door opening into the front room, I could see it.

Reed came in the kitchen, "Boy, it's sure taking you a long time to fry just a few potatoes."

"Well, the kids have been eatin' them as fast as I've been frying them."

So he left. In an instant he returned. He came into the kitchen again and saw me standing there in the doorway holding a potato, "Yeah, hell. You're standing there watching TV. If you want to watch it so damn bad, come in my bedroom."

So after I had taken as long as I dared to fix supper, I went into Reed's room. All the time the show was going on, he was making mockery of the lady's singing. He would say, "I don't know what you see in a silly show like that." All of his comments and distractions made the show almost impossible to enjoy. He kept asking, "Have you seen enough?"

So I said, "Fine, move it to whatever you want. I don't care." I never did get to see it all the way through. I had to stand their while he would watch a little of a show to see if he wanted it switched or to leave it there. It was so humiliating, as he had zero consideration for how valuable my time was verses his.

A new day of work began at Reclaim. Seeing quite a few drums that needed to be welded, I began to weld up the holes while Dale tested them under the water for leaks. I noticed a drum that had "hole" written on the top, but it had a fresh paint job. It looked somewhat suspicious so I stopped welding and went for a bung wrench and removed the plugs. Oh hell. Someone had put this drum to be welded without being washed first. It had acetone fumes in it. I was furious. I gathered my help around me.

"You see this drum?" I asked. "Someone put that there without it being washed and that's just like a bomb. If I hadn't stopped to remove the plugs, my body parts would be blown all over this building. You know what I mean?"

They stood there looking at each other like who could be that stupid. It seemed that if it were not one thing, it was another. We all went about our work again. Boy, the thought was horrible. If someone else had done the welding and had not stopped to question that drum, how could I live with the thought that this place had killed someone.

I was also trying to figure out what to do about the IRS wanting to audit me. I ended up having to spend a lot of time digging up old receipts for the auditor. Then when he finished with the audit, he told me I owed $7,493. I about died on the spot.

"What do you mean?" I exclaimed. "Why, if I didn't have guts enough to run this place, there wouldn't be any money to argue over."

"I know. But since you did make it, the law says you have to pay income tax and this is what you owe."

I had been paying my three helpers in cash, so it looked as though I had kept all that money. I felt like I could chew nails. I went about setting up the pay for the guys so I could take out FICA, state and federal taxes and arranged to make payments on that huge sum with extremely high interest.

As if that were not enough, a week later I was plagued by another run of bad luck. A customer had placed a rush order for 240 excellent lined drums with a baked-on enamel finish inside. Not all lined drums when they are reconditioned turn out in the "excellent" category, so I had Bill bring in over 400 lined drums.

When we got the paint shed full, I got a phone call and the customer said, "Cancel that order."

"Are you serious? This is a joke, right?"

"No, not really. It was an Army order that canceled out. I'm sorry."

"Well, ok." The customer is always right and there is no use making them mad. So I went out and told the guys they had canceled the order. They were the only account I had at that time that would use that type of drum, so I had the guys stack the drums back out in the yard.

Shortly afterwards, Dale came to me and said, "May, the air ball has a crack in it and it's hissing air."

John, the compressor man, saw that I had been using an old Army buoy for an air holding tank. He had told me some time ago that if it burst, it would go off just like a bomb. He told me it could wipe out half the shop by blowing it into kindling wood. I ran to the compressor room and turned off all the compressors. I had hoped to get enough money by now to have replaced it with a regular 500-gallon air storage tank made for the purpose but could not afford it yet. So we moved the drums away from the area and I welded up the crack. I asked Dale if he would set the pressure controls down a little, which he did.

I got busy checking prices on an air tank and ordered one. That was too close for comfort.

Then Bill came to me, "I'm going to need another load of hay. It'll cost about $215."

"Well, ok, but they might need to hold the check a little while."

I was supporting 16 head of cattle at the farm now. The cost of hay and grain was approximately $250 per month. I was coming undone. How could I pay for everything when I did not have many orders? I locked myself in the shop bathroom. I wanted to scream but I knelt there and began to bawl. After having a good cry, I started to pray.

"Oh, Father in heaven. Thank you. I'm sure glad that this whole place didn't blow up. Please help us to get the orders we need so we can meet our debts and obligations. I need guidance and strength. I humbly pray, in the name of our Savior, Jesus Christ, amen."

I leaned against the wall staring at an old rag underneath the sink as I sat down there on the floor. Then I remembered that I had been working on plans to build a bung washer (bungs are the plugs that go into a closed head drum). I wanted to build this machine so, hopefully, I could wash three 5-gallon buckets of bungs at one time, instead of washing them by hand in a bucket as I had been doing.

I jumped up and quickly went to the phone and called Joseph. I asked if he had time to discuss plans for a bung washer and he said, "Sure, come on over."

I hurried to the house. It being around 5:00 p.m., I went to Reed's room, "Can you take me to Joseph's? We're going to design a bung washer so I can wash a whole bunch at a time."

"I want some fried potatoes," he said. "And you need to take care of me before you go."

"Can't I do that when we come back?"

"No, because then you'll claim you're too damn tired."

I hurried to the kitchen, got the pan of grease heating while I peeled and diced the spuds. I fried them in a hurry and fixed him some grilled cheese sandwiches. Then I hurried to the bedroom, got undressed and did enough of what he wanted so we could leave.

When we got to Joseph's, Joseph and I sat down to look over my drawings. "Well, that looks as though it's all right. But instead of using an open head drum, why couldn't you just use a closed head drum on its side held by a shaft running through the drum and bearings on each end? Then mount the bearings on a rack."

"Ok. Just a minute. I need another piece of paper. Now you said the drum was sideways," as I began to draw out what I had understood him to say, while scratching my head. "Ok. What if we use a pipe instead of a shaft? You know what? Hey, look, I got an idea. Why in the heck couldn't we just drill holes all along the pipe and then put a plug in the middle of the pipe and you know what? Heck, we could just use the one side for the water to come in and then when they're through washing and rinsing, we could turn it around and use the other side for the air to come in to dry 'em."

"Yeah, now you're getting your little noggin' to working," Joseph laughed.

"I was thinking that we probably need to use Schedule 80 pipe so it would be heavy enough. That way we could have the ends machined to where we can put the pillow block bearings to mount to our frame."

As we drew the outlines, it looked like a brilliant idea. Then Joseph said, "Yes, I think we have it now. That looks good." Joseph winked at me with the usual sweet smile on his face.

I said, "Let's see now. What are the materials I need," as I began to look over the drum drawing for a parts list. "I'm going to start rounding up everything I need to put this together first thing in the morning," I stood up from the table.

Since Joseph and I were alone in the kitchen, he pushed me gently against the fridge and gave me a big kiss that went right through me. "I'm so proud of you," he whispered. "You sure have a head on those little shoulders."

I hated to leave. We stepped into the front room where Reed and Verda were watching television. Reed looked at me, "You got it figured out?"

"Yeah, I think so."

"Are we ready to go then?"

"I guess," I looked at Joseph. There was love written all over his face. "Thanks for your help."

"Good luck," he wished me, while I shook his hand before leaving.

I worked on this "little" project off and on for nearly two weeks before it was working. I had to get the sprockets, bearings, couplings, and what not. When it was finished and I tried it, man, it worked so slick. Wow! I could not wait to get on the phone.

"Oh, Joseph. Man, you oughta' see these bungs now. They're as pretty as new. And perfectly dry, too."

He laughed, "Yeah, I'd like to see 'em when I come down there."

"It only takes me one hour from start to finish to do three 5-gallon buckets full. But you know, I think if we had a heavier motor and gear box to where it could pull a heavier load, I think we could do five buckets slicker than a greased pig," I laughed.

"What size you got on there now?"

"Three horse. But I think I need a five horse. But I don't want to worry about it until this thing wears out."

"Well, that should do you a good job for quite a while."

"Yeah, really."

Going to the house I noticed the children were running around full of excitement and anticipation talking about how Bill was going to take them all to the canyon for a picnic. Kathleen came up to me all excited and said, "Do you think Reed would let you go with us?"

I smiled, "That would be fun, wouldn't it. I don't know. Do you want to go ask him?" I knew what he would say if I asked.

So when we were in the house and Reed walked by us, Kathleen said, "Bill's taking us to the canyon. Can May come with us?"

"No, she's got too much work to do to be running off to the canyon."

I followed Reed to his bedroom, "What do you mean? Don't you think I've done enough that I could go with the children once in a while?"

Since the door was open, he dropped his voice to a creepy whisper. "Well, if you have time to go to the canyon, why can't you come and be with me? That's not as hard for you to do as work is."

I might have known. "Well, I've got to tighten up the bolts on the de-denter and the chainer along with adding more oil to the hydraulic tank."

I left the room. I walked by Kathleen sitting in the kitchen and just shook my head as I walked outside. While walking to the shop, my mind reflected upon a few weeks ago when Reed's family called a family reunion to be held in the canyon. Reed took everyone except Zella and Mother, but I had long ago given up hope for any happiness around Reed.

On the occasion of the family reunion, I had to stay in his sister's tent for two hours with Reed before I could go play with the children. I would definitely rather be greasing the chainer.

Every time I had a few spare moments between secretarial work, organizing loads coming in, loads going out, repairing breakdowns, and painting, my mind would drift off on a daydream. I would find myself wrapped up in a memory of Joseph's sheltering embrace, filled with the joy that would make the memories of everything distasteful disappear while sweet contentment and peace took its place.

I always thought of myself as an extremely strong-willed person that could suffer just about any torment necessary and still keep my mind on what I was supposed to. But here this 72-year-old man had me in such a dither, it was almost unbearable to go even 24 hours without his presence. It seemed as though everything I would do was just a means of passing time until I could see his sweet face again.

Working around all the equipment with back problems that continually worsened, one day I commenced dressing and all of a sudden, my back muscles tightened. I had a vertebra out of place so far that it was now pressing inward toward the middle of my back between my shoulders making even the slightest movement of any kind extremely painful. As I walked into the kitchen, it became more intense and brought tears to my eyes. What could I ever hope to accomplish in this condition?

Francis said, "Today Reed's sister wants all of us to meet her family in the canyon." Being Saturday, she said to me, when I told her of my problem, "You're probably faking so you won't have to go." She was certainly right about my not wanting to go, but there was no way that I was faking.

I called Joseph. There was no answer. He had been doing the chiropractic adjustments on my back. He was good enough not to charge me, although I would offer him a few dollars each time. I called his daughter. She said he had gone to the cabin. He had a cabin in the mountains 50 miles from Salt Lake near Kamas, Utah.

I begged Reed to take me as I was no good to anyone in my condition. He finally consented and Francis, Reed and I headed for Kamas. Some of the bumps we went over to get there were almost unbearable. The pain would nearly take my breath away, but as I watched all the turns and the roads, then up one hill and down the other, turning to the right, then turning to the left, I was smiling. For truly Joseph wanted to hide away so that he would be hard to find.

We finally arrived. Seeing us arrive, Joseph came out to greet us. Just stepping from the car my focus narrowed to a beautiful person with a red plaid shirt and suspenders fastened to his navy-blue Levi's. His silver hair with delicate waves was gleaming in the sunlight. He looked so handsome, adorable, and dignified. I felt much lighter just to be near him again. He bid us welcome.

He could see I was in pain. He said, "Has this little gal got a problem?"

"I think so," I said. "My back hurts really bad and I don't know what in the heck is the matter. Your daughter said you were up here."

"Let's have you lay on the couch." In a few moments, his loving fingers were carefully moving over my back so as to define the problem. "Ah ha! It's a doozy. This time the vertebra is going in towards your chest and it's a dickens to push that kind out. Now, if I could just roll her over so as to expose her backbone, I could just go pop with a little hit, if I could just put my fist through the front of her rib cage, then her back would be all straight."

Joseph was now laughing. "But it ain't done quite that way. I'll do all I can for her but she'll need treatments every five hours if she's going to be able to manage the place by Monday. Is there any way you can leave her here?"

"Well, we do have a family outing to go to. I wanted to take May with us." said Reed.

"What this gal needs is rest, peace and quiet, not an outing."

"Come on, Reed. Let's just leave her here." said Francis.

Then she asked Joseph, "Can she stay overnight?"

"Oh yes."

"Ok. Let's go."

"May, are you sure you can't come with us?" Asked Reed.

"I'm sure. This is where I can get my treatments so I can work Monday."

"Well, I'll leave you then." They left.

Heavenly days, can you imagine that! What a beautiful thing. Although my back was stabbing with pain, my little soul was so filled with joy. This was just the neatest thing. I had just been transferred from HELL, straight into HEAVEN.

Joseph said in his low, manly voice, "Would you like to take a hot bath, little darlin'? It would relax your muscles."

"That would be nice."

"Ok. Let me help you up the stairs," holding me as we walked halfway up.

It was a pleasant room, the walls a dark honey colored wood with little knotholes here and there, the wood grain an intriguing display of individual patterns. A chandelier, I noted, was a wagon wheel with little lamp lights arranged in it. As I reached the top stair, my eye was caught by a white bear hide spread out on the wall. A little pot belly stove stood in the corner and delicate pink see-through curtains graced the windows.

"What's this? An old-time wind-up record player?" I asked.

"It works, too."

What beautiful furniture. The silverish, cream-colored velvet material on the couch and chair with little flowers arranged among larger flowers reminded me of the pretty little things I had seen coming up there.

The table with a glass top and exquisitely beautiful wood carvings on the legs was truly a complement to the environment. As I turned around, "Oh, and you have a fireplace, too. Isn't that nice."

Joseph wrapped his arms around me tenderly from behind, then kissed me behind my ear. "You're what's nice." His voice went much lower now. "I'd give anything if you could live here with me."

Turning to look into his blue eyes with such love and tenderness, "Oh, Joseph."

We wrapped together like one body, one heart beating for the two of us. His kisses set my soul afire. Can it ever be? It would be worth waiting for.

"If there was even one chance that my prayers could be heard, I would be your wife."

We stepped out on the balcony. Mmmm. What beauty. Tall aspens stood among pine trees with the blue-sky piercing through. A little squirrel, running down the tree, bounced with delight across a patch of wild flowers. Joseph's loving arms were still around me. My pain was forgotten in that moment.

"Have I died and gone to heaven?" I asked.

With a little bit of laughter and him kissing me on the neck again, he said, "I don't know, but I think we're still here."

How would it be to love someone that much and be allowed to marry them. I could not even comprehend such joy. For all the damn hell I had suffered for so many years. I took a hot bath and laid down in the bed upstairs. He called it the "honeymoon suite." Everything was so clean, orderly, and fresh. I soon dropped off to sleep only to be awakened moments later with the sweetest kiss.

"It's time I was working on that little back again. Don't you think so?"

I pulled him down for another kiss, "I think so."

Each time he worked on my back, there was less pain. When he was through, his treatments were working and so was everything else!

"Can I play some of your records?"

"Help yourself. I'm going to go fix you something to eat. I think you may be pretty hungry by now."

When he returned with a sandwich and a bowl of delicious homemade soup, I asked, "May I have this dance?"

I put the Blue Danube Waltz on the record player. As his mighty arms swept me across the floor, I was lost in a joy that I could never imagine, the strongest force I had ever known, taking over.

That day and night flew like a light flashing through space and the darkness descended all too soon. With Reed's knock on the door, the brief moment of happiness ended. I had dreaded the thought of his return and when I saw him standing there, I was filled with an overwhelming depression.

"Are you ready to go?"

The thought traveled through my mind, If I stayed here over a million years, I would not be "ready to go." My heart sunk.

"My back feels better. It's not normal but better."

"Well, let's go then. You can't stay here forever just because your back hurts."

I thanked Joseph and Verda and went to the car with a vacant stare on my face, but a memory of joy was a part of my soul hidden where no one could touch it or mar it or steal it from me. There was not a day that went by that I did not pray, pleading to God for a way to open up wherein I could be free, if possible. To deny my feelings would be hypocritical and to change them would be impossible. When a person is living under a lie, unaware of what the light of truth is, how great and deep is that darkness. But I kept praying for deliverance. I was praying for God to do something. But God was waiting for me to do something.

CHAPTER FIFTEEN

The following Monday in the shop, I went through the motions of working, but my mind was 50 miles away. I could not take it anymore. It was in the afternoon when I went upstairs to the office where there was an old closet I went into. I shut the door so that I was in total darkness where I could be alone with the miseries of my mind. I had no sooner shut the door than I burst into tears. I knew better than to commit adultery but I was coming undone in my feelings. I would much rather commit marriage than commit adultery. I looked at myself as being as honest as they come and this was a form of stealing, lying, and cheating. But I would never steal anything, at least so I thought. How can I marry the man I love when I am married and so is he. The Doctrine and Covenants says "If a woman is found with another man, she shall be destroyed." Oh, hell, I cannot help my feelings. It was like a matter of survival, like a starving person being thrown bits of food. Although stolen, I devoured it as I looked forward to each ounce of love or kindness Joseph could spare me. I tried to look at how one might judge the situation as I wept bitterly.

They're going to call it adultery, I said to myself. I've committed everything in my mind, so what's the difference. And if Joseph wasn't impotent, I'd probably have had sex by now. Not for the need of a sexual relation, but just for the wanting so badly of having children with someone I adored and knowing that he also wanted children.

Before all this I had thought of myself so morally clean that I would squeak. Now, here I was. It was the hardest thing I had ever tried to control, but God help me, it took all the strength from every fiber of my being to control my thoughts, words, and actions. It seemed like I was battling with myself every moment of the day wondering which would win—my intelligence or my feelings. I would ask myself, Why in the world am I fighting myself? I know why I love Joseph. There isn't a woman in this world that wouldn't love a man like that. AND STILL THERE IS NOT A WOMAN IN THE WORLD THAT WOULD NOT HATE AND RESENT HAVING TO GIVE HER BODY TO REED. But because he supposedly held the priesthood, I thought I had to obey. I did not know that men earned women by how much tithing they paid or favors on work projects they did for the brethren. So my religious convictions at that time dictated that I should uphold him.

So you can only imagine how I feel 30 years later knowing all my suffering was just because these men had brainwashed me into thinking their lies were truth. I really had no way of knowing how God would look at Reed and his actions. I knew how Reed made me feel and it was exceptionally difficult to try to uphold him in the position of a husband, the way a woman should treat a good priesthood man. I was torn. What's going to happen? Am I going to hell? I can force myself to be an obedient wife, but I cannot force myself to give up all hope for anything better.

When the council of judges comes into a session to consider my situation, I hope they will consider everything. Am I going to be in the same predicament mother is in? Reed had said that because of her sin, she would be a servant throughout eternity. What should I do? I would be a fool, a total fool, to give up the only sweetness I had ever known. For having sex with Reed felt dirty and sinful. Loving Joseph felt blessed and Heavenly

I continued to cry, the tears streaming down my face. I thought, It's a good thing I'm in the dark so God can't see what a mess I am. Well, he already knows what a mess I am. Oh, God. Have mercy on my wretched soul.

I could not help but have more compassion for Mom. I had thought so much about where it says in The Bible that the sins would go from the fourth and fifth generation, and boy. I did not want that to happen, just because Mom and Dad did not have a priesthood marriage. But they wrote a marriage contract and they both signed it. How is that any different than any other marriage contract? They chose each other and did love each other and were faithful to each other. Reed was never my choice, not in a million years I would have NEVER EVER picked a man so utterly disgusting in every way!

"God, please show me what to do." I got up from the closet, went into the bathroom and threw cold water on my red face. I wanted to center my mind on things that were constructive. I was so thankful to have the business. I made the statement many times, "If I didn't have all this work to do, I'd go nuts." I began sorting out my secretarial work.

The certified public accountant I had contacted told me that it would be better to incorporate Reclaim Barrel. So I began looking into that situation. I told Bill I would need to have him be more diligent in getting and saving receipts for every single thing. He was headed to Church and Dwight Chemical in Wyoming that night. He had always told me that the trip cost $80. The next day when he returned, he had $29 worth of receipts. I asked him for the rest of the receipts.

He sat there on the couch and hung his head and said, "There isn't any."

"What? What in the heck do ya' mean?"

"I've been pocketing $50 every load since we started."

"Oh." My stomach began to churn. I could understand him wanting more money. I could understand everybody wanting more of everything good in life and I wanted them to have this as fast as I could possibly give it to them. What did I ever have that I did not share with all of them anyway? Why, why, do this to me? It could not have hurt worse if someone had kicked me in the stomach to think he would do that to me! Just several weeks before then, I had questioned Bill and Francis on $3,000 worth of missing checks out of the mail. I noticed over a month ago that several outstanding invoices had not been paid. I asked the companies for proof of payment and copies of the returned checks and when they arrived, Bill had endorsed them. I asked Bill and Francis at that time what they did with the money.

Francis said, "Oh, we paid bills with it."

"Don't give me that because I know what bills were paid because I paid them."

But Francis kept rattling on. It was obviously hopeless to expect to see that money. But like the brethren taught in meeting, returning good for evil, I was determined to make myself forgive them. Bill continued to have full rights as my partner in the business. Now I caught him doing this. He did act like he was somewhat sorry. I just assumed that he was sorry. I thought to myself, He probably feels like an ass, so I just dropped it.

For the next several months I was considering the incorporation and getting it set up with my bookkeeper. The papers of incorporation were being discussed and who was going to be the president of the company. Reed and I were sitting in the kitchen. When Reed began, "I think you should let Bill be the president."

"Why should I give him that position when he won't help me half the time unless he just happens to feel like it? I don't think I should."

"I know, May, but he does hold the priesthood, and if he doesn't have a position that is over yours, he will probably just quit and leave it all to you. Then you'll be making the deliveries too. But if you give him the presidency, he might feel like doing more because he is more a part of it."

As I sat there, trying to be open minded on the whole situation, I just had an uncomfortable feeling. I said, "You know very well that if you wasn't pushing Bill, he wouldn't do anything, except maybe take care of cows. I was asking Bill yesterday if he would learn how to weld to help me a little. You know what he said? He said, 'If I learn how to weld, then you'll expect me to do it.' And I told him, 'Well, I guess that's fine for you to have that attitude, but if I had that attitude, wouldn't we be in a hell of a mess.' I just get so sick trying to get him to do anything. It's worse than just doing it myself."

"But that's the point. That's why you ought to give him the presidency so he'll take an interest."

I sat there for a long time. "Well, what the hell, it's just a name. He needs the flattery. Ok, let's do it. Maybe it'll make him feel like getting in and doing something."

When Bill came home, we told him what we decided. We set it up the next day with the bookkeeper, then it was written up that way. We also set up a new account for the corporation with the bank and closed out the old account.

Two days had passed by. Francis and Bill were doing a lot of discussing. Then Bill came to me and said, "I've decided to set it up with the bank so your signature alone will not pass on a check. Mine must be there too." By the look on his face, I assumed he was not joking.

I called the bank and sure enough. That is what he had told them. Is there any end to the shit this guy will pull? It was like I had been hit by another flying brick I was stunned.

I went to Reed and said, "Bill has fixed it with the bank so that my signature on a check alone will not pass anymore. He wants two signatures so I can't do anything without his approval. I've had it Reed. All my incentives are shattered. Every dang time I turn around, he stabs me in the back again. I can't work under those conditions. I built the business without much help from him and now he wants to sit like a little tin god over the top of me and dictate my every move. I wanted to give him some incentive and that's what I get." I rambled on, "If he thinks that he's going to sit there and be my lord and master while I work all my life just to feather his bed, he's nuts."

Reed went to Bill and Francis. Bill was down in his room. Reed told Francis to come down there. "What are you doing so May can't sign checks and have them pass? What's the purpose of it?"

"Well, that way I'll know what the heck she's spending the money for."

"Hasn't she done well on her own? You haven't been hurt."

Francis butted in in a high-pitched voice, "Well, Bill has worked just as hard on the deliveries and cattle. May can account to Bill. He wants to know everything she's doing?"

"Why?" I asked. "What have I ever done that I should come under Bill to that degree? Why should I have to account to him for every little time I turn around? What has he ever done to deserve that position over me?"

"Ha. You're the one that gave him that position," Francis said with a proud look. "He's the head of the company now and he wants to know what you're doing with the money."

"Everybody and their cat and dog know that I built Reclaim Barrel."

"Well, you used my lands and buildings that Reed gave you."

"Don't give me that baloney. If I hadn't earned it, he'd never have signed it over to me."

"It's not just signed over to you. It's Bill's too. You just act like you're the owner and Bill's nothing. Bill will show you he's something and you're going to have to account to him, like it or not."

I sat there by the door on an old milk carton turned upside down while all their words were like jangling noises. I sat there for the longest time trying to sort out my mind and come up with an answer. This went on for better than an hour. When I looked up, and as soon as everyone shut up so I could get a word in edgeways, I said, "I've got an idea. If Bill wants that position, he can have it. He can have all of it. I'll run Reclaim Barrel for two weeks and then I'll hand it over to Bill to run without my help for two weeks. Then if he has had enough, he hands it back to me to be the full owner, 100 percent, without him as partner without him on my account. It will be so far run down, even I won't be able to redeem it. If that happens, I'll just go look for another job."

They all stood there in silence as I walked outside.

Reed followed me. "Are you serious?"

"You're damn tootin' I'm serious."

So for two weeks straight I ran drums through like mad and sold them for C.O.D. prices plus I called in all the money that I could get in that was outstanding. I paid up bills to where all the bills I had incurred under Reclaim were paid. Then I explained to my choice customers what Bill was trying to do and what I was doing. Leon at ChemCentral said, "May, that's nuts! What does he know about the company? Do you think he could run it?"

"I don't know and I don't care. One thing's for sure, I won't continue on with him having any part of it."

"Well, I won't deal with him."

"I really appreciate that, Leon."

Then I explained to my help what was going on.

They all said, "Oh, that's fine. We'll just quit 'til you call us back to work."

One man said, "I wouldn't work for that lazy bum for ten minutes, if I never worked here again."

"Thanks."

Then Friday night September 26, 1981, I said, "Ok Bill, as of Monday morning, Reclaim Barrel is yours. Good luck!"

Things were silent all-day Saturday. No one talked much and silence prevailed Sunday. Then Monday morning at 3 a.m. Bill came knocking on Reed's bedroom door. He was crying.

"I got to talk to you," he said. "I haven't slept the last two nights. I've thought about this over and over," as he continued to bawl. "Francis keeps trying to get me to take over the business, but I can't. I just can't. I don't know anything about it. It's May's baby. I'd rather see her have it than see it go under. I'll sign off my half."

I had tears in my eyes, too. I was thankful that he would rather give it to me than to see it destroyed. With a feeling of compassion, I told him that I would finish paying off his debt to the IRS which was approximately $1,400. I wrote up an agreement and we had it notarized to that effect. I then owned 100 percent of Reclaim, and the land, of one and a half acre that it sat on. I removed his name off my Reclaim Barrel checking account. He was then an employee working for wages.

A few months later Mother stepped on a nail. It went through her work boots into her foot. We were in her bedroom in the basement where I was putting a diced onion poultice on it. I noticed that her toenails needed to be trimmed. Mother had a difficult time doing that job with an old paring knife she had found in a barrel because of her large stomach, dim lighting, and poor eyesight. There was no one she could ask to do this for her because of Reed's teachings. No one wanted to even touch her. The horrible neglect that had taken place was making my stomach churn. I knew if I was caught taking care of this, I would likely be knocked from here to kingdom come. I was quivering and thinking.

In a whisper I said, "I've got an idea. After I put Francis to bed tonight, I'll get the toenail clippers and scissors and hide 'em in the bathroom. Ok? Then if I drink a lot of water, it will make me wake up in the middle of the night to go pee, without waking Reed. Then I'll sneak down here and do this. Ok?"

Mama started to cry. "That would be so sweet of you to do that for me. I'd really appreciate it. I can't seem to do it and they hurt me every step I take."

I finished taping the bag of onions around her one foot. "Maybe it's kinda' a good thing you stepped on a nail, huh?" I smiled.

Mama wiped her tears away and smiled. "Maybe the Lord had me step on it just so I could get this other taken care of."

"Ok. I got to go."

"Thank you, sweetheart," were Mother's words as I was leaving her room.

Choking up with tears on my way upstairs, I stopped there with the scene of injustice before me. Then I went about getting Francis taken care of. All the while I was thinking as I washed her feet with a wet washcloth and massaged lotion on them. I had trimmed her toenails last week. Mother would think she had died and gone to heaven if I could give her this much care. I massaged Francis's back and legs with lotion and pulled down her nightgown. The same pampering that I had given her for over 15 years.

"Is there anything else you'd like?" I asked.

She moved over to the side of the bed, "Yeah, adjust my neck."

Carefully massaging her neck so as to relax her then giving it a slight twist to one side bringing her chin up like the chiropractor had showed me years ago, we heard a pop pop.

"The other side needs it, too."

So I did the same on that side. Then she swung herself around into her sleeping position.

"Is there anything else or may I go now?"

"I guess."

"Good night," as I turned out the light and shut the door with the toenail kit and some medicine for sores in my pocket.

Then at 2:30 I woke up. I quickly sneaked downstairs and woke Mama. I thought, I should have grabbed a brighter light, too. But I managed.

After cutting the nails and doctoring a few sores, Mama said, "Can you raise up a little closer? I want to kiss you."

I smiled., "Ok." Then I quickly made my way back to Reed's bedroom. But for weeks after that I had a gnawing feeling inside of me.

After 15 years of caring for Francis' personal needs, occasionally my mind would ponder over this situation. One morning I had given her a bath and was dressing her. She was sitting on her bed with all but her stockings and shoes on. I dared to speak.

"How come you hardly ever thank me for taking care of you?"

There was silence as I stretched the stocking wide to put over her foot. "Why should I? You're only doing your job," she replied sarcastically. "What do you mean by that?" I waited for an answer.

"You wouldn't do it if Reed didn't make ya'."

I stopped right there leaving one stocking halfway pulled up her leg. I carefully lowered it to the floor. I got up and went to Reed's room. Reed was laying on his bed partly asleep.

"Reed." I shook him a little. "I need to ask you something."

"Huh? What's the matter?"

"Is there someone else who could take care of Francis instead of me?"

"Why? What's the matter?"

Francis was standing at the door. "I told you May didn't love me," she cried. "If she doesn't want to help me, I'll go live with my kids. She was bawling while raving on, "May begrudges every little shittin' thing she does for me. I don't have to live here and put up with it." She slammed the door.

I was shaking my head. "That ain't it at all, Reed. All I ask for is a thank you. You'd think her face would crack or something. It ain't going to kill her."

I sat there dumbfounded. How in the world could she say all that crap when all I asked for was a little appreciation? I hung my head to collect my thoughts then looked at Reed.

"I don't mind doing for her. But if she does appreciate it, why can't she just say so? It would be so much nicer. Maybe I'm wrong, Reed. But I've got just enough gravel in my guts to the point where if she can't afford a thank you, then I can't afford to do it for her. I've got work coming out of my ears, and you figure $10 to $15 an hour for three hours a day, that adds up in a hurry. Hell, if I handed someone $500 or a thousand dollars, I think I would at least get a thank you. Don't you?"

"Maybe I ought to have Zella or Berniece take care of her so you can earn more income."

"What about Kathleen? She's old enough. I think she could learn to do a good job. She's got more time than Zella or Berniece has."

"Yeah, why don't she get Kathleen?" Reed commented while raising up off the bed. He went into Francis' room to find she had put her own shoes on and finished pulling up her stocking when she had always claimed that she could not bend over.

"I want you to get Kathleen off her butt to learn how to take care of you. May's time is too valuable at the shop." I could hear Reed talking as I left the scene.

There was continual contention for about a week. I could hear bits and pieces of the arguments but stayed out of it as much as possible. The next thing I knew Francis was moving to the white house next door.

One day I asked Kathleen, just out of curiosity. She told me Francis was taking care of herself over there. Hmmm. Maybe it was just as well.

With Francis moved next door, Bill helped her fix up the house she was in but Francis left all her boxes of what not in the red house. She was a hoarder. After months of having them sit there, I said, "Look, Francis, tell me what you want me to do with this stuff."

"I'm trying to sort it as fast as I can."

"We've been hearing that for 15 years. Now that you live in a half decent house, we're still in a dump. These boxes are depressing because of the clutter. And there couldn't be anything very valuable in them because obviously, we are getting along just fine without whatever they contain."

Francis flew into a rage, "You're always trying to boss me and tell me what to do."

She raised her hand to strike me across the face. I caught her arm before it made connection. I stared her right in the eye. "I wouldn't try that if I were you. I don't want to hurt you," I said very sincerely.

She lowered her hand and went into Reed, "May's trying to boss me and tell me what to do in my position. I've been working on sorting those boxes in the front room as fast as I can." I could hear her hollering clear in the kitchen.

Francis and Reed came walking toward the front room. Reed hollered at me, "You stay out of Francis' territory. Francis will get it cleaned up."

I said, "Look, Reed. We've been hearing that same damn story for 15 years. She's left this territory and we girls don't intend on living with this crap for another 15 years. The only thing I asked her to do is come with me and we would mark out whatever was valuable so that whatever boxes she wanted taken to her place, we'd carry them over to her. Then whatever was left, I'd sort through them. Ok?"

I stood there with Bill, Francis, and Reed, all hollering at me at once. It was such a massive jangle I could not make any sense out of it.

As I stood there listening to this jangling mess, I said, "Yes. You are all right. You're right for each other. I'm the only one that doesn't belong. But I don't care if you beat me, if you get mad, or what the hell you do. This crap is leaving. Now, she can decide whatever she wants over there. If it's not valuable enough for her to clutter up her house with, then it ain't very valuable, is it?" Then I left

Within a week Francis came over. She knew damn well that if she did not do something, I was going to. Very nicely we went through and I marked a little mark on each box she wanted carried to her house, and I had my guys from the shop carry them over there.

Charlie, Reed's second son, was wearing a pair of pants with a broken zipper. He had a piece of string from a bale of hay around his waist for a belt. I looked at him and said, "Charlie, can't you find a better pair of pants than that?"

"No."

I took his hand, "Come on. Let's go see."

We went downstairs and I looked, but neither of us could find anything better for him to wear. For the next three months I spent long hours sorting through the heap of boxes that were left. Anything that was halfway decent, I threw into a big pile in the middle of the floor to be sorted later according to size. Everything else we loaded up for the dump along with keeping the dumpster from the business chuck full every week. They charged me for dumping 5,000 pounds of garbage by the time I had sorted all there was upstairs and downstairs.

I had all the children trying on clothes and marked their names on the ones that fit. Then I took all the extra clothes that were nice and stored them in a couple of fiber drums in the upstairs of the shop. Then I went to work building a table about 2 feet high, 12 feet long, and 3 feet wide. I put plywood dividers on it, along with a back, so as to make little bins. Then I put each child's name on the front of a bin.

I had been teaching David, Reed's oldest son, to do the washing. He would take the clothes from the dryer and put them in two old grocery carts. Charlie would sort the clothes and pitch them into the bins so the children could find their clothes. They were not ironed, but what the heck! They could at least find what they had.

"Kathleen's job was doing the dishes and tidying up the kitchen. Bill's boy, Guy, had the job of sweeping the floors. Susie and Mary Ann, Bill's children, since they were the two youngest, cleaned the bathroom and helped sweep the upstairs.

I began remodeling the kitchen. I textured and painted the ceiling, painted the woodwork, put up wallpaper and wood paneling about four feet high with moldings on top. My manager and I ripped out the old sink cabinets and had Fashion Cabinets make new ones. We got a Formica counter top from the lumberyard that I installed myself. Then after scrapping all the old flooring, I laid down ceramic tile. The children were so happy to see all this happen. They helped to keep things as good as one could expect from kids who never before had the slightest conception of cleanliness.

Bill became worried that the people from Welfare or Social Services would investigate the house. Francis told the Social Services that she was undergoing a separation from Reed. Also, she had been claiming that Reed's children were living in the white house with her so she could collect Social Services for them, but the children were still living in the red house. So when Reed went in to talk to Social Services one day, the Social Services people found out that Francis had been fraudulent without Reed's knowledge. Bill did not want his family to be caught living there in the red house, so he moved his wife and children over to her father's house to stay for a while. Bill did not know that Berniece had wanted to leave Bill for a long time, but her only reason for staying was because Reed and Francis had told her that if she ever left, she would have to leave her kids with Bill. Now she found herself out of all the mess and with her children, so she immediately filed for divorce. In an effort to protect my business from being involved in a lawsuit, I asked Bill to sign off his half of the business property and I would sign off my half of the farm. I agreed that I would give Francis and Reed a life estate in the white house and that I would finish paying off the balance of over $8,000. They were glad to have it done and we recorded it.

I continued to remodel the red house. The stairway and bedrooms were done. I was glad to have my time occupied as much as possible so I could stay out of Reed's damn bedroom as much as I could.

With Francis gone I moved Mom upstairs from the dingy little room she had stayed in for years. But she caught cold and developed pneumonia. For three days she did not eat much of anything. I asked Dale to help me lift her into the tub as I wrapped a sheet around her to prevent any embarrassment to Mom or Dale. When I had her cleaned and dressed, we took her to the University Hospital. Dale and an acquaintance of mine assisted me. Reed did not even care to help.

While Mom was in the hospital, Reed had an automobile accident and he ended up in the hospital at the same time. Boy, did I see a golden opportunity while Reed was gone. My mind was working a thousand miles a minute. I worked as fast and hard as I could to fix up Mom's room and Francis's old bedroom, upstairs. I redid the ceiling, sanded, and painted the woodwork, put all new wallpaper on the walls and a special wall mural on one wall—a scenery of trees, flowers, beautiful environment with a pond, like that of a canyon with the leaves turning pretty colors as in the autumn. I thought of Mother as being in the autumn of her life and I thanked God for Reed's accident. I knelt down in solitude with tears blurring my vision. "Thank you, Lord. Just, thank you."

Now Mom would have things nice at last. I worked with a feverish passion and determination to complete this before Reed came home. I bought new curtains and painted her bedstead and bought pretty new rugs and a new set of sheets and blankets with a new bedspread.

When Reed came home from the hospital, I was not quite finished as he stepped to the door and looked in. "What the hell is going on? What's all this for?"

I stood there like a little tin soldier and said right back to him, "It's for my mother. I don't know how much longer she will be here but I want it to be nice for her."

What could he say? He went to his bedroom with disgust written all over his face. I had done too much and I had gained too much control over everything for him to stop me.

After all the years of humiliation and degradation, I had finely grown a backbone. And I was not about to take anymore shit from anybody. I went to the hospital to see Mother, but my sisters had found out that my mother was there and they all agreed that no way is she going back to Reed's.

I asked Mom what she wanted to do. "Well, May, I have lived with you for quite a while. Now the other children want me to live with them."

I looked at Mother lying there with her silver, gray hair adorning her stunningly beautiful face. I bent over and kissed her as tears distorted my vision. My mind rolled back in time over all the years I had wanted to see my mother have better things. She was with me all that time and I had never managed to make her living conditions better until now. And now, it was too late. She never would live there again. With the bitter memories that had scarred my soul, I lay across her bosom and uttered, "I understand, so whatever makes you happy, Mother. Whatever makes you happy."

I returned home and over the days and the weeks, Reed became more and more sexually obsessed so that beyond any shadow of a doubt, I could hardly stand him.

Zella had acquired a book called, "The Sensuous Woman." Reed had read it and said to me, "You ought to read this. It's really good."

"I'm not going to read that damn thing."

"This woman enjoys her man. You would too if you didn't have something wrong in your head. I want you to read it."

"NO!"

"Come on." He kept shoving it in front of me. "What can it hurt?"

With fury running through me, I grabbed it and threw it into the garbage container and shouted, "I'm not going to pattern my life after some fucking whore."

"Wait a minute," as he grabbed hold of my arm while I was leaving the room. He went over and pulled out a girlie book from under the mattress. He showed me a picture that about made me throw up. "This is what I want you to do for me."

"I'm not going to do that."

"If you don't do it, it will end up taking you three times longer to take care of me than it would if you would just do it."

"Shit," I exclaimed as I slammed the door.

I continued to work extremely long hours in the business and in the house to stay away from him. I was so tired I could just drop. I felt deliriously sick to my stomach as though I was going to pass out, but I could not lay down anywhere.

One might ask: Why could you not just find a nice little corner and curl up and go to sleep? How could I explain? Reed would never allow me to rest in any other room or place except his bedroom. If I did lay down anywhere else, I would surely get caught. Reed kept a constant watch on me.

One Sunday, a bright, warm beautiful day, I had the children in the shop, teaching them Sunday School. Reed knew that this would last approximately one hour. The children asked questions and it looked like we would be over ten minutes or so. But after an hour's time, he called. Then he kept calling every five minutes. "How much longer?"

"Not much."

He called three different times in approximately 15 minutes. Then after the closing prayer, the children went to play. Being very fatigued, I fell asleep instantly on the couch. When he saw the children at play, he came up promptly to see why I had not come to the house like he had told me to do when I was through. He saw me asleep.

His loud voice woke me up. "What the hell are you doing sleeping up here when I'm waiting for you? You know you're not supposed to sleep anywhere except the bedroom. I knew I should have checked on you sooner to see what you were doing. How long have you been sleeping?"

"I don't know."

In a demanding tone, he said, "You get up to the house and take care of me."

I just sat there, bearing up under the heat and impact of his voice.

Several weeks later I went in the kitchen and picked up two oranges then walked outside where I sat on the cement edge that encircled the lawn in the back of the house. While I was sitting there, Reed came out, walked up to me, and asked, "What are you doing out here?"

"Just eating an orange."

"Why are you eating it out here?"

"Well, why not?"

"Are you enjoying yourself?"

"Yeah."

"Huh." And he walked back into the house.

Less than two minutes went by when he came out again and a similar conversation ensued. He went back into the house and came out again three times while I was eating those two oranges. Hell, I thought and shook my head, as I stared off into the weed patch next door. I looked at the cat running over in the field and thought, Goll, that cat has more freedom than I do That's not right. Then I thought for a minute. What in the heck, Lincoln freed the slaves a long time ago.

The long hours continued but I dared not pass even one hint how fatigued I was. My body felt like it was made of marshmallows and wax waiting to melt under the workload and heat of the day.

Reed came down to the shop while I was working. "Aren't you tired?"

"I've got all this that's gotta be done tonight." I was so tired I could have fallen over right then, but I tried to put momentum in my movement.

"Yeah. You're so damn tired. You'd better get up to the house and get some rest."

I avoided going as long as I possibly could. I went up there, but there was no rest to be had. I took the pillow and put it behind me as I sat up in bed to ask Reed a question "Why do I have to take care of you just because you say so?"

Highly provoked, his eyes had a nasty glint. "What do you mean, 'cause I say so'? That's a stupid question. The woman is meant for the man, not the man meant for the woman. You're to do what I want, not me having to do what you want. You get that?"

I looked away from him toward the window. "No, I don't get it. I don't get it at all."

"Let me show you something," he said as he pulled out The Bible, "The woman's desires should go to her husband and he should rule over her," he shoved The Bible in front of me with his finger pointing to the word 'rule'. Then he put The Bible on the dresser and pulled out The Doctrine and Covenants and read where the Lord told Emma Smith that she should administer to Joseph Smith and be a helpmate to him. "You're in the same position to administer to my wants and needs and these are my wants and these are my needs, whether you like it or not."

"I don't care about Emma Smith's position. I don't want that position. Can't you get someone else?"

He grabbed my shoulder and shook me then yelled so loud they could hear it across the street, "NO! You belong to me and you will never get away from me. Never! Never! No never! Unless you break your marriage covenants, and I'm the one who will say whether you are allowed in the celestial glory or not. I hold the keys over you and I'll tell you right now, if you don't bring yourself into submission, you'll go into dissolution."

I was so damn sick of hearing all this shit. I sat there with a blank stare on my face and thought to myself, I don't know that I won't go to hell. With tears filling my eyes, I believe I'm at God's mercy anyway. But before I get there, I'm going to do all the good I can for people, so that just the very moment when Satan is ready to grab me Jesus will reach out and shout, OH NO YOU DON'T! SHE IS MINE!

Later that day after servicing Reed, I went over the damn statements in my mind that he had made. Feeling bewildered and sick at heart, when I lay myself to rest, I went into a dream or a nightmare.

There was a large room—it looked like a cave. The ceiling was about 25 feet high. Some of the rocks were broken out on the one side close to the ceiling so that some daylight came through a small opening. The cave looked about 40 feet by 80 feet and the opening about 4 feet wide and 6 feet high. I was toward the back of the cave with a steel ankle bracelet fastened around my ankle and hooked to a chain that was fastened to an object in one side of the floor underneath the top opening. I could look out toward the entrance of the cave and see a beautiful fantasy, like country scenes of the kind that Walt Disney created: a town, beautiful green hills, trees and flowers, and everything nice, so as to promote happiness.

Reed was walking around in the cave near me. He would do whatever he wanted to do to me. I could not see any way to free myself but even so my attention was focused toward the entrance. It seemed that there was so much darkness between me and the opening and that I could never escape. I woke up. I had that same dream for several nights.

I contemplated over the things of the gospel and what they meant to me in my life. I thought of the sufferings of our Savior. He suffered for God and his religion to save the world. The early Saints, too, suffered for God and their religion. Now I was suffering for God and for my religion but there was no good to come of it just continual humiliation and the disgrace of my innermost feelings by having to do things below my dignity. I always believed that if I kept my mind looking toward the Lord for answers and not give up, He would help me find them. I was just totally confused.

One Sunday afternoon I called up Joseph when I got home from meeting and told him what the brethren said, also some of the things Reed would say and do.

Joseph, with a very sober tone, said, "I know he's not justified. And boy, I know what I'd do if it was me. I'd take a sharp knife and chop off his dick."

Two weeks later I went to Sunday meeting and a man, Alfred Osheskey, whom I had much respect for, was talking and he said that it was a correct principle that when your leader tells you to do something, you should take it before the Lord. If the spirit of the Holy Ghost does not bear witness to you that it is of God, do not accept it. He said that Joseph Smith taught that people place too much confidence in their leaders instead of finding out what the truth is for themselves." Then he picked up one of The Journal of Discourses and began to read from it.

"What a pity it would be if we were led by one man to utter destruction? Are you afraid of this? I am more afraid that this people have so much confidence in their leaders that they will not inquire for themselves of God whether they are led by Him. I am fearful they settle down in a state of blind self-security, trusting their eternal destiny in the hands of their leaders with a reckless confidence that in itself would thwart the purpose of God in their salvation and weaken that influence they could give their leaders, did they know for themselves, by the revelations of Jesus, that they are led in the right way. Let every man and woman know, by the whisperings of the spirit of God to themselves whether their leaders are walking in the path the Lord dictates or not.' Then he continued, 'Let all persons be fervent in prayer until they know the things of God for themselves and become certain that they are walking in the path that leads to everlasting life."
The Journal of Discourses•, Vol. 9, p. 150

Did I hear what I thought I heard? I sat there numb. Is this the truth? Is this our religion? Whew! That's quite a statement. I want to read that again when I get home.

Then Alfred went on to say that one person should not want to lord it over another. It sounded so good I could hardly stand it.

We came home from church. I rode with Bill because he would drive much faster and I could make a phone call first thing. Reed came in the house while I was talking to Joseph and I quickly changed the subject.

"Who you talking to?"

"Joseph."

"Well, hang it up or I'll hang it up for you."

"Well, I best be going. Good bye."

"You ready to go to bed?"

"No."

"Why?"

"I need to go to the bathroom."

"Well, hurry."

While I was in there, I knelt down and prayed quietly. I poured out my heart, "Oh, God. Don't you see me? Don't you hear me? How long must I suffer this ungodly oppression? Can't you do anything?" as I wept bitterly.

Bang, bang, bang on the door. "What are you doing in there?"

I turned on the tap quickly. "I'm washing my face."

"Well, how much longer are you going to take?"

"Not much."

"Well, hurry."

I splashed cold water on my face to try to remove the evidence of crying. Then I came out.

He grabbed me by the arm and shoved me into the bedroom.

"Reed, can't we go see Brother Guy and let him counsel us?"

"NO! It's none of Brother Guy's business how I run my family, and if you dare tell him anything, I'll just deny it. You'll be looked upon as a liar. The priesthood always sticks up for the man, not the woman."

"Do all men treat their wives the way you do?"

"That has nothing to do with it. Any man who would have you would treat you exactly the same way I do. You'll never get away from me," he repeated. "Never!

Never! Never! So you'd better get over your hang-ups and bring yourself into submission or you're going to go into dissolution," as he raised his hand into the air, supposedly to the square. "I can promise you that in the name of the Lord."

I said nothing but I resented that damn lingo I had heard for so many years. I thought, I don't believe it because I know that Joseph wouldn't treat me the way you do.

The next day Joseph came over to work on the boiler. As we sat down at the kitchen table in the office, I told Joseph about the horrible way Reed treated me at the time I had worked on the de-denter for two weeks and came in needing some rest. I described it to him in detail.

Joseph looked down at the floor, shook his head, and wept. He drew me close to him. We looked into each other's eyes. He had the most loving expression, then he spoke.

"I can't even imagine a man treating a woman as sweet as you are with such inconsideration." With tears still in his eyes as his broken voice continued, "I know what I would have done. I would have just held you in my arms while you slept."

I cannot explain how I felt. I put my head on his chest with my arms around him. I thought what a beautiful spirit, as I wept with joy. Then I told him what Reed's attitude was to this day.

He said, "May, you have got to do something. Can you make an appointment to see Brother Guy?"

"If I make an appointment and his wife Margaret happens to call and tell Francis, I'm dead meat. But if we just sneak away and go see him, then nobody will be the wiser. Ok?"

"You bet. I'll take you."

"Could you be here early tomorrow morning?"

"All right. How about 3:30 a.m.?"

"Sounds perfect so we can be there by four o'clock."

CHAPTER SIXTEEN

Early the next morning I met Joseph and he took me to see Brother Guy Musser. When I knocked on the door, the girl that answered said, "He's not here right now. Can you come back later?"

"I can't come back later," I exclaimed. "But I'll tell you right now, if Brother Guy knew the reason why I came, he would want to see me."

"Just a moment," as she shut the door.

A few minutes later Brother Guy came to the door and invited us in. I introduced Joseph and Brother Guy and we sat down on the couch. I had not talked even five minutes to Brother Guy explaining the way Reed treated me and the things he would say and the things he would do, when Brother Guy threw his hands in the air crying, "Stop! Stop! I've heard enough. I can't stand it anymore. That's worse than anything I have ever heard of in Las Vegas".

I asked, "What I want to know is if I can have a divorce?"

"If that's what you want, you certainly have grounds for a divorce. Yes! No man in his right mind should treat a woman in that manner."

"How soon could I get a divorce? Today?"

"Well, I would recommend that you wait six months."

"Six months? I'll try. But what can I do to stop him from abusing me sexually?"

"Just stop having sex with him."

"Just stop?"

"Yes, stop. Don't do it anymore."

I smiled, "Ok." I thought, That sounds good. I'll surely see how it goes.

We talked a little about Reed's background. Then I said, "I'd like to ask you something. Reed has always told his family that you are behind him 100 percent in the things he teaches his family."

Guy shook his head while looking at the floor then raised his eyes to meet mine. In a casual voice he spoke, "That man is one of the biggest liars in the state of Utah."

"Why then did you marry me to him?"

"He said that you wanted to marry him and we feel that the woman should have her choice."

I looked at him as though I was stoned. I thought, All this was an 18-year misunderstanding. I felt sick but regained my composure.

I said, "I appreciate your taking the time to see me."

"That's all right. Good luck. Let me know how you're doing."

"Thank you," as we shook his hand.

"And I'm pleased to meet you, Mr. Tanner."

Joseph replied, "I'm pleased to meet you, too."

While on our way home, I said to Joseph, "Boy, that will be the neatest thing that ever happened to me to be free from that hell hole."

Joseph commented, "That was sure something that Brother Guy knew Reed's father and said that he was pretty much the same way."

"Reed always told me that when he was a little boy, his father would beat him up all the time. In fact, he said that his father wanted to kill him when he was two days old. He said that that was the reason for the scar across his forehead. His father took a razor blade to him. Reed's uncle took Reed to the hospital. He said that his father was always beating up and smacking his mother around all the time, too. I'd always felt so sorry for Reed. Anytime he had a dog or a rabbit or anything for a pet that he liked, and his father learned that he had something like that, his father would just go kill it. So considering a childhood like that, I've tried to understand him rather than condemn him. But I don't know, Joseph. It's been 18 years and I still don't understand him and I can't see where spending another 18 years would help him one ounce more."

Joseph let me off at the corner of the driveway. "Good luck, little darlin'," he said as he squeezed my hand.

"Yeah, I need it." Then I stepped from his car and he left.

I went into the house. Reed was coming down the stairs to meet me. "Where have you been?"

"Uh. Joseph took me to see about getting in on a good deal with some cheese at one of the stores, but we got there too late and someone had bought it already. It was going for 50 cents a pound."

"I don't care about it," he snarled. "You had no business leaving for anything unless you have asked me and got my sanction."

"Well, Joseph heard about it last night, and you were sleeping and I didn't want to disturb you. I knew it would only take a few minutes to run right there and back," I went on hoping to emphasize the change of subject. "Gee wouldn't it have been nice if we had got in on a deal like that? They even had bacon, too. But it was gone also." I knew Reed liked bacon.

"Well next time, you ask. I don't care if you do wake me up. You understand?"

I slapped at the wall, killing a cockroach, "Yes."

I hurried in and changed into my work clothes. Then I went to the shop. About 4 p.m. Reed came down, "Are you going to quit early so you can come up and take care of me? You left this morning without doing anything."

"No, I don't think so."

"What do you mean, 'no, you don't think so'?"

"Well, I'm tired of the battle Reed. You won't go with me so we can talk it over with Brother Guy. Last Sunday at meeting Uncle Marion got up and said a woman's body is her own, and I don't want to do it. So, by that I'll take it that I don't have to."

"Oh, yeah? Well, your body is your own but you're supposed to serve me with it."

"Well, I don't look at it that way and I'm not going to. That's all there is to that."

He walked back to the house like he was in some big hurry. Some of the guys said that Reed walked like a penguin.

He brought back some of the "good books" again. I was cutting a piece of metal with the torch. He turned off the oxygen, "Now, you're going to listen to me and get this in your head." He read me the same stuff he had read to me time and time again about how I was supposed to submit, and how I was supposed to believe, and administer to his wants and his needs.

As he read, he kept looking up from the book at my face to see if I was getting convinced or not. I purposely tried to express that he was boring me to death. His intensity picked up as he kept thumbing through the book, grabbing at any straw that he could find.

I leaned up against the tool shelf while sitting on the work table listening. I had a c-clamp in my hand that I was turning in and out. All of a sudden he said, "There now. Are you going to repent?"

"Repent of what?"

"Your damned disobedience to the laws of God. Here are the laws of God," as he shook the book in the air over my head. "Now, are you going to follow them?"

"Reed, that's your interpretation of the law."

"Well, you're to take care of me. It's not my fault I need a woman. You're the one with the crack between your legs. I can't take care of myself."

"Well, I don't know what you're going to do but I'm through with it."

"I could die with blood pressure and you'd be guilty of murder. You know that? What if I have to go to some whore on the street, the sin of adultery would be on your head, not mine because you're the one that drove me to it." He was poking me in the shoulder with his drilling finger.

This type of reasoning went on and on, Reed not allowing me to work, just standing in my way. I got up, turned the oxygen tank back on, and he turned it off. There was no point in trying to accomplish anything, so I went to the house. It was late anyway.

Later on that evening I lay there trying to sleep. He was hovering over me, shaking me, and holding onto the book in one hand while hollering at me. Needless to say, I got very little rest that night, perhaps two or maybe three hours.

For an entire week, this same routine went on. Exhausted, I finally said, "Ok. I'll give you 15 minutes."

"Fifteen minutes? I need more than that."

"Tough. It's 15 minutes or nothing."

"Well, ok."

So after 15 minutes was up, he asked, "How often do I get 15 minutes?"

"Once a day."

"I've got to have more than that!"

For three more days this went on. Then when I was at the shop, he said, "I want you to come upstairs in the office." I did.

He locked the door, pointed to the rug, "Now kneel down. I want to pray with you."

As we knelt there, he put both arms as to the square. His prayer was, "Eternal Father, in the name of Jesus Christ, and by the holy Melchizedek priesthood invested in me, I ask for the powers of heaven to bring a curse upon May that her back will come out of place so as to give her intense pain and that her friends, Joseph Tanner, Dale Wayne Hunter, and Myra Mackert, will have accidents even unto death, if necessary, to bring her into submission. This I ask in the name of Jesus Christ, amen. Now, you pray."

"If I pray, I'll pray the way I want to pray. I won't pray the way you want me to pray."

"Go ahead."

"Oh, God, my eternal Father in heaven. I humbly come before you at this time to give you thanks for all the blessings you have given me. I want to dedicate everything that I have unto you, including my life. And in exchange, I pray for guidance at this time that I may know the path that you would have me pursue that my course may be pleasing in thy sight. I pray for your spirit and ask for strength, mentally, physically, and spiritually. I ask this humbly in the name of Jesus Christ, our Savior, amen."

We looked at each other and without speaking went downstairs. "Well, are you going to submit yourself now?"

I shook my head as I said, "Reed, I can't see why, even if I am in disobedience, how could that have anything to do with Joseph, Dale, and Myra? Why should they suffer for anything that I do or don't do? Why would the Lord punish them for a sin of mine?"

"Oh, don't worry. He would if that's what it takes to bring you in submission to me."

The combination of every single thing that was upon me that I was suffering mentally, physically, and spiritually at that time was so great every moment of the day, I felt so physically sick and weak. It was as if every step I took, I knew not whether I would fall on my face. I could not bring myself to do for him when I knew I did not have to. How could I go for another five months?

He refused to take me to Joseph's for a chiropractic treatment. I could hardly stand the pain. And although I only weighed 115 pounds, I lost 12 pounds. I looked and felt like a bag of bones.

When the pressure was so great, he came to me suspecting that my back was killing me, though I had not said anything. "If you'll take care of me for three hours, I'll take you in to get a treatment."

Reed had told Joseph not to come on the yard anymore and Joseph was trying to honor his wishes. To think of having one glimpse of Joseph's sweet smile, oh how blessed that would be. What a price I would have to pay. I cried inside. Reed had me where he wanted me. I hung my head and sought the support of a nearby tree.

"Well, do you want to go or not?"

"I left the welding tanks on. I'd better shut them off."

"Well, hurry and let me know what you're going to do."

I went straight to the shop bathroom and locked the door. "Oh, Father. If you're up there, I'm telling you, if I'm going to have some help or inspiration, I've got to have it in a hurry." My heart was so heavy. I walked to the house.

"Are we going?"

"I suppose," as I walked toward the car.

"Now, remember. You promised."

When we got there and I laid on the couch, it felt like heaven. Joseph's touch was sweet on my back.

Later that night after we had returned home, as I entered the bedroom, I looked at Reed, his eyes beating upon me with the most sickening smile, as though to say, "I've won. Now, I'll get my way!" His hairy belly was protruding out from his dirty underwear. My mind was racing 100 miles an hour. If I had a way to run or a place to go without him ever catching me, God knows, I would have gone.

"Come on. Show yourself," he commanded.

My mind was petitioning heaven, Oh, God. Please stop this. As my mind was repeating this, I stood there with my clothes on.

"Get undressed," he shouted. He fondled his privates as he reached over to turn on the red light. I felt the presence of evil spirits so thick in the blackness of that night. "Get your clothes off." He reached over and grabbed a handful of material from my blouse and shook it back and forth, accelerating my already trampled feelings.

"I will. For hell's sake, give me a minute," I hollered.

"What for?" he yelled.

I undid my clothes and stood there naked.

"Put on your black see-through robe." I took my time.

"Come on. Dance! Lift your legs. Show me your privates."

I looked at him and at that very moment, the red light shone on the left side of his face and the blackness of the night on the other. The look of agony was mixed with the triumph of hell. The exact same face I had seen in the dream when I was being abused at 15 years old. My feelings were exactly like those when I had that horrible nightmare. His face was an exact picture of the demon. Artists throughout the ages have drawn their conceptions of what a devil looks like, but they have drawn a handsome man compared to this face before me. If I had been in the very depths of hell, naked, so that every freak, bastard, and whoremonger there could see my body and fondle me, I would have not felt one speck worse. The desperate need to escape consumed my being. Gritting my teeth as tears were streaming down my face, I said inside my mind, Oh, God. I'm sorry but I can't wait any longer. I'd rather lose everything. I don't want to go against priesthood direction, but I cannot stand this. I would rather be dead. I'm going to get out from under this freaking oppression.

Just then, Reed's loud voice said, "Lay down now. I've seen enough."

I thought to myself as I laid down, Do anything you want but it won't be for long.

Paper and pencil can never describe the horror of that night. As soon as he was satisfied enough so I could leave without being noticed, I quickly got dressed and ran down to the shop. I called Brother Guy as soon as I dared to. It was five o'clock in the morning. I let the phone ring about 65 times until his wife answered.

"Hello."

"Hello. This is May. It is urgent. I must speak to Brother Guy."

"Well, he's still asleep."

"I can't help it and I'm sorry. But I've got to talk to him right now. I can't wait. I'm sorry." I was shaking and crying.

"Well, let me see if I can wake him."

"Thank you."

"Hello." Said Brother Guy.

"Hi. This is May. I'm sorry to bother you at this time of night. But I've got to tell you. I can't stand it here any longer. What do you suggest?"

"Well, I guess you'll need to stay there until he dies."

"Until he dies! I can't! I can't wait that long. I can hardly stand it another day."

"Well, what are you going to do?"

"I feel like running away."

"Well, there's nothing to stop you from doing that."

"Oh, yeah. The moment I do that, he will ask God to curse me."

Brother Guy said in a very jovial way, "Well, it won't have any effect."

I gasped, "It won't have any effect?"

"No," he said almost with a laugh in his voice. "It won't have any effect."

"Well, all right. That's what I'm going to do."

"Ok. That's fine. Let me know where you run to."

"I will. Thank you. Bye."

As I sat there, I felt a heavy cement yoke I had carried on my shoulders lift straight up leaving me feeling so light, I felt as though I would float up and hit my head on the ceiling. Whew! I sat there for a long time with a blank stare on my face. Oh, that was the neatest thing, oh. I went over and knelt down on my rug.

"Oh, God, my eternal Father in heaven. Thank you. That's the answer." I felt so good I could hardly contain myself. I was overcome with tears of joy. "Bless thy holy name forever."

I could never contemplate such a thing without knowing it would be with priesthood sanction. But now I felt I had finally received that sanction. My whole body tingled with joy, like little electric shocks all through my system. I clapped my hands, "Thank you. Thank you. A million times thank you." I've got a lot to do. Now, let's see. Get my head on track. What have I got to do before I can run? Let's see, I must plan this really well. Uh, Dales got to be able to run this without me then I'll call in several times a day 'cause I don't know where I'm going or when I'll be back. Now, let's see. I sat down and wrote out directions on everything I could think of that Dale would need to know to keep things running without me. When Dale arrived that morning, I told him the plan. I would leave one week from that day. It was perfect because I had just started my period. I would not have to have intercourse for this week. I worked with a zeal that would not quit.

During this time I imagined that maybe I would have to move to China and I could see myself working in the rice paddies. Or maybe I might move to some other far away city and get a job as a scrub woman, cleaning a hotel or motel. Whatever or wherever, I had to go, and the 'where' seemed irrelevant. I counted nearly every second until I could have my freedom.

CHAPTER SEVENTEEN

On the day of my escape I brought Zella and Kathleen together and told them I was leaving Reed. And that I would never return. And I wanted Kathleen to know a secret. I said I was there the day you were born Zella is your mother. Kathleen looked dumbfounded. Sweetie, look in the mirror at your features, consider how tall you are, look at your legs. Perhaps now you can give your real mother the love and respect she deserves. I told her all of the beatings Zella had endured was just so she could be with her children. You must keep this secret for me.

I hugged and kissed them.

Zella and Kathleen with tears in their eyes asked, "Don't you love Reed?"

"No I don't." I replied.

Tonight is my last in hell, May 13, 1982. This thought had been running through my mind over and over again. Reed was in the kitchen talking to Zella. I thought, I must hurry. I took a bag into Reed's room and very quickly lifted the mattress and shoved the things into the bag that I always had to wear to please Reed, except for one pair of panties. I quickly went through the kitchen passing by Reed.

"I forgot to turn off the compressors," I said. "I'll be right back."

I hurried out into the blackness of the night and went straight to the tool room and locked the door behind me. I put the clothes in a pile on the cement floor then quickly grabbed the torch and the striker and turned on the acetylene and oxygen tanks. Then I knelt down as a cool breeze chilled me through a crack in the door. With feelings of resentment and disgust, I said out loud, "This is what I think of all this damn stuff," as I lit the torch and threw the hot flames upon it until every speck was black ash. Then I turned off the torch and scooped up the ashes between two thin pieces of metal and then took the ashes to the mud holding tank where I threw them in, and said, "There, that's where you belong."

I hurried over to wash my hands and walked out proudly as I said to myself, Tomorrow at this time I will be out of his clutches forever. Then I hurried into the house.

That night while doing Reed's bidding, my eyes kept focusing upon the clock each time a few more minutes had passed. That night seemed like a small eternity. While in my mind I was saying with teeth gritting and tears flowing, Come morning, I will have the victory. You will never lay one finger on me ever again.

About a quarter to four in the morning, Reed looked as though he was asleep and I quietly got up and got dressed. I went to the shop with a feeling of exhilaration running through me as the fresh air kissed my face. Thank God I made it through that hell for the last time. I'm coming down to the finish line now. Nothing can go wrong. My mind was racing. I thought, He must not know even the slightest of my plans. For I fully knew Reed believed in blood atonement, with a fear that something could go wrong but trusting that he would not know. I conducted business as usual to the best of my ability for the day. I had everything I planned to take with me in a grocery bag: two skirts, two blouses, underwear, my patriarchal blessing along with my baby pictures, an old coin collection, a little money, my coat, and a Mosiah Hancock Journal my mother had given me, then I grabbed my cat. Wayne Hunter had offered to let me stay in a room in his basement. I wrote a note to Reed and had Dale take it to the mailbox. It read something like:

I have gone and I will never, ever return to stand your oppression. And if you want any of your children to stay with you, you had better learn to rule with something besides force and beatings.

That was May 14, 1982, the day I will never forget, the day of my escape.

I had made previous arrangements for a man to come and get my little goats and take care of them. He was busy loading them at the time I left.

It was five o'clock in the afternoon. I had Wayne's other son, who worked for me, drive down the back alley to pick me up. I huddled down in the seat so I would not be seen.

Dale was still working there at the shop when Reed came down and started hollering for me all around the yard. According to what Dale told me later, he said that when Reed could not find me, and the office door was locked, he flew into a rage, then broke out the shop kitchen window and asked his boy Charlie to go in and unlock the door. After Reed had searched the office and upstairs, Dale left.

I had arrived at Wayne's alright, and Wayne had just shown me my room. As we stood there talking, the glass in one of the windows suddenly fell out and lay on the lawn unbroken. Somehow it seemed like a sign of bad things to come. Dale arrived and Wayne asked him to go after putty to secure the window back in place.

We walked upstairs and were talking in the kitchen when a knock came on the front door. Someone answered it, and there was Reed forcing his way through the front room toward the kitchen. In a flash I opened the door to the basement and stood behind it for a moment. My heart was pounding.

I heard Wayne and Reed outside the door. Wayne said, "You're not going down there."

"She's my wife and I demand that you turn her over to me. You're committing adultery by even having her in your home."

"I never even thought of such a thing, said Wayne, why I haven't even had sex with my own wife for six months!"

"You turn her over to me. She must answer for what she has done."

Hearing all this screaming, I began to shake.

"I don't know what you've done to her but she told me that she would rather rot in hell before she'd ever go back to you. So whatever you've done to the girl, it must be pretty bad."

Wayne later told me that Reed put his hands up to the square to try and put a curse on Wayne. I heard Wayne say, "Get your hands down. You're out of order."

I could not take it anymore and seeing the window was out, I grabbed my coat and sack with my little bit of money and took off out through the window. I crossed the lawn, over the fence, ran across the road and down through a subdivision. A couple of children were along the street and I asked them, "Do you live here close? Could I please use your phone?"

"Sure." They answered.

From there I called Wayne's and told Bonnie, his wife, I was far away from there and that I knew Reed would not leave until he searched the place, then I called someone else to come get me to stay at their house. Reed called everyone's place that he knew I was familiar with, including where I was at. He called there seven times. They told him they had not seen me.

With all the disturbances of that night, I retired around 2:00 a.m. After a long, sound, uninterrupted sleep, I awakened to Freedom. My eyes glanced over the light yellow and white designs on the wallpaper and the lace curtains dancing from a gentle breeze. I yawned. The thought occurred to me, What are you going to do today? I smiled as I answered the thought, Not a cotton pickin' thing! I reached for the pillow next to me propping myself up for a lazy day. I reached over into the sack I had brought. After fumbling through its contents, I pulled out a pink paperback book. "Two dollars and fifty cents" was scribbled in pencil in the upper righthand corner. I was holding The Mosiah Hancock Journal.

I closed my eyes as my mind wandered back several months. My sisters had brought Mother over to see me and she handed me this history saying, "May, as soon as you can, you need to take the time to read this story of your grandfather on your father's side."

I opened the cover to cast my eyes upon a faded photograph of a man who appeared as though he had been through hell and back. A sense of gratitude that this picture had been preserved added to my feeling of wonderment as I snuggled into a comfortable position for a good reading session.

For hours, I found myself entertained with an appreciation that grew stronger with every page. I came to a part where his poverty had kept him from having a pair of shoes even though his duties required him to go to the canyon through deep snow for firewood. His feet were badly frozen. He wrote, "Who can imagine the pain and suffering of frozen feet. In three days' time every nail came off my toes." He wrote further, "Could I find fault with God or any of his servants or even my innocent brother who ran away and left me? Not that I know it to be so."

I clasped the book, bringing it to my lips and kissing the lines he wrote. Then holding this precious record to my bosom, I lay with tears wetting my pillow. This is my ancestry. I could not help but notice that some of his experiences were similar to mine. But what really disturbed me was the way things turned out. Maybe he was helping me, I wondered. Who knows? But what a joy I felt to know I had come from his lineage.

The following Monday, I went to the West Jordan Police station and explained the situation briefly so they could understand what the circumstances were. They accompanied me to Reclaim and one officer went to the door.

"Is Mr. Stratton home?" Reed came to the door. "Would you step out here, sir? We'd like to talk with you. May has been talking with us. Do you know what it is about?"

"No, I don't know. She won't even speak to me."

I said, "I'll tell you what it's about. I don't want to see you. I don't want to talk to you. I don't want you to come within 50 feet of me ever again. You no longer work for Reclaim Barrel Supply Company and I just want you to leave me alone."

The officer said, "Is that plain?"

Reed answered, "Yes."

The next day I was outside working with a plastic drum. Reed spotted me. As he walked toward me, I walked through the shop and outside over to where Wayne was working and stood by Wayne. Reed came through the building to the doorway. He saw me standing by Wayne. He stood looking at us and we looked at him, then he turned and left.

The next day was Wednesday. When Dale and I came to work, there were police cars around the red house where Reed was staying. I wondered what was going on and could see that Celia, Francis' sister who was Billy's mother, was there. We had always liked each other. She was standing on the lawn so I walked up to her and asked, "What in the world is going on?"

"Oh, May. It was horrible. Reed was praying in his room when Francis came to the door. Reed's eyes were bloodshot and he was delirious, completely out of his head! When he saw Francis, he thought she was you, and commanded her to come in. He yelled at her, 'Get in here. I'm your god! You have got to ATONE for what you have done to me.' Francis was scared and ran over to her house and called Brother Musser to ask him what to do. Musser told her to call the police and then when the police arrived, they went into the house to get him and Reed said to one of the officers, 'Don't touch me or you'll freeze.' The officer said, 'It's plain to see you need help, Mr. Stratton.' Two of them took hold of him. I think they took him to the hospital."

"I see. Well, how are you doing?" I asked Celia.

"Oh, I'm just fine. But I've sure been wondering about you. Are things working ok for you?" She asked.

"Yeah. I'm all right."

"I sure hope so," she said as she leaned towards me. "I've always thought a lot of you, May."

I gave her a hug. "I've always liked you, too."

"I'm glad you left. I wouldn't tell them that, but I am glad."

"Thank you."

Bill came up to my office about ten days after I had left and said, "Reed wants me to ask you a question. He wants to know if you're going to come back or are you going to be destroyed."

"I'm not coming back. Not now, not ever. And as far as going to hell is concerned, I've already been there and there's only one way to go and that's out."

"That's not the kind of answer I want."

"Well, that's the only kind you're gonna get."

He left. I watched out the window as Bill walked over to the red house and then Reed, along with all the members of the family, walked over to the white house.

Just guessing, I suspected that some kind of ritual went on to bring curses on me because after that, Bill would not drive my diesels. After three days of his lousy excuses, I fired him and hired a dependable truck driver.

Seeing Bill in the yard, I went to him and said, "Bill you ask them which house they want to live in either the white one or the red one. Because if they want to live in the red one, then I can transfer Francis' and Reed's life estate to that one."

He came back to me the next day. "Well, what did they decide?" I asked.

"We've decided we're going to have them both."

I sent them an eviction notice. In return I received a notice that I was being sued for half of all that I had for a settlement. Or in other words they were asking that the court grant that I should have to return everything to them.

One day while leaving the shop Reed was watching me. And as I drove out, he was right behind me. He kept on my tail until I moved to make a left turn, then I ran through a red light and gunned it for a right turn. He dared not to do the same.

Even though I was away from there, my mind could not believe that I had finally gotten away safely. Every night for weeks I would have nightmares. I had a dream where I was in the bedroom by the door with my clothes on and my shoes off. I was thinking, How do I get to my shoes? They were right by Reed. I can't travel fast without them. Then I carefully walked over and slipped them on then walked back toward the door. 'Where are you going?' he yelled. Just then I grabbed the doorknob and took off, running through the house and outside, across the driveway into a tall green wheat field. As I ran, I was scared to death because his legs were longer than mine and maybe he would catch up. But I ran with all my might. I was so scared and sweaty that I would wake up.

Then the next night I dreamed that I was by the kitchen door, and Reed was in the kitchen. I was fidgety and nervous. My adrenalin was getting worked up as my strength increased for what I was about to attempt. Then I slipped out the door, hopefully without him knowing that I had left. Then I took off as fast as I could, running across a country-like area with trees, bushes, and weeds. After I had run for what seemed to be half an hour, I looked back and I could see Francis and Reed running after me. I was near a canal so I jumped in. There was a heavy embankment and I burrowed in under the dirt and roots near some willows with only my head out of the water. I stayed as still as a mouse, hoping to God they would not have the slightest idea where I was. I heard them run past but I stayed put because I was afraid to get out because I had no idea how close they might be. I woke up in a cold chill.

Another night I dreamt I was running through a city or a well-populated area. As I ran through the city blocks and around buildings near apartment houses, I did not know where Reed was or how close. As I ran near a house where the window was open, I jumped in quickly. It was a little girl's bedroom. I quickly hid in her closet while she looked at me. I put my fingers up to my lips as if to say, "Shhh". Then I woke up.

I went to seek counsel from one of the priesthood brethren because I did not want to do anything that would not be according to the priesthood's approval. I sat there before him like a scared, whimpering child, not knowing what to do or if I dared to say anything. I could not keep my face from twisting from all the agony that was going through my soul.

This man sat me down, pulled up a chair in front of me, picked up my hands and put them in his, and said, "It's ok, sweetheart. Now just tell 'daddy' anything you want to."

I could not hold back my emotions anymore and I burst into tears.

He said, "Just take all the time you need. It's ok."

So for three hours I gave him a brief description of the last 18 years.

He said, "Oh, my hell. I have never heard of anything that horrible going on even in Las Vegas."

I said, "What I would like to know is, according to the laws of God, what are my obligations to Reed, or anyone in that situation?" I explained to him all that was in my name so that I could carry on my business.

He said, "Thank the Lord. It should be yours. You have earned it 20 times over."

I said, "They want a settlement."

"You owe him nothing. You have your own life to live now."

"If Reed would just admit even to any degree that he had done wrong in anything, my heart could be softened with compassion, but no. Not only all that he's stolen but now he wants more. He wants to force me to support him for the rest of his life. Did you know that?"

"Oh, that's ridiculous."

"But it's true. You know what though? I feel as if it would be worth $100 a month to me if he could bring himself to do one thing."

"What's that?"

"Well, the grapevine has it that Reed and Francis are spreading it around that I'm having affairs with all the guys that work for me."

"Yes, I've heard that, too."

"They're not only insulting my integrity but also that of all the men that work there." Laughing, I added, "They don't just pick one guy. No, hell, I'm supposed to be having it with all of 'em like I'm running a regular whorehouse up there or somethin'. I'm so sick of it. I'd just like to see him eat crow. If he wants anything out of me, let him come to you and to those people that he's spread those lies to and tell them there's no backing for it. Then perhaps I could consider giving him five cents."

"I doubt that he'd ever do that."

"If he doesn't, then I'll do nothing more for him. I'll hire an attorney and I'll just keep fighting it all the way to the Supreme Court if I have to. I'm just thankful that the priesthood council isn't against me in this."

"Well, bless you. Do what you have to. I think the Lord's on your side. Let me know how it's going, ok?"

"You bet," I said, as I gave him a hug. "Thank you."

A few months went by. I made an appointment to see him at a later date to obtain a priesthood release of my marriage (divorce). When I arrived, Reed and Francis were just leaving his house. Reed was approximately eight feet away. He turned to me and hollered, "You'll never get a divorce from me, and if he gives you one, it won't be binding in the heavens."

I stepped into the house and shut the door. "Yuck," I said. "He'd just love me to believe that shit."

"Oh, please. Don't talk that way in my home," said the man excitedly.

"I'm sorry. But I just can't stand his lies."

"I understand."

We went to another room where an ordinance was performed to release me from Reed according to priesthood law. I was very happy, and thanked the man then left.

I purchased a .38 revolver for security, also a blue heeler dog I called Miss Piggy. Although the business had an apartment where my office was in the shop, I did not have enough nerve to live there. The creepy feeling, combined with fear, would keep me paying rent and driving 15 miles to have a room to sleep in at night where I would beg the Lord to let me have a night's rest without a nightmare. The nightmares continued night after night for over a year, all different types of nightmares of my getting away. Then one night I dreamed I was running down a darkened street. There were only a few lights and I could just barely see the road ahead. I had my loaded .38 revolver and I was running as fast as I could. Reed was only 100 feet behind me. I was so fatigued and I felt I could not run much farther. I turned and commanded, "Stop! Or I'll shoot. I mean it. I'll shoot." He kept coming and when he was about ten feet way, I shot him. As he was falling, I shot him again, and again, and again, until I unloaded all six shots in him. Then I woke up. I have had fewer nightmares since.

After about a year and a half, I asked a friend to dedicate the office apartment to remove the evil spirits. He did, and I could feel a definite difference, so I then moved in. After I moved in, however, I started having a whole new set of nightmares. It was like I ran away then I came back and then I was trying to run away again. I could not figure out why until it dawned on me, Well, it's because you moved back here. Even though I was away from Reed and had the protection of a bolted door, my dog, and my loaded .38, I was still scared.

One day Billy came up to my apartment and knocked on the door.

"Hello," I said.

"Hi. I come to let you know some good news." said Bill

"Oh?"

"Kathleen just had a baby. You knew she married me, didn't you?"

I had heard that she had.

"Well, I just wanted to tell you."

I was unable to fake a smile, feeling as though I was about to lose my lunch. "Whatever," was my only comment.

"Ok. Well, I'll see ya' around." He left.

I thought to myself after he left, What a waste of a life. The girl didn't have the chance of a snowball in hell. I shivered and again thanked the Lord that I was out of the mess.

I had taken a driver's training course and was now driving everywhere. I hired an attorney to fight my case, but he kept asking me, "What do you think is a fair settlement?"

I answered, "I don't think giving him anything is a fair settlement."

"Well, look, you walked out of there with everything and left them with a home and Billy's farm, but no income from the business. What they want is so much a month out of your income."

The thought went through my mind as the attorney talked, Reed wants a reward? After what he has stolen from Mother and made her suffer along with what I have suffered? As I remembered Reed's words, "You'll never get away from me. Never, never, no, never." As these echoes went through my mind. I sat there sick.

Then my attorney said again, "Well, think about it? What are you prepared to offer them?"

"I can't reward them with anything and I don't feel I owe them anything. Not one dime. I tell ya', if I worked all day long to earn $50 and I thought I had to give Reed one dime, I'd feel so sick I wouldn't be able to work."

"With all that you're making on Reclaim Barrel, don't you think it would better to offer even $100 per month and avoid a lawsuit of this magnitude rather than all the expense this is going to cost you? And even then, the judge might grant them so much of your income, or they might have the whole thing returned to them. You never know how it could go."

"Well, I can't help it. I can't reward him. I know I've earned everything I have."

"How can we prove that?"

I had been hedging about telling him very much, but how could he possibly represent me if I did not tell him anything. Then I said, "I will go and give this some thought and I'll get back with you."

"Ok."

On my way home I asked the Lord in my mind how to proceed. I know nothing of these matters, I told the Lord, with a weak and sick feeling. But I just cannot see rewarding them. I thought about this issue almost constantly. I felt the necessity of preparing a document of explanation describing briefly those 18 years of my experience. I handed it to my attorney then said, "Maybe when you have read this, you might have some understanding as to where I'm coming from. All I am asking for is to be able to keep that which I have. Had I not earned it, they would not have put it in my name and I built Reclaim after all. I don't hate those people, but if I never had any encounter with them again, it would be too soon."

I sat there while he read the document. When he came to the part where Reed said he saved my life by killing a shit eating dog that was headed my way, this attorney laughed and laughed in a hideous way. I thought, And this man is representing me? Oh, no. Needless to say, I switched attorneys.

After several months with the second attorney, the case was ready to come to court and he kept hitting me with the idea, 'What are you going to do for a settlement?'

Saying, 'Come on, now. We've got to give them something. Now, how much?' I looked at him and thought, Man, you're sick.

Three days before it was to appear before the judge, I went to see the judge to ask for an extension.

He asked, "Why?"

"Because my attorney has been spending time on other people's cases and I feel like he's ready to wash me down the drain, and I want to hire another attorney that I can have more confidence in."

The judge said, "Ok, kid. I'll give you a bite of the apple just this one time, but that's it."

"Thank you, Judge." Then I hired Peter Ryan.

The preparation for the case went on for many months.

During that time, I went to pick up Mother on a lovely summer morning, about 10:00 a.m. We had made plans to go to the canyon. We took off and as we came around the mountain at Parley's Canyon on our way to Oakley, I breathed a sigh, "Isn't this nice. Oh, yeah, this is why I came. Ummm. I love the fresh mountain air."

"Yes, this is nice," Mother commented.

When we arrived in Oakley on our way up to Mirror Lake, I stopped at a little store. "What would you like, Mom?"

She sat there thinking and finally said, "Let's see. I believe I'd like some ice cream and root beer. Do you think they have that?"

"Ice cream and root beer coming up!" I grinned as I skipped away into the little store.

I felt so good about being able to give her these little treats. I returned with the goodies, and we sat there enjoying the warmth of the day and looking into the green pasture ahead of us.

"Life is so nice," I sighed, as I laid back in my seat with a slight breeze coming through while I ate a Fig Newton.

I looked at Mother as I asked, "Why did you stay there all those years? Heck, you weren't married to him. You could've left."

"Yeah, I know, but I felt that if you didn't have me to help you, you wouldn't have been able to endure under the load."

I sat there in silence and stared at the steering wheel. Tears came to my eyes, I said, "I wouldn't have."

I was so sorry about Mom's sufferings. "Mom, sometimes children are fools." I said, "But, the love of a mother is as enduring as time."

I remembered how, even as a child, I had prayed for God to keep Mama alive because I felt I needed her for my strength. I said, "I'm glad that God chose a spirit like you to be my mother. I do love you. I hope I can live so that you and Daddy can be proud of me from here on out."

"Oh, May. I am proud of you."

I thought to myself as she said that, That's just because you're so loving and so forgiving, but I'm not very proud of myself.

I said, "You know that book you gave me, The Mosiah Hancock Journal? I've been reading that. And Mama, I'm so happy that he was my grandfather. I didn't know he was a bodyguard to the Prophet Joseph."

"Yeah. Your father was his last child and you're my last child," she said smiling, "So you just barely got in on that bandwagon."

I bent over and kissed her on the forehead. "We're going to have a good life." As I started up the car, I felt a warm, contented glow. "I just love to come to the canyons. It seems to me like its God's home. I like to come up here to study the gospel."

We continued on our way and after a while we arrived at one of the beautiful lakes. I stopped the car and helped Mother out so we could sit under a shade tree by the lake. I saw a couple of little chipmunks dash out of sight.

"You know what, Mom? Joseph Tanner has a pet chipmunk."

"Oh, yeah?" she laughed.

"Yeah. And it comes right up and eats right out of his hand. He calls it Funny Face. I've seen it and it's really cute."

"How is Joseph anyway?"

"He's just fine."

"Is he ever going to marry you or what? How did that turn out?"

"Joseph knows that I love him very much but he told me that he had been praying for the Lord to send someone in my life that was younger that could for sure give me children. He said he didn't think he would be able to give me all the blessings that he wanted to see me have. I 'bout cried my eyes out. I begged him not to talk like that. He said, 'No, little darlin. You deserve the best and even though it means my giving up something that's very precious to me, I want you to have all that this life has to offer you.' Mama, I believe that Joseph was a Godsend to help me out of that prison. There's no way I could have ever done it without his help. I needed him to lean on. There will always be a deep love, an appreciation, one little part of my heart, that man will always have."

I turned to get my camera. "I'm going to get a picture of that cute little wild flower right there."

I was gone for a few minutes taking a few pictures. When I returned, Mama said, "Well, May. What do you think of the priesthood work? Are you going to live the principle? Do you still believe it's the work of the Lord?"

"I do. But you know what? Alfred said in meeting about the Holy Ghost being our guide. It seems to me that that's the most important thing right now. Because if I can't have the Lord's guidance in something, then I've failed already. One must know for herself and that's something that's so precious, sacred, and secret, as the convictions that a person has with their God. I can't see anybody being pushed into any type of marriage if they don't know that God is with them. Do you know what I mean?"

"Yeah, I know what you mean."

"Because you know, Mom," I said, as I reached over the seat to pick up a book I had in the back. "All that damn suffering we went through that's not part of our religion."

I had not yet read the bible where I would realize the words of Jesus. Jesus said, 'Know the truth and the truth will make you free'. And when God makes you free you are indeed free.

"I've not lost my faith, Mother. And I've not lost my testimony or my desire to serve God. But I feel I've got a lot of sorting out to do to separate the things that are true from that which is not. I feel weak but maybe in time the Lord will make me strong again."

My spirit was overwhelmed with the desire to sing. I gave way with enthusiasm.

I know that my Redeemer lives.
What comfort this sweet sentence gives!
He lives, he lives who once was dead.

I Know That My Redeemer Lives, words by Samuel Medley, music by Lewis D. Edwards, Hymns, p. 95.

Mother was now singing with me. Hearing Mom's sweet voice just made me feel good all over.

After two years of depositions and a great deal of expense, my case was scheduled to meet before a jury at trial.

One day I was talking to Peter, my lawyer. "What their attorney is trying to emphasize, for all it's worth is that I came in the family with just the clothes on my back. And seein' as how the original property on 5th East was Francis', which she shared with Reed, they want it returned to her because that property, when it was sold, was used to buy the farm and the Reclaim Barrel property which was one and a half acres on Redwood Road. That is what I wound up with after 18 years. They're not denying that I built Reclaim Barrel?"

Peter commented, "Yes, I can see what it is. Because you're the bread winner, they figure you're in the position that the man would be in wherein a wife would sue for support. That's why he's trying to claim disability and now they want you to support him."

"Right!" I exclaimed, "But more than that they're trying to say that just because I had food, clothing and shelter, I have had my pay." I sat there shaking my head while staring at the floor. "It's going to be a doozy how to prove what I've told ya'. It's like one person over here could testify to one thing and another one over there could testify to another. The evidence is all over this whole cotton pickin' valley. But the most important thing is that it's recorded in the heavens where no one can erase or lie about the facts. We can only pray for heaven to help us win this case."

"Well, while you're praying, get me the names, addresses, and phone numbers of all the witnesses that you can think of and list the things they could testify to. Can you do that?"

"You got it!" I said as I sprang up off the chair. We shook hands. "I'll have that for you in the morning."

All that I had witnessed of Zella being beaten, and her children all given to Francis, who then received welfare assistance for each child. My mother being beaten into silence, forced to sign power of attorney to Francis, who then confiscated her Social Security checks. Plus the value of Mother's home that they received all the monies from. Then treated her like hell. I was in a battle for something to show for 18 years of hard work. And the hundreds of thousands of dollars of earning all put in Reed and Francis names. I rounded up letters of witnesses that I had built something—Reclaim Barrel from Reclaim Bottle.

The months passed quickly while we gathered evidence to support my position. Three days before the court day, I met with a very close friend, Doug Jordan an art instructor at the college on Redwood Rd, at his place of employment. The snow was falling heavily as he opened my car door to sit down. I began telling him about the court date.

I said, "I think maybe I should fast for these three days that we might have power from heaven to fight my battle."

He thought for a moment then picked up my hands and said, "No. I want you to be strong and valiant when you walk into that courtroom. I will fast for you."

Years later he became my choice for a husband.

I looked at him as I beheld the face of a true friend. Sweeter words I had never heard. "Bless you," I said, as I gave him a kiss on his cheek.

He looked at his watch. I must go now or I'll be late for work. But don't worry, ok?"

"Thank you."

He got out and shut the door. I sat there pondering over the last two minutes as I thought of all my assets. My friends are the most precious.

The night just before going to court Peter asked me if I was willing to give them anything. Sarcastically I answered I will go home and think about it, pray about it, and I will let you know in the morning.

Peter said, "Yea you do that.

When I stood in the doorway in the morning Peter asked, "Well?"

I looked at him and said, "If I have to go to work and earn a dollar a day and if he will be getting a dime of it. I will NOT GO TO WORK! DO YOU GET THAT?"

Peter straightened out his shoulders and said, "Well ok then. Let's go kick ass."

I met Mother in the hall. She kissed me and said, "I've been praying for you. We all have." We hugged.

"I wish you could come in, too," I said.

"I wish I could, too, but they said I have to stay out here, so it's ok."

We took our positions in the court room. I sat next to Peter, my attorney, and Mary, his secretary. Mary bent over to whisper in my ear. She was looking over at Reed as she said, "You know, the first time I saw Reed a couple of months ago, when Peter was going to take his deposition when he walked in the room, no one needed to tell me who he was. I just knew. He looked like death warmed over, with the most evil countenance. It sent a shiver through my whole body."

When asked by the court to expose what I had gone through in front of the whole courtroom full of people it seemed greater than I could bear. I looked around me and felt such shame, as though someone was about to dump a bucket of sewer water upon me. I sat trembling. My mouth could not speak to reveal the offenses, the humiliation. and degradation. Some things are not even written in this book. I fought to control myself. Drying my eyes and steadying my voice, I proceeded to utter words from a tormented soul. Describing what one might expect to see in a house of the damned, and what I had suffered, supposedly to serve God. But in fact, God had nothing to do with wicked men lusting for power, money, and sex.

It was when Joseph Tanner took the stand. For he had served as a Deputy Sheriff and on Search and Rescue for over 30 years. His words convinced the jury. He testified that when work was being done, equipment being repaired, or built, Reed or Francis were nowhere around. Only me and

Joseph did the work.

A jury of eight voted. Six said that I should give them nothing more. Two said I should give them something.

And so I won.

I finished paying off the $11,000 balance on the white house and gave them a life estate in it. For I would not have it on my conscience that I had left them homeless. It all comes back to the words of Jesus, "Know the truth and the truth will make you free!" Mathew 23.

But people don't seek the truth if they think they already have the truth. I attended a funeral, and there sat a row of young girls, like they were frozen in time. Long hair, long sleeves, long dresses, long faces. Listening to blind guides leading the blind. I had awakened to see others still asleep. These women were still in a prison in their minds.

So I was told by Rulon Jeffs, one of the "Brethren", that God wanted me to consecrate Reclaim Barrell. That is their way to "confiscate" what I had. In my gut I thought, If you men want something like I have, then go work for it. Spend years of blood sweat and tears to earn it.

So when Rulon Jeffs (who by the way is the father of the rapist child molester, Warren Jeffs, who now sits in prison) realized that his request was denied, he told my manager to quit working for me because I was an apostate. So sweet obedient Dale took a $3 per hour cut in pay to go work for a business in the group.

My book keeper called me while doing my taxes and asked, "What happened?"

I answered, "What do you mean?"

Well, last year you grossed $180,000. This year you grossed $235,000."

I said, "Oh that. My manager quit!"

I have had to grow some guts. And I keep loaded weapons handy, to kill or be killed if need be. But I will never live under tyranny, oppression, and degradation ever again.

There is a pattern if a person knows enough about polygamist cult history to connect the dots. In the marriage ceremony the man is told he will become a God, to have wives and concubines, and posterity as numerous as the sands upon the sea shore. They will occupy worlds without end, and will become kings and queens. But women and children are property, kind of like cattle or sheep. Women and children are put on the welfare system to be supported. Yet at the same time the women and children are exploited, and put to work, to build very successful businesses on free labor. This is why the Kingston's are so rich.

It is young female flesh that is the grease to keep the wheels of child abuse spinning. The young boys, like my brother Joe, who refused to give free labor, well they want their asses thrown out. They do not want competition from the young boys for the young girls. You may have heard of the Lost Boys of Short Crick.

All the God wannabes that have use the words, "Thus saith the Lord," with a lust to lord it over others for gain of money, power, and sex when God had not spoken to them, are all examples of this pattern.

Not many ever escape out of the coocoo's nest. But because God is real, I did. Nothing is more important to me than freedom, except God, Jesus, and the truth.

I think of Jesus saying they are like "whitened sepulchers, beautiful on the outside, but inside full of dead men's bones. They make long prayers to be noticed of men, and love the praises. Then they lay burdens on men's backs, grievous to be born that they would not lift with even the flick of their finger. The holy pretense of these rulers who demand obedience are lazy asses who secretly devour widow's houses." Then Jesus added, "Generation of vipers, how can you escape the damnation of hell?"

I am a Christian, I have accepted Jesus as my Savior, and he has forgiven me of my sins. I study the Holy Bible diligently to know what God really said.

CHAPTER EIGHTEEN

Weekends would always find me in the canyons, breathing the fresh air of freedom. I parked in a place with a gorgeous view. I would crawl in the back of my Subaru station wagon and read the Bible, and sometimes the Book of Mormon. I remember when I read where Jesus forgave the harlot. I wept believing Jesus forgave me also. As the days and months went by, I felt cleaner, as though emerging from a sewer. And I began to feel a sense of dignity and self-respect.

I was still staying at Myra's when I wondered if I could pull off a likeness of a face as I had done 19 years ago. So, I tried drawing my beloved Joseph. Well, it was someone, but not him. So I tried again.

I then showed it to Myra. She said, "You know why you did this?"

I said "Tell me".

"Because you can."

Feeling encouraged. Every week I would do a sketch of a friend or employee, but still, not knowing nothing about nothing in paintings. I bought some oil paints and canvas anyway, trying to figure it out. Then a personal friend to Doug Jordan told me I should go take the art classes from Doug at the college.

I replied, "I can't do that. Reclaim Barrell takes up all of my weekdays."

He suggested maybe I could do private lessons.

I asked, "What would it cost me?"

He said he would find out for me. So an appointment was made. And this man with salt and pepper gray hair, knocked on my door. He looked a lot like Conway Twitty. This was 1985, and a whole new life began for me.

He began kinda like a drill sergeant. "What all do you want to learn?"

I said "Well, drawing. Painting people, scenery, animals, sky, water... pretty much everything."

"And how long do you intend to use this information?"

"Probably the rest of my life."

"What is the main reason you want do this?"

As if to say, "woman don't waste my time!"

I took a deep breath, "Well actually I would like to represent stories in the Bible. You know, like Daniel in the lion's den, so the viewer would pause and reflect on the word of God."

Doug was silent as he then sat back into the chair. The air had gone out of his balloon. After a few minutes, tears came to his eyes.

He said, "That is the same reason I wanted to become an artist."

We then agreed on three hours once a week at $25 an hour, every Friday at 4:00p.m. I made cassette tapes of the lessons so I could listen and memorize everything. I always had soft music playing down low in the back ground.

I began offering him a loaf of my homemade whole wheat bread to take home. Then he told me he had pulled off chunks of it to eat as he drove home. Then I began to offer him supper before the lessons. He accepted. All of this morphed into us eventually discussing everything under the sun. But he was a married man. Then one day he told me that his wife had threatened to divorce him three times. And I thought, Dang if she is going to throw him away, I'm going to catch him.

The music from Ann Murray's song, "May I Have This Dance" was playing, and in that moment, I gestured, may I? He accepted. A slow waltz ensued in my office. Like a feather being sucked into a vacuum, I had zero resistance. As our lips met, my world was changed.

I started four 10-hour days a week, and anyone wanting overtime got 25 cents more per hour. And I organized loads of barrels, coming in as well as going out. We were knocking them out. So with record profits, I had no problem finding buyers so I could sell Reclaim Barrell. I was sick of the environmentalists bugging me all the time. And even though I was making real good money, something deep in my soul said. I have to sell this place. I have to pursue my dream of being an artist. And if I don't, something very beautiful and sacred inside of me will die. And I can't allow that to happen.

So in June of 1988, I sold Reclaim Barrel to Ray McCune for a song, way cheap, and bought 57 acres in a little place south of Salt Lake City called Indianola. I had just enough to build a log cabin, as a dried in shell. And the day I moved in, in February of 1989, it was 20 degrees below zero every night for two weeks straight. I was freezing my butt off, but happy. And my finances went from $3000 to $5000 a month to less than $500. Like having chicken one day and feather's the next. I began thinking I better find a job before the unemployment checks ran out.

A rebuke crossed my mind YOU HAVE GIVEN UP A HELL OF A LOT TO BECOME AN ARTIST. NOW BY GOD, YOU BETTER BECOME ONE.

And I could paint and still get P. G. And I wanted to become a mother. All the kissing and fun lovin with Doug, we would not have intercourse, we were saving that for marriage. But turning forty my window to have a child was closing and I was not waiting.

So I said to Doug, "Look you say you want to marry me. And I want to marry you. So how about we have a friend witness us reciting marriage vows? And if you do not feel married then we will just keep on without intercourse."

He smiled the burst out laughing, "You are one crafty woman."

"Well shit. You either will marry me or you won't. You either do or you don't."

So we made covenants on my birthday.

I had a dream of a 10-year-old boy, with Doug's beautiful gray-blue eyes, and my nose. He was behind like a glass wall. I could see him but not touch him. I wept with tears of joy.

I went through boxes of pregnancy tests. But shit was about to hit the fan. Doug's wife heard that he had married Kaziah Hancock and she confronted him.

She said to him, "What's this that Kaziah is going around telling people that she is your wife?"

Doug told her, "I don't know. I will have to ask her."

Hell, I had not been going around telling everybody and their cat and dog. But the secret was out.

Doug had written a list of all the things the L.D. S. church had changed from what Joseph Smith taught. He gave the list to his wife. She gave that to her Bishop and the Bishop told her to divorce Doug. So she did. And like the song says, she got the gold mine, he got the shaft. She got the house, the kids, and half of his retirement.

Doug retired from the college then he came to live with me in our cabin in Indianola. Monogamy is such a beautiful thing. One man, one woman. The two become one flesh.

One year on the opening day of the deer hunt. Doug was fixing his lunch. I said "Sweetheart, you know there's a herd of deer in our alfalfa patch every morning. Why don't you just shoot one of them?"

Doug, sounding sarcastic said, "Well, that's not a hunt."

I said, "Oh, ok."

So Doug spends all day in the mountains and came back with blood hot eyes, and was extremely tired as he plunked down on the couch in despair. So I knelt down beside him and said again, "Honey, the deer were in the alfalfa again this morning right after you left."

He snarled at me, "If you think it's so damned easy, why don't you go do it yourself?

The next morning, I always woke to pee around 4:00 a m., so I woke Doug up and said, "The deer are in the alfalfa.

He grabbed his binoculars searching for horns. He shouted, "Where's my gun? It's in the truck. Go get it."

Me in only bra and underpants, ran out the door, only to see our neighbor parked, looking at the same herd. I ran back in, grabbed clothes, and got the gun. Doug took aim but he missed. Fired again, missed, fired the third time, and missed.

Tibbs the neighbor hollered out "My hell Doug, if you can't shoot better than that, shit go down and throw rocks at it."

The fourth shot hit.

An hour later, I brought a bowl to get the heart, kidney, and liver. Then about an hour later, I went back to tell Doug breakfast was ready.

He said, "What are we having?"

"Liver and onions."

"Where did you get the liver"

"What do you mean where did I get the liver? Shit, you just handed it to me."

He said, "NOOO!"

For years we worked hard on the farm—me milking goats, and us feeding baby lambs and baby calves, moving irrigation hand lines in the alfalfa patch and feeding oat hay to our horses.

One day I came in the house and Doug was sitting at the kitchen table when I pulled down my pants looking for something in my underwear that was scratching me.

Doug started laughing and said, "I just love it when all that happens."

"Well dang there's a little prickler that is scratching me."

"Yeah I know," laughing more, "I put it there."

I began taking Lydia Pinken's vegetable compound that is supposedly as they say, 'Have a baby in every bottle' and still I was not getting pregnant after four years.

One day I got a call from a man in a book club. They had been reviewing my first printing of my original book "Prisons of the Mind." He wanted me to come and speak to, as he called them, "Dyed in the wool Mormons". I tried to talk him out of it but he insisted. So I went. Instead of being a half an hour it lasted over two hours. We had a good time. And there was a gynecologist there and I asked him if he knew why I was not getting pregnant. We made an appointment for an examination.

A week later he called and told me I had ovarian cancer, and that if I did not have my ovaries removed, I only had three months to live. This was in 1992.

I cried "But then how can I have children if you take out my ovaries?"

He said, "It's not a matter if you have children or not. It is a matter if you live or die.

With a broken heart, reluctantly I had the operation.

In prayer I poured my heart out. "Why God, could I not have even one child. My sisters had all had eight or more," as I sobbed, red faced, snot running, as a steady flow of tears came out. I was a mess. Bewildered, when I pulled myself together I asked Doug if we could adopt a child. He shook his head negative.

Although I loved Doug with all my heart. He was, as his sister had called him as a small boy, a little shit. For instance. whatever money he made he would buy fun stuff. Antiques, or a saddle, or horse. Me, well what I brought in paid bills, and boring stuff, like gas, groceries, and home repairs. So, when I sold some penny stock and got $20,000, I paid to have the natural gas brought to the cabin, and a furnace put in. That was nice to have a steady temperature in the winter.

Mother had married a man in the polygamous group as his second wife. They were living in a dot on the map, po-dunk town called Modena, Utah by the Nevada border. I went to visit, only to find out the jack ass had two trailers. A large one for the first wife, and a tiny little camping trailer for Mother, who was in her eighties. She had to get up at all hours of the night to stock a 30-gallon drum, homemade stove, to try to keep warm.

When I came home from the visit, I told Doug, "I want to kidnap my Mother so she can live with me."

He replied, "You can't do that."

"Why not? She's my Mother."

"But she is his wife."

I wish I would have kidnapped her way back then. She later died from pneumonia in 2006. The jack ass she had married sold her burial policy, that I had bought, for over $3000.

And I asked him what was his plan to bury Mother.

He said, "I have a friend with a backhoe that could dig a hole on his property in Modena, and bury her there."

My Mother

"The hell you will!" I said.

I told the nurse at the hospital to have that man removed from the premises, and that he should be told nothing of where Mother's body was. So, I made a casket for Mother using lumber purchased from the Anderson Lumber store, who was kind enough to let me use a space in the back of the store. I had her embalmed and brought her home in the back of my pickup truck. She is buried in the Manti Cemetery, where I can go visit and take flowers.

One of Doug's old friends from the college called him one night and said, "I hear there is a prophet of God speaking tonight in Manti. You want to come?"

Doug said, "Sure, why not?"

Doug asked me if I wanted to come. I said, "NO."

Kaziah, the Goat Woman

ESCAPE PRISONS OF THE MIND

Kaziah Hancock—Self Portrait

Kaziah's Kids

Goat Girl

259

Circle of Friends

Cowboy Ways

CHAPTER NINETEEN

Doug came home from listening to James Harmston who would speak on what he called "The Models," like the things a person must do to climb the stairway to heaven. For ten hours these lessons would go on and on. Well that is not a lesson. That is programming. There is a pattern in cult leaders. They love to be the object of attention and worship. They view their followers as sinners, and/or suckers. They want total obedience. They refuse to accept responsibility for anything bad that happens as a direct result of their radical teachings. Harmston claimed he was following Joseph Smith's original teachings, but it was his own interpretation...

All of this really had Doug's undivided attention.

Doug told me, "This really is a prophet of God."

I asked, "What did he say?"

Way too much for me to try and repeat. You have to go listen for yourself. I'll find out when the next meeting is.

Harmston claimed that these are the last days. And that his mission was to gather up the elect, that would prepare themselves to meet Christ upon his return. He would read straight out of the Book "Teachings of the Prophet Joseph Smith," and then out of the 132nd section of the Doctrine and Covenants. So the latter consists of repentance, baptism, and the laying on of hands. Become a member, pay tithing. These are standard. But Harmston went further, claiming a person must live polygamy and consecrate everything to the Lord, to be born again.

It reminds me of words in the old Hank Williams song, "They want you to give your money to the Lord. But they give you their address."

Then Harmston, hammering on consecration brought up in the Bible, Acts 5:1-11 on Ananias with Sapphira, that God had struck dead because they held back a portion of the money from selling land. Harmston was selling this as a united effort. People who held all things in common. You know like Jim Jones and the story of 'just drink the damn cool-aid to meet Jesus'.

Let me say right here this is opposite of John 3:1-18 which says: "For God so loved the world that he gave his only begotten Son, that whosoever believeth in him should not perish, but have everlasting life." PERIOD.

But people are lazy. We want someone else to read scriptures and tell us what they say, not realizing that Satan himself is a scripture lawyer. Like when he tried to tempt Jesus by quoting scriptures. But the thing is, Satan twists things just a little. And if a person is not well knowledgeable in the word of God, they fall into the trap. 'Cause you don't know what you don't know till you know it.

Harmston asked me directly "Jesus is on his way. What will you give to meet him?"

I said, "Don't ask me that. It's anything and everything. Nothing is more important to me than Christ."

So in one meeting Doug turned to me and said "See those women over there? I want you to go ask them if any of them want to come into our family."

Now think back. He was against me having Mother come to live with us. And he was against me adopting a baby. But now I was supposed to ask five women if anyone wanted to marry Doug. Just a sick feeling, like a kick in the gut.

I answered, "Who? Which one?"

He said, "Any, or all of them."

Here we go again. Like Daddy had believed the bullshit on this numbers game. That but for the Grace of almighty God, we would have all perished on the desert.

So two women approached Doug to take him up on his offer. Rose and Laprell. Doug asked me to choose one even though he wanted both, so he could move up the ladder faster.

I replied "How would you like it if I wanted two more husbands?"

I should have said "Hell No! I want a divorce."

See, men don't like it when the shoe is put on the other foot. But I was being forced to choose. And Doug was the love of my life and I love Jesus more than my own life. So I reluctantly said Laprell.

And when she moved in, she kept giving me the looks, that if looks could kill I would be dead. Then Doug told me I need to get a revelation and consent to having Rose marry him also.

I ended up saying "I don't care anymore. Whatever makes you happy."

My heart had been ripped to shreds already.

I sold the farm in 1995. It had doubled in value and there was enough to buy a home in Manti where Doug could live with Laprell and Rose, and I could have a piece of land and build a small cabin for myself. But of the three women, I was the only one willing to work to pay bills and Doug knew it. And he was determined to have us all live in the same house.

I went up into the canyons to pour my heart out in prayer.

"Oh God, righteous and eternal. I know you see me. I know you hear me." Tears streaming, snot flowing, flies stinging my face as they landed to drink my tears. "What am I? Am I a freak? Am I a malfunction? No matter what I do I cannot make Doug happy. Haven't I worked hard enough to deserve a little piece of land and a cabin by myself where I can have my goats. Is this asking too much? All I have, I have dedicated to you. For your honor. Your glory. Not mine. For your kingdom to come, for your will to be done, on earth as it is in heaven. I will lay it all on the altar of sacrifice. But if you can find it in your heart and have compassion on me. Please Lord. I love my goats and I need land. Even if I live in a little sheep camp trailer, I could be happy. Those two women hate me, and they hate each other even more. This is my prayer God. I ask humbly, in the name of Jesus Christ, your holy son. Amen."

Doug was supposed to hold the holy priesthood, to be the head of the household, and I always tried to honor him. But the day would come when enough is enough.

The first chunk of land was sold. And one acre, with a home with five bedrooms was purchased. Doug, Laprell, Rose, and Rose's son Rubin moved in. I stayed in Indianola cleaning up the yard, and improving the home so it would sell for an additional $30,000 more. Every day I was praying to God, dedicating everything to him and singing hymns. And at the end of this prayer, I put my hands in the air and shouted, "Hosanna, blessed be the name of the most high God." I repeated that three times. And in a flash the Spirit of Christ showed up. I could not see him. But in a loud voice into my brain, he said," WOULD YOU GIVE YOUR LIFE FOR ME?"

I shouted "YES."

"THEN LIVE FOR ME!"

And he was gone. Wow!

I went over and sat down thinking. How? How Lord can I live for you?

What I have witnessed men doing that claim to hold the same priesthood as Jesus is just opposite from our Lord, Jesus. He was the most humble man that ever walked the earth. These men were prideful and self-centered. Didn't Jesus say something like "he who exalteth himself will be humbled. And he who humbles himself will be exalted."

Well when the monies came in from the last piece of Indianola property, what do ya know? Doug was the big man in town. Shit, he was handing out rolls of hundred-dollar bills. Harmston got approximately $200,000. And Doug would walk into the pizza parlor and say, all drinks and pizza are on me.

Isn't it something how easy it is for a person to give away money that they did not earn? Doug was on a high like a cocaine addict. And when all the monies were gone the air was out of his balloon. And he hated the withdrawal pains.

I had sold artwork, and my horse and saddle. I scraped up enough to put a down payment on 15 acres with irrigation water and a well. $5,000 did it with payment of $500 a month. Harmston agreed to make the payments.

Laprell said to me "I am sure glad that it's your name on the contract and not mine."

I answered, "I am, sure glad it's my name and not yours too."

The 15 acres had a $65,000 balance.

Then Doug, wanting to get his hands on more cash told me, "We need to sell this home and divide the money five ways."

I asked, "How do you get five ways?"

"Well there's you, me, Laprell, Rose, and Rubin."

"Look, one person's money bought Indianola and only one person is going to own the monies when this house is sold."

"Well I am going to get half."

"Oh, and am I going to get half of your retirement?"

"No."

"Then you're not getting any money from this house!"

As Doug was walking out, he shouted, "You are the most selfish person I have ever known," and he slammed the door behind him.

I had finally made a stand and would not back down. Within the week Doug said he was going to file for a divorce. The Harmston cult that used their interpretation of Mormon doctrine for their own personal gain had ruined a good man.

I said "I would never suggest divorce, but if that is what it takes to make you happy," but then said, "By all means, go for it."

I also left the group of Harmston's in 1997, then all of them moved out. I was by myself, crying myself to sleep every night. But I would not be used a as mop anymore.

When Harmston was working on Doug to get $250,000 from the sale of my property in Indianola, he indicated that he would make sure that the payments of $500.00 a month were made on my 15 acres. Well what do ya know, I should have had all that happy bullshit put in writing, because after I left his cult, the group made one payment and refused to make any more. My thoughts were I'll see you in court... Then I heard through the grapevine that Harmston and his puppets would hold prayer circles where they asked God to curse me, to have accidents and sickness, even unto death.

Okay, well I was saying prayers also. My prayer was this, "Oh God, righteous and eternal Father in Heaven, I come before you to bless whoever in the Harmston group that has a pure heart and love truth, that they can repent and read the Bible, and come to a knowledge of the truth, and can come to know the real Jesus, that even they might not be lost. In Jesus Christ's name, Amen."

I prayed that way because in Harmston's twisting of scriptures, he said he was sent as a prophet to prepare a people to meet Jesus. Then when Jesus didn't show up, he switched to "Well, what if I am Jesus?" Well, shit! That was it. I'd had it.

Remember when I said that at the time Doug divorced me and I left the Harmston cult, prior to me having my name removed from his church, Jim Harmston had promised to pay the $65,000 balance on my 15 acres. But when I "apostatized" he refused to honor his commitment. So I brought a law suit against him, for over $250,000 he had received. So him and his "elite" as he called his members, began to hold prayer vigils asking God, while they were all dressed in their special underwear with holes, and white attire, with their green or white or whatever the hell color of their aprons were, holding hands in a circle, they prayed that God would curse me, that I would have accidents, even unto death. They even fired bullets into my dried in shell cabin, while I was not there.

Hell, I had to leave the cult. Harmston was completely nuts. He claimed that a person came back to earth many times, and that he was in fact Enoch, Abraham, Moses, Noah. And yeah, of course, he was Moroni and Joseph Smith. Gads, talk about someone having a screw loose. But of course he is dead now. He would tell 16-year-old girls that they had been his wife in another age, and time. And if they believed him, well the old fart in his sixties would buy lots of Viagra. So he died of a heart attack. No tears here.

But while his members were praying for my destruction, I was praying for them, that they might get their eyes opened and come to Jesus, to find truth that they would repent and be forgiven. Some did, and came to apologize to me for having been part of the prayer circle to curse me. I forgave them with hugs.

You know folks, when stupid people hate you, you must be doing something right.

So in 1998, I sold the home and acreage to finish paying off my land and I built a cabin as far as the money went, I had a dried in shell, but it was not livable. So I bought an 11'X14' Tuff Shed and lived in that. This is where I created the large painting, "Circle of Friends." That was how I imagined my life at 72, surrounded by the animals that made me happy.

Life became fun again, raising and expanding my goat herd, flying by the seat of my pants. I got the nickname of, "Kaziah the Goat Woman, the Artist," painting landscape portraits, animals, and fun stuff.

The painting of "Cowboy Ways," with the muddy boot on the table like he doesn't give a damn what others think, it's what makes him happy, his can of peaches, and his dog... is one of my first large paintings.

I remember a prayer to God when I said.

"Lord, God, creator of heaven and earth, I ask forgiveness for having ever being stupid enough to believe in 'Mormonism.' I want all of that removed from me. Like emptying a bucket full of mud, I want a new start, a clean bucket. And I only want you, God, your son, Jesus, and the Holy Spirit Jesus talked about. That's it! Please remove everything else from my head to my toes. In Jesus name. Amen."

I took my Book of Mormon, Doctrine and Covenants and all the books I had read, and filled the trash can.

One day in 2000, I was painting and singing along with Bryan White's song, "Lord, don't you have just one more miracle left," when a knock came on the door. A man was looking for land that was going to be auctioned off at fire sale prices. I told him I knew nothing about it, and he left.

The thought crossed my mind maybe I could buy it, resell it for a profit. I rebuked that idea with Oh yeah sure. Hell, I am so broke I can hardly even pay attention. I don't have a pot to piss in or a window to throw it out of. And I'm going to go buy land, forget it.

But a strange thing happened in a dream that night. An angel came and said come with me. I always had dreams that I could fly. Anyway, so it was the angel and I, hovering close to the ceiling watching the auction. The land went for $20,000 and the man sold it for $50,000, Making a $30,000 profit. Then the angel said to me, "See that could have been you. But oh well the blessing will go to someone else because you won't even look at it."

When I woke up, I was pissed, $30,000 would finish my house so I could move in. So I began to investigate. I found the land and researched how many times it had been divided. Where was natural gas, telephone lines, and the electricity. Was there culinary well permits? The auction was being held that very day, and a friend was on his way from Salt Lake City with an $8,000 down payment on five acres I was going to sell him.

With a sober mind, gravel in my guts and spit in my eye, I went to where the auction was to be held. I asked the auctioneer "What culinary water do you have?"

He said "I am not guaranteeing any culinary water."

"Your sign says 'Cabin Lots'... and you can't build without water."

"I'm not guaranteeing any culinary water."

"Well that's false advertisement. What about the irrigation shares?"

He said "I have 56 shares of North Six Mile."

I went home and called the friend bringing me the $8,000 and asked him to stop by the bank. I called the bank and asked them to convert the unsecured funds to secured funds. They said "We don't normally do that, but for you, we will."

This piece is next to Highway 89 north of Sterling, Utah. When the auction started, the 250 acres with 56 irrigation shares started at $80,000. I knew the water shares alone valued over $130,000. When my hand went up, I asked "Where is the culinary water?" I wanted everyone there to hear his answer. So as he repeated himself about not guaranteeing water, I hollered "Then that's false advertisement."

Just then, a man on the sideline said "I have culinary water." I asked him in a whisper "So what do you have?"

He was the former owner and said "I have three well permits."

"How long are they good for, and will you sign them over to me if I am the successful bidder?"

"Yes," was his answer.

I sat back down, and at $120,000 I won the bid. I was told that they needed 10% down. I showed the $8,000 certified check, and asked if he would take a personal check of $4,000.

"Well we don't normally do that, but I will this time."

I went home and called my bank and said "Listen, I have bid and won on a 250 acre piece of ground. I have just written a $4,000 check. Whatever you do, don't let it bounce."

The bank manager asked "Until when?"

I told him "Until I can get you to grant me a $120,000 loan."

The manager exclaimed "Kaziah, what do you think we are? Your partners in investment?"

"Well yes. Yes I do. Look, you will have collateral to the hilt. You will have all this plus my 16 acres and home, and all the water from both places. You want to give me this loan."

"Well come on in and fill out the application."

They granted me the loan. The angel left off a $100,000 in the dream – a good thing, or I never would have given it a second thought.

So, for months, I worked to have it surveyed into 9 building lots. I got the well permits and bought 6 more permits. I cleaned up the boundary lines, and got the perk tests done. Then I hit a brick wall when I asked for the power company to bring electricity to the lots. They wanted $20,000 up front!

I went back to the bank to get the additional $20,000.

The manager said "Absolutely not. We already went out on a limb for you. There is no way we will even consider loaning you more."

I called other loan places to ask for a $140,000 loan.

I was stressed to the max. If this did not work out, I stood to lose everything, all while the Harmston group was praying for my destruction.

I got on my knees to plead my case to a kind, loving, compassionate God. This was my exact prayer:

"Oh God, righteous and eternal Father in Heaven. I come before you in the name of Jesus Christ and by the power of the holy Melchizedek priesthood that only Jesus Christ holds. I command the angels who love and serve Him to come to my rescue. Everything I have is on the line. What do I do? In the name of Jesus Christ, Amen."

For three days, I prayed this exact same prayer. Then on the fourth day, I marched into the bank and said to the loan manager, Melba "You have to give me a loan for the other $20,000."

"Why would you say that?"

"Because if you don't, you will force me to go to another loan institution to borrow $140,000 so I can pay you off and have the $20,000 to bring in the electricity. And if I do that, you will lose over $1,000 a month in interest.

She said "We already pulled off Mission Impossible for you. I don't want to even ask."

"Well ask anyway!"

So, reluctantly, she called the loan headquarters.

"Kaziah's here again. She is insisting that we give her a loan for another $20,000 on top of the $120,000 we already granted her, to bring in the electricity."

She put the call on speaker so I could hear. He said "What has she done with the land so far?"

Melba answered "She has subdivided it into 9 lots. She has secured more well permits. She has the perk tests, and the letters from the police and fire department that they will service the area and she had alfalfa planted on 4 lots. But she can't start selling lots until she brings power to them."

The man at headquarters said "Okay have her fill out the application."

Melba let me fill out the papers. Then at the loan headquarters in Provo, around the table, I was told later how the conversation went...

One person "What is Kaziah's income?"

Answer "Well she's a portrait artist."

"Does she have any other income?"

"No."

"Well how can we possibly grant her more?"

Then a voice at the end of the table asked "Do we even know this woman?"

"Yes."

"Has she had loans with us before?"

"Yes."

"Well what is the status of those loans?"

"They are all paid off."

"Well then, WHAT IS OUR PROBLEM?"

And the loan was granted!

I started selling lots. I also brought the phone and natural gas to all the lots. I paid off all I owed to the bank. I had money to finish and furnish my home, and had one lot of three acres, a well permit, and one irrigation share, left to sell.

Then what do you know, who came knocking? Ivan Douglas Jordan, love of my life. Little shit. He asked if I would sell him the lot. I was asking $30,000.

I said to him "Sure but only for a cash out. You see Doug, all the work I have done to make it sellable, this one is my profit."

As he stood at the door, he could see the beauty of my kitchen area. He was humbled. He had thrown me in a garbage can because I refused to be "obedient."

But almighty God had picked me up and gave me the land and cabin I prayed for. And I was totally out of debt.

He said, "I understand."

No hugging, no hand shake, no I'm sorry for the way I treated you. Nope. None of that. Just silence. And he left.

Even weeks after I moved in, when walking from the art studio to the kitchen in the most beautiful home I had ever lived in, I would burst into tears of gratitude. It was free and clear. I even bought back 5 acres I was selling, and had money in the bank. This was truly a miracle, by a loving and compassionate God. God is very real.

I had serious reflection about what paintings do I want to leave with my signature on them. I had been studying the paintings of J.C Leyendecker, Nicolai Fechin, Rockwell, Van Gogh, and even Picasso. I decided it was time to start a series called "Unsung Workers."

When I found a person to paint to go into this series, I offered them $10 to let me take their picture. I remember when I finished the painting of Nadia, the street sweeper. It was then I had a thrill, that I had arrived. I could imagine a choir singing in heaven, "She's got it, she's got it, by George. She has got it."

I painted other workers like, the 'Farmer', the 'Baker', the 'Cleaning Lady', the 'Waiter' on the Amtrak Train, the 'Greaser', the 'School Teacher', and the 'Coal Miner'. I was having a blast! And what do ya know, I lit on my own style. But in my heart, I knew that I owed God for saving this little goat herder girl.

Continued on page 317

KAZIAH MAY HANCOCK

Street Sweeper

Good Shepherd

KAZIAH MAY HANCOCK

Lady Hog Farmer

ESCAPE PRISONS OF THE MIND

Dairyman

KAZIAH MAY HANCOCK

Cowboy

Farmer

"Homemade" Baker

ESCAPE PRISONS OF THE MIND

Cy's Market

KAZIAH MAY HANCOCK

Coal Miner

ESCAPE PRISONS OF THE MIND

Mother

Nurse

Ministering Angels—Mother Teresa

School Teacher

Waiter

Artist Ted Wasmer

ESCAPE PRISONS OF THE MIND

Everybody's Mom

KAZIAH MAY HANCOCK

Cleaning Lady

ESCAPE PRISONS OF THE MIND

Grandpa Santa

Dog Groomer

Flower Girl

Garbage Collector

Greaser

ESCAPE PRISONS OF THE MIND

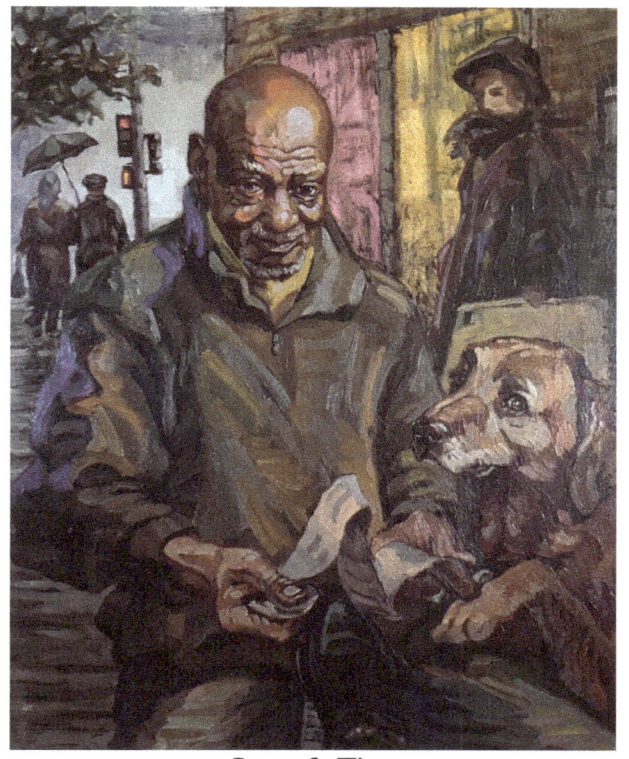

Izzy & Tizz

Milkmaid

Secretary

Waitress

291

Born to Paint

ESCAPE PRISONS OF THE MIND

Onion Soup

Mocha Days

ESCAPE PRISONS OF THE MIND

Movin' em Up

Going Home

North Carolina Wetland

ESCAPE PRISONS OF THE MIND

Six Mile Creek

Bare Necessities

My Impression of Spring City

ESCAPE PRISONS OF THE MIND

Rio Grande

Sanpete Winter

Commitment

Abraham Lincoln

Military Muscle

Compassionate Listener

New Beginnings

Spirit of Independence

Stand with Integrity

ESCAPE PRISONS OF THE MIND

That Will Be $9.33 Please

KAZIAH MAY HANCOCK

The Blues

The Kiss

What to Fix for Kids

Wolverine Drilling — Summer

Fairview Mill

Fields of Gold

Bug Collection

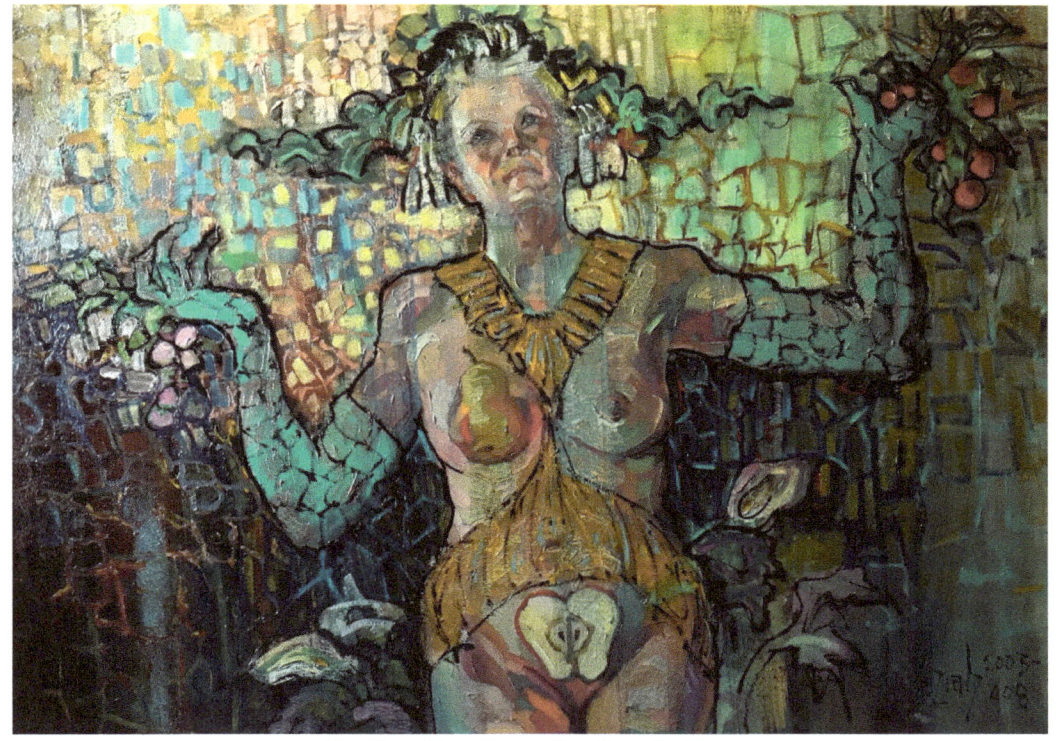

In the Garden of Adam's Eve

Firefighter

Guardian Angel

Helen

ESCAPE PRISONS OF THE MIND

Mother and Baby Nursing

The Duke

Two Mothers

Hun, Is that You?

Just You and Me, Molly

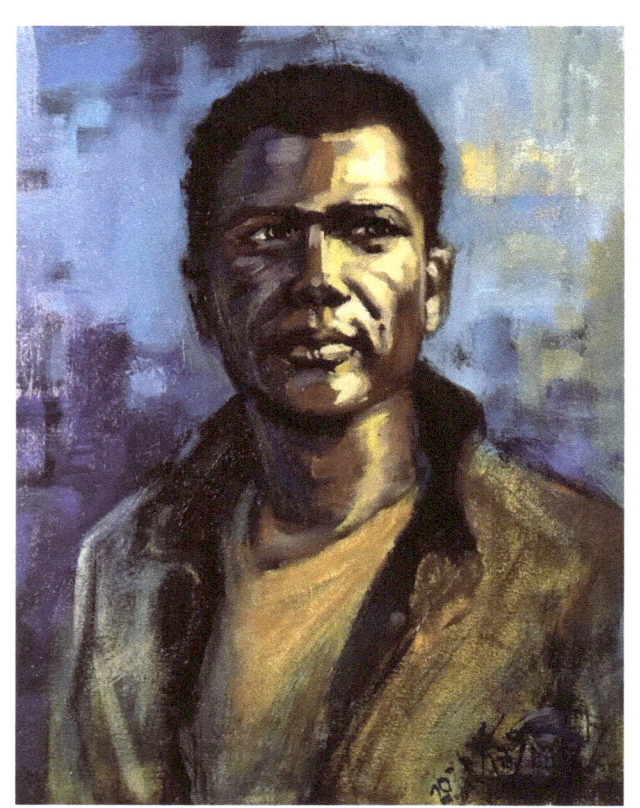

Sid

Soup's On

ESCAPE PRISONS OF THE MIND

Continued from page 271

Then on September 11, 2001, the Twin Towers of the World Trade Center were brought down by terrorists, and the Pentagon was attacked too, and our nation went back to waving our flag, and flocking to churches. The fear of an enemy, so intent on killing Americans, they would even kill themselves to do it... my hatred for Bin Laden, the head of the terrorist that killed thousands, and not knowing what he would do next.

Before March of 2003, as an artist I was flying by the seat of my pants, painting anything and everything that was a worthy subject. But when I heard a radio broadcast telling of the loss of American soldiers fighting Al Qaeda, I was reminded that freedom is not free, and I was moved with compassion. I began just a simple act of kindness to paint fallen soldiers as a gift to their families. I had no idea how this project would change my art for the next 18 years, putting soldier portraits as priority.

In that radio broadcast, I learned of the soldier James W. Cawley, his life, and death. As President Bush had declared war, and this was the first casualty I had heard of, I stopped and sat on the floor, with my back braced against the base of my couch. I had tears streaming, but felt so grateful for all the men and women who enlisted to go find and kill Bin Laden, so I could live in peace. A person feels quite stupid and helpless, enjoying the American dream, while beautiful men and women were dying to secure my dream. At least I did. But I am not stupid so I thought, Well shit. Don't just cry. Why don't you do his portrait as a gift for his family. So I contacted the newspaper to have his family contact me. Then I was told about John D. Smith, that had been killed. I was asked, "What about him?"

I replied, "Yes, I will paint him too."

This was the beginning of what would become a 501C3 Project Compassion Soldier Fund in 2005, where other artists would help me paint thousands of our nation's heroes. I started a movement nationwide where artists heard about Project Compassion, and began to do some art—some pencil portraits, some painting. Even President Bush began painting soldiers' portraits, but he really should get some art lessons. But a movement was created from just a simple act of kindness, and I finally felt like I had found what Jesus wanted of me, when he asked if I would die for him and I shouted "Yes," and he said "THEN LIVE FOR ME!"

Then a request came in to paint an Army soldier, Brian Alex Vaughn. The mother told how he had become a medic, and when he could have come home, he wrote to her. "Mom, I can't leave. I have too many men that I am doctoring. I need to try to get as many of them back home to their families as I possibly can. And I know that no one here will take as good a care of my guys as I will. But I will come visit as soon as I can. Tell everyone how much I love and miss them."

As I looked at the images the mother had sent, I was a mess, in tears. Bryan looked so much like the son I always wanted, with Doug's beautiful eyes and my nose. I was thrilled that his mother had this quality human being, but so sad now he was gone. The mission that killed him was not even his. He was filling in for a friend, always going above and beyond, going the extra mile. God knows how I love this kid. One photo of him looking calmly out of a window—I chose that one to paint, even though I had to go with a larger canvas to a 24"X36". And I wrote his mother a letter.

She called me when she got the painting and said, "This painting is wonderful! But your letter is priceless."

The father of Dustin DeCol came home and found a package for him. He opened it and called me. With tears in his voice he said, "How can I tell you how much this means to me? I just came home from sitting in the hospital where my son lay dying from his wounds. And outside there were protesters of the war. Shouting so loud my son could hear them calling him a baby killer and a terrorist. So horrible that he had to endure such a thing until he breathed his last breath. I drove home with the biggest broken heart. Then to open the package and see the love you have put into his portrait. I cannot possibly thank you enough."

I replied, "God bless you. And your precious son."

James W. Cawley

John Daren Smith

ESCAPE PRISONS OF THE MIND

Brian Alex Vaughn

Dustin Decol

CHAPTER TWENTY

After a couple of years (it was the year 2006 at this time) I had only painted 250 soldiers. But Boyd Huppert from KARE 11 TV out of Minneapolis, Minnesota wanted to film me painting a soldier, Dale Panchot, and then his parents receiving his portrait. So, knowing he was coming, I began feeling a bit nervous. Then I thought, Why? Why be nervous? It's only a few minutes. And hell, no one watches the news anyway. And if they do, they can't remember anything.

So putting my fear of the camera aside I told myself, I am going to use this open window of opportunity to send as much love out to soldiers and their families as I possibly can. So I did just that.

The clip was only six minutes long, and my love for our soldiers is real, and people seeing this small clip of news could feel it. Although it is only like putting a band-aid on a broken heart, for the families, at least someone gave a damn. I couldn't let it be like the soldiers that came home from Vietnam, who were spit on, called baby killers, and terrorists. Hell no! I am opposite of all that shit.

The clip went onto the Today Show, CNN, and even The View invited me to present a portrait of a soldier to a mother who had lost her son.

Because of the KARE 11 news clip being seen by tens of millions of views nationwide, other TV stations came and filmed me painting a soldier, and the family receiving the portrait, for the evening news. I don't know, it's like 15 or 20 stations. It was a lot.

During the time the KARE 11 News clip was racing across the nation, it was seen by Fed-Ex's founder Fred Smith. (There was a Fed-Ex truck delivering the painting in the KARE 11 video.) I was contacted by Fed-Ex in 2007, and was asked "What can we do for you?"

My answer was "Well anything you can do will help."

The Fed-Ex contact person said "Alright, I will get back to you."

After about 3 hours, I called him back and left this message, "I was just thinking, when you guys are around your table to decide, well it just seems to me that if you come up with anything less than 100% free shipping, then, well, when you look in the mirror, you just might see egg on your face, 'cause it seems to me, it's just something you oughta wanna do anyway."

The Fed-Ex rep called back and said "I laughed so hard when I listened to your message, and was going to play it at the round table, but they had already voted 100% Free Shipping for Project Compassion."

Then I burst into tears of gratitude. "Thank you! God bless Fed-Ex."

Then military organizations began contacting me to give me an award. For a girl that had only been on a plane twice prior to Project Compassion, well then, they were flying my fanny all over the nation. The Veterans of Foreign Wars, the American Legion, the Disabled American Veterans, the Military Order of the Purple Heart, the Daughters of the American Revolution, the Sword of Ignatius Loyola. Then the Local Awards, XO Award, Utah National Guard, Red Cross, Governor's Mansion Award, The Utah Arts Counsil Humanitarian Award. All this was so amazing to me.

I even had speaking engagements, like speaking before our nation's Generals in the heart of the Pentagon in 2008.

I also spoke at the Air Force Academy in Colorado Springs. I started out with something like this, as I was looking over the sea of Cadets.

"I have a goat ranch and sometimes I need help. So when the local kids show up, there is the wannabe cowboys, that when asked to catch a 60-pound goat, they will make a dash and just barely miss it. Like I'm supposed to be impressed. Well I'm not impressed. Then there is the real cowboy. He locks his eyes on the critter and says, 'You are going down.' He grabs ahold of it running and it may flip his ass over. He may emerge covered in blood, mud, and crud. But he's got it." I paused to look at them and said, "That's you. God bless you I love you with all my heart."

Well a man from West Point was sitting with the Cadets and I was contacted. "We want you to come to West Point." So on September 11, 2008, I spoke there also. It was such a grand honor to let these kids know how much I love them.

Well folks, my desire to adopt a child is real. And I adopted a whole nation. When soldiers would see the KARE 11 clip, once in a while my phone would ring. A man with tears in his voice would say "You don't know me ma'am but I love you," then hang up.

My last words to the Generals were, "Well if we ever see a day when there is no longer young men and women, willing to risk life and limb for this great nation, then our ass is grass, and the lawn mower is fast on its way."

The Generals gave me a standing ovation. And as I stepped away from the podium to shake their hand, they would put a military coin in my hand. All of those honors and blessings were so unforeseen.

In 2008, I also hired a local woman named Kenna to be my secretary for Project Compassion. Ironically, and unfortunately, she abused my trust and stole funds from Project Compassion, and forged my signature. Over the next 5 years, she stole more than $130,000 and I fired her in 2013.

In 2012, the Greenbaum Foundation, who had been funding Project Compassion so that I could retain the help of other artists, pulled their funding. Project Compassion has been funded mostly by donations since then, and I have been the sole artist.

None of these unfortunate events have stopped me from showing my gratitude for our nation's heroes through painting.

I will continue to honor the honorable, to serve the few who serve the many.

Continued on page 340

Bowman

Clay

Butcher

Culbertson

Dooley

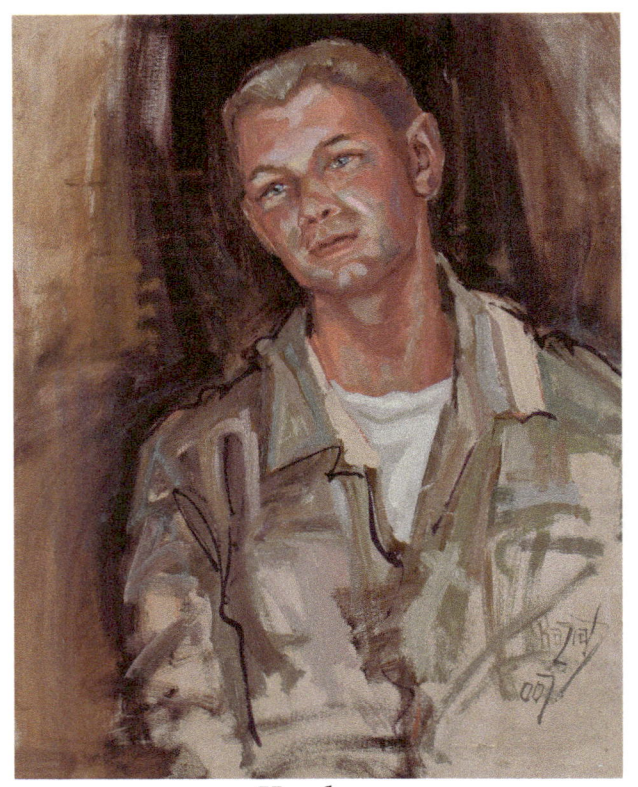

Herzberg

Hicks

Holler

ESCAPE PRISONS OF THE MIND

Kazsynski

King

Kirven

Kuglics

Langarica

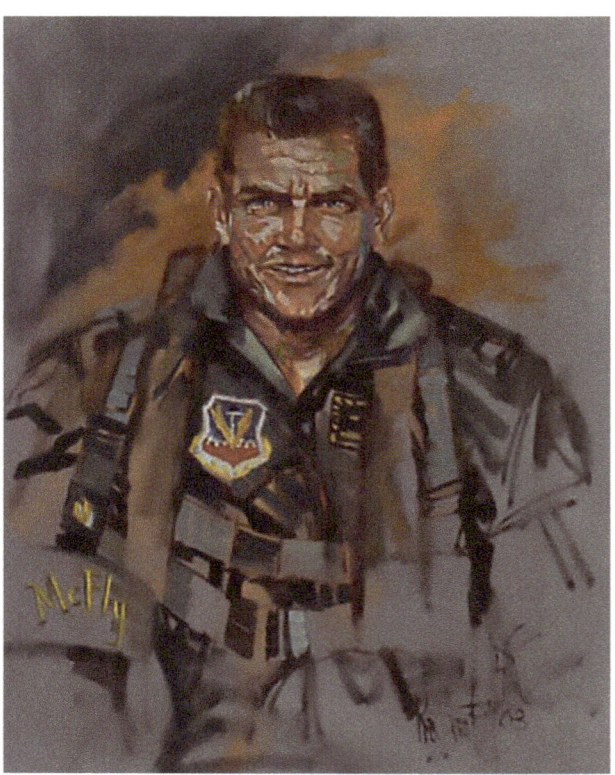

Lapinski

McFarland

ESCAPE PRISONS OF THE MIND

McGinnis

Moore

Mills

Monsoor

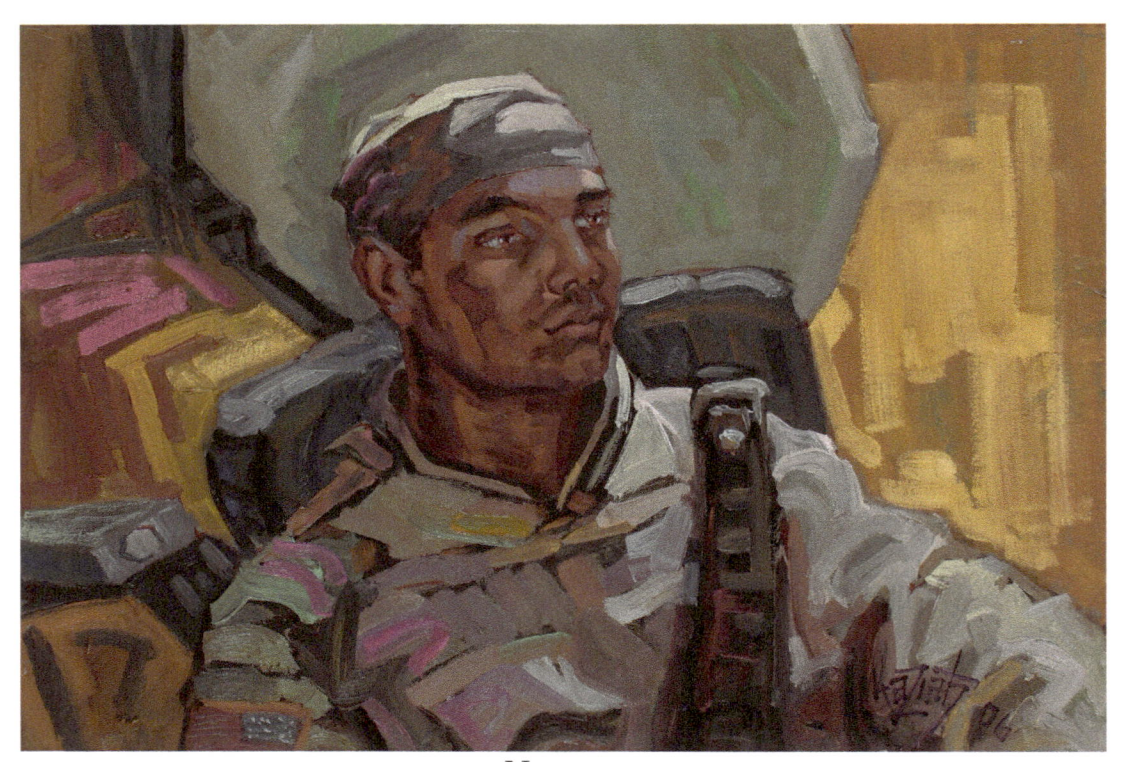

Navarro

ESCAPE PRISONS OF THE MIND

Owens

Roberts

Richardson-Below

Pursel

KAZIAH MAY HANCOCK

Rogers

Rojas-Gallego

Rode

ESCAPE PRISONS OF THE MIND

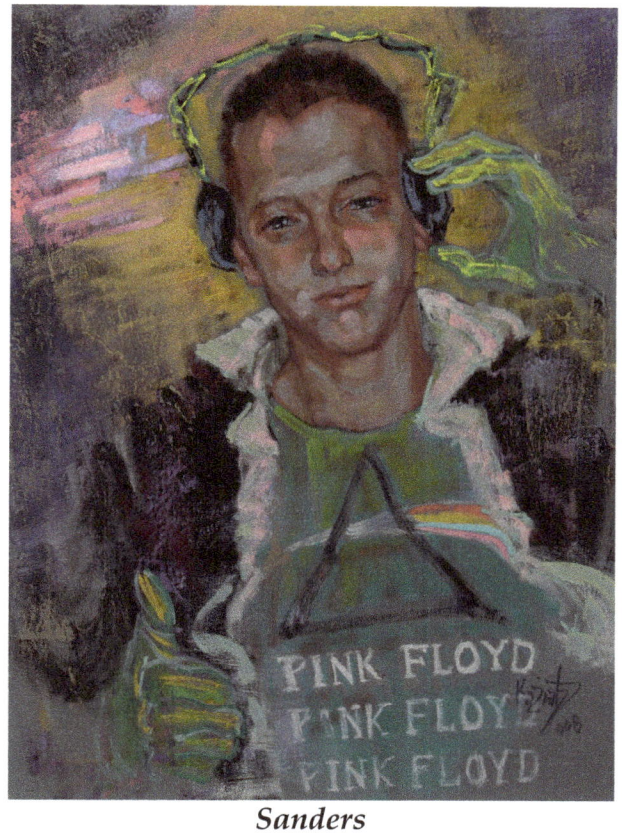

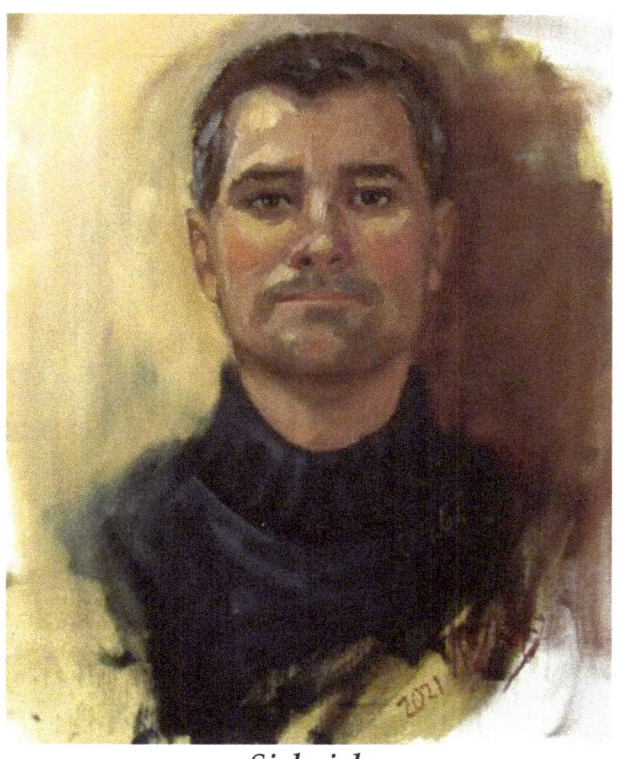

Sanders

Schwartz

Sicknick

Simmons

Songy

Swanson

Vaillant

ESCAPE PRISONS OF THE MIND

Valdepeñas

Washington

Wallace

337

White

Williams

Wood

Yashinski

ESCAPE PRISONS OF THE MIND

Yrure

Zaun

USAF to Honor the Living

Continued from page 325

In 2012, my sweet sister Ester passed away. The chapel was filled with friends, family, and many grandchildren. One of ger grandsons, Christian spoke of his love for his grandmother. Then when the service was over, he was standing on the sidewalk. I came up and said "Ya know, Ester always made people feel loved."

Christian said "She was always encouraging me, but for a while I was smoking weed, and that's all I wanted to do. Then I realized I was just wasting my life, so I got a guitar, and have been learning to play. Ya know we all have artistic abilities because we are all related to Kaziah."

Then as his ride approached, he shook my hand and asked "And you are...?"

"Kaziah!"

His head went back as his mouth dropped open. "Oh my gosh, I love your paintings."

When I told Sarah and Carol about this, I laughed so much.

In the years since all that, I have continued to paint fallen soldiers, firefighters, police officers, first responders... all as gifts for the families. I had painted 2,499 of these heroes by October 2021. Then I decided to do a fun one for the 2,500th hero painting, and did my favorite homicide detective, Joe Kenda, although he is still living. I painted a portrait of the real Joe Kenda, beside the actor who plays Kenda in "Homicide Hunter" on TV.

Sometimes I just paint for fun also. Flowers, landscapes, butterflies for each of my very closest friends. I've done portraits of some of my dear friends, or their children as gifts, and even some of their beloved animals. I was born to paint, and I try to bless others with the gift God gave me.

I am a Christian. I study the bible, for about a half hour each morning. I read out loud. My dog and cats were in attendance for many years, until my sweet dog passed away. Now it's just me and my kitties. And we love God and his only Son, Jesus. And we are blessed.

THE END

ESCAPE PRISONS OF THE MIND

Joe Kenda—Homicide Hunter

Basquiat

ESCAPE PRISONS OF THE MIND

Basquiat

Art and Intrigue with the Image of Man

Lietenant Dan

Matt

Sign Painter

ESCAPE PRISONS OF THE MIND

Hobo

Billy Idol

Warhol in Me

The Crucified — Abstract

ESCAPE PRISONS OF THE MIND

Wired for Genius — Steve Jobs

Rush Limbaugh

ESCAPE PRISONS OF THE MIND

Calla Lily

Easter Lilly

Iris

Poppy

KAZIAH MAY HANCOCK

Flags of Peace

A NOTE TO READERS

Just a few images of the soldiers, police, and firefighters are shown in this book.
But if you go to www.heropaintings.com you can see more.

For more go to: www.theartofkaziah.com
To request that a fallen hero be painted, and to see more,
visit www.kaziahhancockheropaintings.com
And also: www.heropaintings.com.
There are also many videos online of me painting,
plus my audio book "Kaziah Born to Paint."

CPSIA information can be obtained
at www.ICGtesting.com
Printed in the USA
JSHW011128240722
28463JS00002B/5